- 上海紧缺人才培训工程教学系列丛书
- 金融英语专业技能证书

金融英语教材编写委员会 ◎ 编写

基础类 FINANCIAL ENGLISH

# 金融英语（第2版）

清华大学出版社
北京

## 内 容 简 介

本教材系上海紧缺人才培训工程金融英语岗位资格证书考试用书。由上海国际金融学院、外交部高级译审、上海外国语学院翻译学院、花旗银行、美林集团、博思艾伦咨询公司等权威机构代表组成的金融英语项目专家委员会,经反复修订,历时两年精心完成。

本教材根据金融混业经营趋势和中国入世后需要编写。具有实用性、实务性和实战性特点。适应范围为银行、证券、保险、期货、基金、外汇等金融服务业。

本教材共有4部分:商业银行、投资银行、金融衍生品和保险。共21个单元,包括实例阅读、对话、听力、模拟试题、术语解释、练习、案例分析。另附两部分选修内容:金融职业伦理和反洗钱知识。

本教材适用于有一定英语基础并有志于金融职业生涯者和高等院校金融专业学生及教师。

本书封面贴有清华大学出版社防伪标签,无标签者不得销售。
版权所有,侵权必究。举报: 010-62782989, beiqinquan@tup.tsinghua.edu.cn。

**图书在版编目(CIP)数据**

金融英语/金融英语教材编写委员会编写. —2版. —北京: 清华大学出版社,2011.10(2023.1重印)
 ISBN 978-7-302-27052-2

Ⅰ. ①金… Ⅱ. ①金… Ⅲ. ①金融－英语－教材 Ⅳ. ①H31

中国版本图书馆 CIP 数据核字(2011)第 204480 号

责任编辑:刘志彬
责任校对:王荣静
责任印制:沈 露

出版发行:清华大学出版社
网　　址:http://www.tup.com.cn, http://www.wqbook.com
地　　址:北京清华大学学研大厦 A 座　　　邮　编:100084
社 总 机:010-83470000　　　邮　购:010-62786544
投稿与读者服务:010-62776969, c-service@tup.tsinghua.edu.cn
质 量 反 馈:010-62772015, zhiliang@tup.tsinghua.edu.cn

印 装 者:三河市科茂嘉荣印务有限公司
经　　销:全国新华书店
开　　本:185mm×230mm　　　印 张:26.5　　　字　数:416 千字
　　　　　附光盘 1 张
版　　次:2011 年 10 月第 2 版　　　印　次:2023 年 1 月第 16 次印刷
定　　价:45.00 元

产品编号:037091-01

**主办机构：**
    上海国际金融学院
    上海市紧缺人才培训事务服务中心

**主　　编：** 陆红军

**编　　委：** 王荣华　　Neil Benson　　姚忻华

**专家委员会：**

  Neil Benson
    花旗银行多伦多分行前总裁
    美国沃顿商学院金融硕士

  柴明颎
    上海外国语大学翻译学院院长、教授

  王荣华
    上海国际金融学院副院长
    中国驻冰岛前任大使

  王琦凌
    上海国际金融学院CFA培训中心总监
    特许金融分析师

  姚忻华
    上海国际金融学院教授
    美中投资集团公司副总裁

  胡荣禄
    美林（亚太）有限公司执行总监
    新加坡发展银行上海分行前行长

  谢国诚
    博思艾伦咨询公司大中华区
    金融业务总监

# 序

改革开放以来,中国取得了举世瞩目的成就。随着中国加入世界贸易组织和现代服务业的快速发展,金融市场进一步对外开放,外资银行代表处、外资金融机构纷纷在华开办业务,并逐渐从货币经营发展到资本市场和金融服务各个领域。与此同时,中国的企业也开始走向国际、融入世界。在全球金融竞争日趋激烈的今天,金融英语的普及和掌握,已成为非英语国家人力资源发展水平的重要内容,也是衡量金融中心城市的一个指标。应该说,中国在这一方面人力资源建设中存在着不足之处,尚有很大的发展空间。

《金融英语》教材在这一背景下出版,十分及时。首先,国际金融体系基本上是以英美金融体系为基础确定游戏规则的,这套教材从策划、编写到培训、考试,也基本上遵循这一体系。这与目前国内不少同类教材有所不同。同时,这套教材力求符合国际金融混业经营的特点和新巴塞尔协议的原则,注重实务,涉及商业银行、投资、金融衍生品、保险等多元化金融业务,不仅可帮助银行从业人员、金融专业学生及其他金融行业工作者提高金融专业英语水平,也可帮助人们更好地理解金融创新和新的金融理念。

《金融英语》教材的编者均为来自著名跨国金融机构和金融教育机构的资深专家。他们精心编写,经典选材,避免了从本土市场的角度来理解与开发金融市场的局限性,也有利于提高金融人才与国际接轨的程度。

希望该书能够成为帮助读者和学者更好更快地掌握金融英语和金融知识的有用教材。

世界银行常务副行长

# 再版前言

在 2006 年 12 月中国入世的金融业保护期即将到来前夕，为改变我国金融业面临混业经营的严峻挑战，而又缺乏以适应综合金融环境为基础、以提升实战能力为目标的专业金融英语教材的局面，在清华大学出版社的支持配合下，《金融英语》问世了。

2007 年次贷危机爆发、2008 年全球金融危机全面升级，此起彼伏的金融事件和词汇充斥人们的视线。金融尤其是国际金融，以前所未有的程度被世人所关注。善于学习的中华民族懂得一个道理，掌握金融英语是把握财富安全和金融主动权的基础国民能力，因而学习热情也空前高涨。与之不相匹配的是国内同类教材尚存在着三大不足：即实用性不足、新颖性不足与规范性不足。造成目前的教材往往游离国际金融变化的现状，使学生学的与实际用的差距太大。所以，从最初就以实际为研发方针的《金融英语》教材，根据最新变化、应广大读者的要求，我们编写组专门对《金融英语》教材进行了再版修订。

《金融英语》系列教材是与我国建设国际金融中心的国家战略相匹配的重要战略性教材之一。国际经验表明，作为世界商贸与投资理财通则统一语言的英语水平是形成一个国际金融中心的重要语言环境，也是当今经济强国软性基础设施的必要能力建设。1994年,上海国际金融学院建院时就立下了"通金融、精外语、善实务、严自律"的院训。十多年来,学院设立了金融英语专业与课程,培养了大批适用人才,学员范围包括中国银行、花旗银行和美洲银行等国内外金融机构,成为我国20世纪90年代紧缺人才工程在金融人才培训领域的先行者和推进者。

2003年,经上海紧缺人才培训工程联席会议办公室批准(沪紧人培〔2003〕35号),上海国际金融学院负责开展金融英语项目培训。学院花了两年多时间组织国内外金融界、学术界知名资深专家设计与编写《金融英语》系列教材,经过精心策划、市场调研、专家咨询和多次反复修改,已初步形成包括《金融英语(基础类)》、《金融英语(专业类)》和《金融英语(管理类)》系列教材。世界银行时任常务副行长章晟曼先生在百忙中为教材作序,是对我国人力资源能力建设的关注和支持。本教材在清华大学出版社出版后,金融英语不仅列为上海市紧缺人才培训工程的岗位资格证书,而且作为上海市银行同业公会仅有的两个专业培训证书之一在银行业推广。同时,还将本教材作为上海世博金融英语100句的基础教材。几年来通过这一教材的专业培训与自学,受益的金融业高管、员工和大学生已近5万人。金融机构与学员们反映:这本教材不仅能学到金融英语,还能掌握国际金融的最新业态、知识、体系与实务技能。中国人民银行周小川行长和苏宁副行长在2008年陆家嘴论坛期间对金融英语在长三角地区的推广予以关心与支持,充分显示了我国对这一软实力工程的高度重视。

《金融英语(基础类)》教材能使学员在金融基础业务中较熟练地运用英语,熟悉国际金融的基本业务概念、术语及一般的业务程序与原理;听懂日常会话和一般的业务交谈;看懂与金融业务有关的一般文字材料,拟定一般的业务文件;在基础业务中掌握英语基本语法知识;掌握金融英语写作的文风要求,信函和报告的写作方法、规范、跨文化差异和应注意的问题;掌握阅读的技巧,提高学员的理解能力,并掌握各门类中专业词汇的用法;牢固掌握英译汉和汉译英的技巧;掌握金融英语口译的基本技巧,胜任高级别会谈、重大场合即席讲话等类金融活动的口译工作。

教材编写组以上海市紧缺人才培训工程金融英语岗位资格证书考试和金融银行专业技能资格考试为目标,通过先搭建框架,然后在国内外相关专业机构深入调查和开发研究教材,力求体现权威性、专业性和通俗性的统一。教材中以应用型金融英语为主、应试型金融英语为辅,主要突出实务、实用、实战的特点,将读、写、听、译融会贯通。

本教材涉及金融的各个主要领域,理论与实践并重,专业与一般兼顾,金融与英语并举,具体包括商业银行、投资银行、金融衍生品、保险等金融业务的理论与实务,并配有英语听力材料、模拟试题、对话练习、词汇练习、知识测试等专业练习,使教学深入浅出,通俗易懂。

本教材具备培养"金融+英语"双重紧缺人才的特色,在同类教材中处于领先水平。这套教材的出版,在我国东部和南部沿海城市的进一步开放中发挥了较良好的作用,同时对我国西部开发、东北振兴和中部崛起所需的金融英语人才的培养也是十分必要和及时的。

本教材是上海紧缺人才培训工程教学系列丛书,也是金融英语专业技能岗位资格证书考试用书,适合银行、保险、证券、基金等金融从业人员,各类大学金融专业及有志从事金融业务的人员学习、参考之用,也可作为报考金融专业研究生和特许金融分析师(CFA)、注册金融理财师(CFP)、注册金融风险管理师(FRM)的辅助教材。

本次再版中我们根据后金融危机时代的特点作了若干修订。同时为方便学员,将原为网上下载的听力材料改为CD随书。作为一种新的尝试与探索,本教材难免存在诸多不足与疏漏之处,恳请同业专家和广大读者斧正。

《金融英语》考试培训教材编写组
2011年2月16日

# 目录

## Commercial Banking
## 商业银行

**Part I** **The Banking System 银行体系** ········ 1

Introduction 导语 ························· 3

Section A—The People's Bank of China 中国人民银行 ············ 7

Section B—Bank of China 中国四大国有商业银行之一：中国银行 ······ 10

Section C—Bank of America 美国商业银行之一：美洲银行 ······ 12

Listening Material 听力材料 ··········· 14

Sample Examination Questions 模拟试题 ························ 21

**Part II** **Retail Banking: Bank Accounts 私人业务：银行账户** ············ 24

Introduction 导语 ························ 25

Section A—Deposit Accounts 存款账户 ························· 26

Section B—Foreign Currency Deposits 外汇存款 ························· 27

Section C—Deposits by Correspondence 邮寄存款 ························· 28

Section D—Deposit Collections in Different Places 异地存款 ⋯⋯⋯⋯⋯ 28
Section E—Loss Reporting 报失 ⋯⋯⋯⋯⋯⋯⋯⋯⋯⋯⋯⋯⋯⋯⋯ 30
*Listening Material* 听力材料 ⋯⋯⋯⋯⋯⋯⋯⋯⋯⋯⋯⋯⋯⋯⋯⋯ 32
*Sample Examination Questions* 模拟试题 ⋯⋯⋯⋯⋯⋯⋯⋯⋯⋯⋯ 39

**Part Ⅲ    Retail Banking: Loans 私人业务: 贷款** ⋯⋯⋯⋯⋯⋯⋯⋯⋯⋯⋯ 40

Introduction 导语 ⋯⋯⋯⋯⋯⋯⋯⋯⋯⋯⋯⋯⋯⋯⋯⋯⋯⋯⋯⋯⋯ 40
Section A—Housing Loans for Individuals 私人住房贷款 ⋯⋯⋯⋯⋯ 41
Section B—Auto Loans 购车贷款 ⋯⋯⋯⋯⋯⋯⋯⋯⋯⋯⋯⋯⋯⋯ 42
Section C—Education Loans 教育贷款 ⋯⋯⋯⋯⋯⋯⋯⋯⋯⋯⋯⋯ 42
Section D—Secured Personal Loans 以定期存款/国库券做担保的
　　私人贷款 ⋯⋯⋯⋯⋯⋯⋯⋯⋯⋯⋯⋯⋯⋯⋯⋯⋯⋯⋯⋯⋯ 45
Section E—Other Type of Loans 其他私人贷款 ⋯⋯⋯⋯⋯⋯⋯⋯⋯ 47
*Listening Material* 听力材料 ⋯⋯⋯⋯⋯⋯⋯⋯⋯⋯⋯⋯⋯⋯⋯⋯ 49
*Sample Examination Questions* 模拟试题 ⋯⋯⋯⋯⋯⋯⋯⋯⋯⋯⋯ 57

**Part Ⅳ    Retail Banking: Foreign Currency 私人银行业务: 外汇** ⋯⋯⋯⋯⋯ 58

Introduction 导语 ⋯⋯⋯⋯⋯⋯⋯⋯⋯⋯⋯⋯⋯⋯⋯⋯⋯⋯⋯⋯⋯ 59
Section A—Currency Conversion 汇兑 ⋯⋯⋯⋯⋯⋯⋯⋯⋯⋯⋯⋯ 59
Section B—Collection from Abroad 托收 ⋯⋯⋯⋯⋯⋯⋯⋯⋯⋯⋯⋯ 59
Section C—International Remittance of Foreign Currency 国外汇款 ⋯⋯ 60
Section D—Foreign Exchange Dealings for Individuals 私人外汇交易 ⋯⋯ 60
Section E—Automatic Banking of Savings Deposits 自动储蓄
　　存款业务 ⋯⋯⋯⋯⋯⋯⋯⋯⋯⋯⋯⋯⋯⋯⋯⋯⋯⋯⋯⋯⋯⋯ 61
Section F—Multifunctional Debit Card 多功能借记卡 ⋯⋯⋯⋯⋯⋯ 62
Section G—Personal Cheque Deposits 私人支票存款 ⋯⋯⋯⋯⋯⋯⋯ 62
Section H—Safety Deposit Box 保险箱 ⋯⋯⋯⋯⋯⋯⋯⋯⋯⋯⋯⋯ 62
Section I—Fee-based Business 收费业务 ⋯⋯⋯⋯⋯⋯⋯⋯⋯⋯⋯⋯ 62
Section J—Automatic Deposit Service 自动存款服务 ⋯⋯⋯⋯⋯⋯⋯ 63
Section K—Transfer Service for Security Firm 为证券公司提供
　　转账服务 ⋯⋯⋯⋯⋯⋯⋯⋯⋯⋯⋯⋯⋯⋯⋯⋯⋯⋯⋯⋯⋯ 63

*Listening Material* 听力材料 ·················································· 64

*Sample Examination Questions* 模拟试题 ··········································· 74

**Part V Corporate Banking：Loans 公司业务：贷款** ····················· 75

Introduction 导语 ·················································································· 76
Section A—RMB Working Capital Loan 人民币流动资金贷款 ················· 77
Section B—Fixed Asset Loan 固定资产贷款 ············································ 78
Section C—Foreign Currency Loans 外汇贷款 ········································ 79
Section D—Project Financing 项目融资 ················································· 80
Section E—Bill Discount 票据贴现 ······················································· 81
Section F—Syndicated Loan 银团贷款 ·················································· 82
*Listening Material* 听力材料 ································································· 85
*Sample Examination Questions* 模拟试题 ··············································· 95

**Part VI Corporate Banking：Credit Lines；Trade Finance 公司业务：信用额度；商业信贷** ··············································· 96

Introduction 导语 ·················································································· 97
Section A—Credit Line 信用额度 ·························································· 98
Section B—Worldwide Credit 统一授信 ················································· 98
Section C—Export Buyer's Credit 出口买方信贷 ····································· 99
Section D—Export Seller's Credit 出口卖方信贷 ···································· 102
*Listening Material* 听力材料 ······························································· 103
*Sample Examination Questions* 模拟试题 ·············································· 114

**Part VII Corporate Banking：Other Services 公司业务：其他服务** ············ 115

Introduction 导语 ················································································ 115
Section A—Agent Bank Business 委托行业务 ········································ 117
Section B—Trust Loan 委托贷款 ························································· 118
Section C—Financial Advisory Service 财务顾问 ··································· 119
*Listening Material* 听力材料 ······························································· 121
*Sample Examination Questions* 模拟试题 ·············································· 125

# Investment Banking
# 投资银行

**Part I**  **Introduction 导语** ·········· 127

    Section A—The Basics 基本定义 ·········· 129

    Section B—Setting Goals 设立目标 ·········· 131

    Section C—Needs and Money 需求与货币 ·········· 132

    Section D—An Overview of Markets 市场概览 ·········· 133

    Section E—How Suppliers Make Their Money Available? 如何供款 ·········· 139

    Section F—What Suppliers of Money Expect— The Profit Motive 供款人的期望——盈利动机 ·········· 142

    Section G—Buying and Selling The Right to Use Money 买卖货币使用权 ·········· 143

    Section H—How Long Can The "Buyers" Use The Money? 货币"买家"可以使用货币多长时间呢? ·········· 143

    Section I—Can Suppliers Always Be Sure of Getting Their Money Back? 货币使用权的归还 ·········· 144

    Section J—Words and Expressions 术语及解释 ·········· 145

**Part II**  **The Financial Marketplace 金融市场** ·········· 148

    Section A—Introduction 导语 ·········· 148

    Section B—The Participants 入市者 ·········· 149

    Section C—The Places 交易场所 ·········· 149

    Section D—The Products 金融产品 ·········· 152

    Section E—The Term 金融产品的期限 ·········· 152

    Section F—Marketability and Liquidity 适销性及流通性 ·········· 153

    Section G—Words and Expressions 术语及解释 ·········· 153

**Part III**  **Debt Securities 债务型证券** ·········· 159

    Section A—Introduction 导语 ·········· 159

    Section B—General Characteristics of Debt Securities 债务型证券的共性 ·········· 160

    Section C—Short-Term Debt 短期债务 ·········· 163

Section D—Long-Term Debt: Bonds and Debentures 长期债务：政府债券及
　　　　公司债券 ················································································· 165
　　　Section E—Words and Expressions 术语及解释 ·········································· 168

Part IV　Equity Securities 权益型证券 ····························································· 171
　　　Section A—Capital Structure 资本结构 ····················································· 171
　　　Section B—Preferred Shares 优先股 ························································ 172
　　　Section C—Common Shares 普通股 ························································ 173
　　　Section D—Words and Expressions 术语及解释 ·········································· 178

Part V　Research 研究金融市场 ······································································ 180
　　　Section A—The Research Department 研究部门 ········································· 180
　　　Section B—What Buying a Share of Stock Gives Us? 购买股票的意义 ·········· 181
　　　Section C—The Company Under a Microscope 显微镜下的公司 ···················· 182
　　　Section D—How Much Money Is Company Earning? 公司收益情况 ············· 184
　　　Section E—Earnings Available for the Common Shareholders 可分给普通股
　　　　股东的收益 ·········································································· 185
　　　Section F—What Are the Earnings Worth 收益的价值 ································ 186
　　　Section G—Consider the Dividend 股息 ··················································· 187
　　　Section H—Words and Expressions 术语及解释 ·········································· 190

Part VI　Trading 股票交易 ············································································ 191
　　　Section A—Putting Our Knowledge into Action 变知识为行动 ···················· 191
　　　Section B—Opening an Account 开户 ······················································ 191
　　　Section C—What the Client Should Expect from the
　　　　Securities Firm? 证券公司提供的服务 ······································ 193
　　　Section D—Stock Symbols 证券交易代码 ················································· 195
　　　Section E—Where Are The Company's Shares Traded? 交易场所 ················· 196
　　　Section F—The Quote 报价 ···································································· 198
　　　Section G—Placing an Order 下达买卖指令 ·············································· 199
　　　Section H—The Reporting 公司报告 ························································ 201

Section I—Measuring Movements in the Overall Market 交易指数 ……… 205
Section J—Words and Expressions 术语及解释 ……… 205

**Exercises 练习** ……… 209
Listening Comprehension Exercises 听力综合练习 ……… 209
Speaking Exercises 对话练习 ……… 210
Skill-building Exercises—Research 阅读与研究练习 ……… 212
Skill-building Exercises—Writing and Speaking 说写练习 ……… 212
Skill-building Exercises—Writing 写作练习 ……… 212
Building Vocabulary Exercises 词汇练习 ……… 213
Test Your Knowledge 知识测试 ……… 219
Case Study 案例分析 ……… 223
*Sample Examination Questions* 模拟试题 ……… 225

# Derivatives
# 金融衍生品

**Part I** **Introduction 导语** ……… 227
Section A—A Common Business Problem 一个普遍的商业难题 ……… 231
Section B—What Are Derivatives? 金融衍生品的定义 ……… 235
Section C—Uses of Derivatives 金融衍生品的用途 ……… 236
Section D—Words and Expressions 术语及解释 ……… 240

**Part II** **Options 期权** ……… 242
Section A—The Basics 基本定义 ……… 242
Section B—Options Are Binding Contracts 期权是契约 ……… 243
Section C—Equity Options 股权期权 ……… 243
Section D—Buying Options 买入期权 ……… 246
Section E—Selling Options 卖出期权 ……… 247
Section F—You Bought an Option and Now You Want to Get Your Money Out 套现 ……… 251
Section G—You Have Written an Option (Original Seller) and You Want out of the Contract 赎回 ……… 252

  Section H—Time Decay of Put and Call Options 期权买卖的
    时间衰减 ················································································ 254
  Section I—Valuing Options 期权估价 ··············································· 254
  Section J—Why We Use Equity Options? 使用股权期权的原因 ········· 256
  Section K—Words and Expressions 术语及解释 ······························· 258

**Part III  Futures and Forwards 期货及远期** ········································· 263
  Section A—The Basics 基础知识 ······················································ 264
  Section B—Futures Contracts 期货合同 ··········································· 264
  Section C—Forward Contracts 远期合同 ·········································· 271
  Section D—Margins 保证金 ······························································ 271
  Section E—Long and Short 多头及空头交易 ····································· 273
  Section F—Foreign Currencies 外汇 ················································· 274
  Section G—Futures and Forward Contracts—Similarities and
    Differences 期货合同与远期合同的相同与不同之处 ·················· 275
  Section H—Words and Expressions 术语及解释 ······························· 278

**Exercises 练习** ······················································································ 286
  Listening Comprehension Exercises 听力综合练习 ··························· 286
  Speaking Exercises 对话练习 ··························································· 287
  Skill-building Exercises—Writing and Speaking 说写练习 ················ 288
  Skill-building Exercises—Vocabulary 词汇练习 ································ 289
  Test Your Knowledge 知识测试 ························································· 291
  Case Study—The Impacts of Subprime Mortgage Crisis 案例分析——次贷
    危机的影响 ················································································ 294
  Sample Examination Questions 模拟试题 ········································ 297

# Insurance
# 保　　险

**Part I  Introduction 导语** ···································································· 299
  Section A—What Insurance Is and Why We Need It? 什么是保险？
    为什么需要保险？ ···································································· 303

Section B—How Insurance Works? 保险的作用 …… 304
Section C—The Fundamentals? 基础知识 …… 305
Section D—Words and Expressions 术语及解释 …… 313

**Part Ⅱ　The Insurance Market 保险市场** …… 316
Section A—Who Supplies Insurance? 谁提供保险? …… 316
Section B— Who Buys Insurance? 谁购买保险? …… 316
Section C—Where Do We Buy Insurance? 何处购买保险? …… 316
Section D—What Do We Pay for Insurance? 保险的成本(保费) …… 317
Section E—How Do We Buy Insurance? 如何购买保险 …… 318
Section F—Words and Expressions 术语及解释 …… 323

**Part Ⅲ　Life Insurance 人寿保险** …… 324
Section A—Introduction 导语 …… 325
Section B—Life Insurance That Provides Protection Only 只提供保障的寿险 …… 326
Section C—Life Insurance That Provides Both Protection and Savings 提供保障兼储蓄功能的寿险 …… 328
Section D—Some Additional Features of Life Insurance Policies 其他种类的寿险 …… 329
Section E—What Does It Cost? 决定保险费的因素 …… 329
Section F—The Pay Out 赔付 …… 330
Section G—Words and Expressions 术语及解释 …… 331

**Part Ⅳ　Personal Property and Liability Insurance 个人财产及责任险** …… 333
Section A—Introduction 导语 …… 333
Section B—Insuring the Building 房屋保险 …… 335
Section C—Protecting Yourself Against Liability for Damage Caused to Others 第三者损失赔偿责任险 …… 336
Section D—Insuring the Contents (of Your Home) 家庭财产保险 …… 337
Section E—What Is not Covered? 家庭财产保险中不包括的项目 …… 340
Section F—Words and Expressions 术语及解释 …… 343

## Part V Automobile Insurance 汽车保险 ········································· 344

Section A—Types of Automobile Insurance 车险的种类 ················· 344

Section B—Who Is at Fault? 谁承担过失 ····································· 345

Section C—Protecting Yourself Against Liability for Damage Caused to Others 公共责任保险 ········································ 346

Section D—Covering Medical Costs 投保医疗费用 ······················· 346

Section E—Protecting Your Vehicle 车险是汽车的保障 ·················· 347

Section F—Other Kinds of Coverage That Are Readily Available 其他种类的车险 ························································ 348

Section G—You've Had an Accident, Now What? 车险的索赔步骤 ···························································· 348

Section H—How Much Will Auto Insurance Cost? 车险的成本 ······· 350

Section I—Words and Expressions 术语及解释 ··························· 352

**Exercises 练习** ·················································································· 355

Listening Comprehension Exercises 听力综合练习 ····················· 355

Speaking Exercises 对话练习 ···················································· 356

Building Vocabulary Exercises 词汇练习 ···································· 358

Test Your Knowledge 知识测试 ················································ 360

*Sample Examination Questions* 模拟试题 ··································· 362

# Elective Course A Ethics
# 选修内容 A 金融职业伦理

1. Ethical Behaviour ········································································· 365
2. Politics ························································································ 366
3. Good Ethics Means Good Business ················································ 367
4. Ethics and Decision-making ··························································· 369

Case Study Lincoln Savings and Loan Association ···························· 374

Questions for Discussion ································································· 382

## Elective Course B  Money Laundering
## 选修内容 B  反洗钱

1. Money Laundering and Crime ································································ 383
2. Benefits of Laundering Money ································································ 384
3. Some History ···················································································· 385
4. Money Laundering Schemes ··································································· 388
5. The Money Laundering Process ······························································ 392
6. Preventing Money Laundering ································································ 394
7. Customer due Diligence—Know Your Customer ········································· 397
8. Effects of Money Laundering ································································· 398
9. Case Studies ····················································································· 398

# Commercial Banking

## 商业银行

## Part I

### The Banking System  银行体系

Commercial banks are the foundation on which a successful economy is built. They finance growth and facilitate trade and commerce.

## Commercial Banking　商业银行

We use our bank accounts to save money and pay our bills.

Banks help us get the money we need to build houses, apartments, offices and factories and to buy the raw materials we need to produce our goods.

International trade is made much easier by services provided by banks.

Part Ⅰ—The Banking System  银行体系

## Introduction  导语

Whether we are the president of a Fortune 500 company, a school teacher, a housewife or a taxi driver, a strong and smoothly functioning banking system will help make it much easier to do our everyday business and accomplish our goals.

Banks help us manage our money, save for retirement, and finance our homes, cars and businesses. Our government uses a special bank to help manage the economy so that our standard of living will be going up steadily.

### Money, Banks and the Economy

We need money to build new homes to live in and new factories to produce the goods we need in our everyday life and to trade with other countries for their products. Banks are one of our most important sources of money for these purposes. However, when our desire to buy goods and services exceeds our economy's ability to produce them, the prices of those goods and services rise. We call this inflation.

If prices start to rise too fast, it would create problems for individuals, families and businesses. If left unchecked, inflation would stop an economy from growing and lower people's standard of living.

When this happens, the government usually moves to control prices (inflation) by reducing demand until the country's ability to produce improves. One of the tools is the banking system. The government uses its central bank to reduce the amount of money that commercial banks have to lend, and to increase the cost of money that they lend.

On the other hand, if an economy is not growing fast enough, the government can use the banking system to encourage people to expand their businesses by lowering interest rate so that more money can be borrowed.

## FM 96 Breaking News

We interrupt our regularly scheduled program to bring you this important development. In a surprising move, the country's central bank raised the interest rate it charges on loans made to commercial banks. It also announced sweeping changes to the rules governing lending by commercial banks for the purchase of homes and apartments.

We now go to Sally Chan, our reporter in Beijing, who has just come out of the news conference about the changes.

**Announcer:** Sally, these seem to be rather dramatic moves on the part of the People's Bank. What prompted such sudden actions?

**Sally:** The spokesman for the Bank told us that there was great concern that the property market was becoming overheated by rampant speculation. According the Governor, the sharp rise in real estate prices in major cities like Shanghai and Beijing was creating unacceptable inflationary pressure.

**Announcer:** Was everyone caught off guard by this action or was it expected?

**Sally:** The changes were completely unanticipated by the market. Despite the widespread publicity about rising prices, no one believed that the central bank would move so quickly and decisively. The supply of new

## Part I—The Banking System 银行体系

|  | apartments had been increasing steadily. It was generally believed that the oversupply would limit rising prices. |
|---|---|
| **Announcer:** | Did you learn why the Bank felt so important to make the move now? |
| **Sally:** | The Bank seemed to be mainly targeting at speculators who were buying up a large amount of real estate in the hope of flipping it for quick profits. Unfortunately, the ordinary home buyers got caught as well. |
| **Announcer:** | What would be the effect on a young couple trying to buy their first home? |
| **Sally:** | Two things. First, they have to come up with a much larger down-payment. This means that saving money to buy that first home would be longer and harder. Second, the commercial banks would undoubtedly raise the interest rates that they charge on mortgage, so the monthly payments would be more, and the amount of interest they have to pay for the loan would increase higher. The cost of home ownership is, therefore, going up sharply. It might put many people's dream of homeownership out of reach. |
| **Announcer:** | What would happen to the real estate market? |
| **Sally:** | Several commercial bank officers with whom I spoke after the press conference explained that we could see some problems as speculators facing with higher borrowing costs, experience difficulties in cash flow. |

### Costs Are Going Up

The company which built this factory will face higher construction costs as a result of the decision made by the central bank to raise interest rates.

In addition, it would cost more to borrow money from the bank to pay for the raw materials to its suppliers and wages to its workers.

## Dialogue: Borrowing money to buy a home

**Mr. Roberts:** We are really anxious to move into our own home, but Glenda and I are very concerned about the announcement this morning by the People's Bank. What do you think we should do?

**John:** Your concern is quite right. The action by the central bank means that the cost of mortgage is going up. This means that the monthly payment and the total amount of interest you will have to pay over the 20-year term will be much higher.

**Mrs. Roberts:** I don't understand how this would affect us. I believe that the People's Bank just raised the interest rate it charges on commercial banks!

**John:** That is true. However, when our bank's cost of money rises, we have no choice but to increase the interest rate that we charge our customers.

**Mrs. Roberts:** Has your bank raised mortgage rates?

**John:** No, nothing has been announced yet, but I expect that it will happen in a day or two. The commercial banks usually respond very quickly to actions taken by the central bank.

**Mr. Roberts:** How much do you think the increase will be, and how will that affect our monthly payment?

**John:** The mortgage rate will probably go up by 0.05%. Your loan is for RMB 1,000,000 and the term is 20 years. Your monthly payment will go up by about RMB 300 per month (about 4%). Not too much really. Your monthly payment is still quite reasonable.

This unit is about the structure of bank organizations and how to describe them. We will hear three bankers describing the structure of their organizations respectively.

Part Ⅰ—The Banking System  银行体系

John Gilbert, a mortage specialist, explains to Mr. and Mrs. Roberts, who plan to buy a new home, the effect of the central bank's decision to raise interest rates and increase minimum amount of down payment.

## Section A—The People's Bank of China  中国人民银行

Listen to the introduction to the People's Bank of China.

### Skill-building exercise #A1—Vocabulary

Look at the words in the left-hand column taken from the text. Match them with the words from those in the right-hand column.

1. A central bank      a financial institution designated by the central government to formulate and implement monetary policy and to supervise and regulate the financial industry
2. Function      a special activity
3. Formulate      supply and distribute
4. Implement      official document giving permission
5. Monetary policy      create in a precise form
6. Issue      carry out

## Commercial Banking  商业银行

7. Administer — a general term for banks, securities, futures and insurance companies
8. Circulation — policy for currency
9. License — control and direct
10. Supervise — put into action
11. Financial institutions — of or related to government money
12. Regulate — go round continuously
13. Financial market — a government body to oversee foreign exchange
14. Foreign exchange — information in numbers
15. Gold reserves — pay what is due
16. Fiscal — gold put aside for later use
17. Payment — system of buying and selling foreign money
18. Settlement — paying or being paid
19. Statistical data — market for money and finance
20. State Administration of Foreign Exchange — watch or check

### Skill-building exercise #A2—Listening comprehension

1. Listen to the passage again and tell us what departments there are in the People's Bank of China.

2. What supporting departments are there in the People's Bank of China?

3. How many branches, sub-branches and county-level offices are there in the People's Bank of China? What other affiliates can you name?

### Skill-building exercise #A3—Reading comprehension

Put most simply, the Federal Reserve System is the central bank of the United States. The Congress created the Federal Reserve through a law passed in 1913, which was charged with the responsibility to foster a sound banking system and a healthy economy. This remains, today, the broad mission of the Fed and its component parts: the 12 Federal Reserve Banks nationwide, each serving a specific region of the country; and the Board of Governors in Washington, D.C., set up to oversee the Fed System. To accomplish its mission, the Fed serves as a banker's bank and the government's bank, as a regulator of financial institutions and as the nation's money manager, performing a vast array of functions that affect the economy, the financial system, and ultimately, each of us.

### *A bank for banks*

Each of the 12 Fed Banks provides services to financial institutions that are similar to the services that banks and thrifts provide to businesses and individuals. By serving as a "banker's bank", the Fed helps ensure the safety and efficiency of the payment system, the critical pipeline through which all financial transactions in the economy flow.

### *The government's bank*

Another important Federal Reserve responsibility is serving the nation's largest banking customer—the US Government. As the government's bank of fiscal agent, the Fed processes a variety of financial transactions involving trillions of dollars. The Federal Reserve also issues the nation's coin and paper currency.

### *Supervisor and regulator*

As a regulator, the Fed formulates rules that govern the conduct of financial institutions. As a supervisor, the Federal Reserve examines and monitors institutions to help ensure that they operate in a safe and sound manner and comply with the laws and rules that apply to them. The Fed's supervisory duties are carried out on a regional basis.

### *Money manager*

The most important of Fed's responsibilities is to formulate and carrying out monetary policy. In this role, the Fed acts as the nation's "money manager"—working to balance the flow of money and credit with the needs of economy. Simply stated, too much money in the economy can lead to inflation, while too little can stifle economic growth. As the nation's "money manager", the Fed seeks to strike a balance between these two extremes, or, in other words, to foster economic growth while maintaining price stability.

The control lever that the Fed uses in this process is the "reserves" that banks and thrifts must hold.

The Fed has three tools for affecting reserves:

### *Reserve requirements*

Altering the percentage of deposits that institutions must set aside as reserves can have a powerful impact on the flow of money and credit. Lowering reserve requirements can lead to more money, which will be injected into the economy by freeing up funds previously set aside. Raising the requirements freezes funds that financial institutions could otherwise pump into the economy. The Fed, however, seldom changes reserve requirements because such changes will have a dramatic effect on institutions and the economy.

*Discount rate*

An increase in the discount rate can inhibit lending and investing activities of financial institutions by making it more expensive for institutions to obtain funds or reserves. But, if the funds are readily available from the sources other than the Fed's "discount window", a discount rate change won't directly affect the flow of money and credit. Even so, a change in the discount rate can be an important signal of the Fed's policy direction.

*Open market operations*

The most flexible, and therefore most important monetary policy tools are open market operations—the purchase and sale of government securities by the Fed.

Assignment: Discuss among yourselves on the following three questions:

1. What is the role of the Fed?
2. Compare the Fed with PBC and tell the similarities and differences between them.
3. Tell us about the revised role of PBC.

## Section B—Bank of China  中国四大国有商业银行之一：中国银行

Dialogue:

In this section you will hear a dialogue between a reporter and a vice governor of BOC on the organizational structure of BOC.

Look at these headings while listening. Which ones does the Vice Governor talk about and in which order?

- The Supervision Departments
- Top Management
- Supervisory Committees
- Business Division
- The Board of Directors
- The Supporting Division
- The Management Division

## Skill-building exercise #B1—Listening comprehension

Listen again to the vice governor. While listening, write in the boxes the names of these three operational divisions and list the main responsibility for each division.

## Skill-building exercise #B2—Vocabulary

Look at the terms in the left-hand column. Match each with its correct definition in the right-hand column.

1. Board of directors          finding a solution for...(funds)
2. Top management              management of non-performing asset
3. Asset liability             banking department to control funds
4. Budget                      obedience
5. Audit                       banking service for the general public
6. Remuneration                a way in which something works
7. Operation                   banking service for corporations
8. Corporate banking           pay or reward for one's work
9. Retail banking              official examination of accounts
10. Compliance                 a group of people controlling a company
11. Treasury                   the state of being responsible for debts
12. NPA management             the highest management authority
13. Workout                    a plan of how money will be spent over a period of time

### Skill-building exercise #B3—Speaking

Listen to the interview of the vice governor on the history of BOC. Discuss with a partner on what impresses you the most.

## Section C—Bank of America  美国商业银行之一：美洲银行

You are going to listen to the spokesman of the Bank of America (Asia). Look at the following list of banking services. Put a tick next to those he mentions.

### Skill-building exercise #C1—Listening comprehension

| | |
|---|---|
| Deposit accounts | |
| Individual and corporate loans | |
| Trade finance | |
| Factoring | |
| Leasing packages | |
| Insurance | |
| Investment | |
| Foreign exchange | |
| Online banking service | |
| Bullion | |

### Skill-building exercise #C2—Listening comprehension

Listen to the extracts of the speech by Ken Lewis, Chairman and CEO of the Bank of America. Work with a partner and note down what you think Ken says, fill in the blanks instead of the words in.

1. What is happening in our market is _____.

2. To that point, the industry has been adding _____.

3. Expansion of choice and access at the local level is the result of new and growing delivery channels, as well as _____.

4. The ability of banks to expand into new markets through de novo branching or

## Part I—The Banking System 银行体系

interstate merger has _____.

5. While the number of commercial banks dropped by almost half over the past 70 years, the number of bank offices has increased _____.

6. Obviously, the proliferation of other channels, such as ATMs, telephone banking and online banking _____.

7. As our industry consolidates nationally and expands locally, the dual banking system has been a key _____.

8. That uniform regulatory standard provides tremendous benefits to national banking companies, their customers and shareholders, including _____.

9. Support of uniform national standards must not be confused with _____.

10. We require our own associates to uphold the highest standards of _____.

### Skill-building exercise #C3—Reading comprehension

Read the text of the extracts from Ken Lewis's speech. Consult dictionary on those words you don't know and present your findings to the class or group.

### Assignment: Class presentation

You are going to make a short presentation on your bank or company. Look at the list of points below and decide the order you will use in your presentation. Then compare your order with that of a partner and discuss the differences. Now make a short presentation of the structure of your bank or company. Use any visual aids, such as diagrams, to help you.

- Range of services
- Specialized products
- Financial performance
- Geographical representation
- Structure

Commercial Banking  商业银行

## Listening Material 听力材料

### The People's Bank of China

The People's Bank of China (PBC) is the central bank of the People's Republic of China. Its chief mandate is to formulate and implement monetary policy and supervise and regulate the financial industry. The PBC was established on December 1, 1948 based on the consolidation of the former Huabei Bank, the Beihai Bank and the Xibei Peasant Bank. In September 1983, the State Council decided to endow the PBC with the power of a central bank. The Law of the People's Republic of China on the People's Bank of China passed on March 18, 1995 legally confirmed the PBC's central bank status. The PBC's main functions include: formulating and implementing monetary policy; issuing and administering the circulation of the currency; licensing and supervising financial institutions; regulating financial markets; managing official foreign exchange and gold reserves; acting as fiscal agent; maintaining payment and settlement system; collecting and analyzing financial statistical data; participating in international financial activities at the capacity of the central bank; and overseeing the State Administration of Foreign Exchange. Located in Beijing, the head office of the PBC consists of 13 functional departments, namely, Governor's Office, Legal Department, Monetary Policy Department, Banking Supervision Department I, Banking Supervision Department II, Department of Non-Bank Financial Institutions, Department of Cooperative Finance, Statistics Department, Accounting and Treasury Department, Payment System and Technology Development Department, International Department, Internal Auditing Department, and Personnel and Education Department. In order to ensure scientific formulation and implementation of monetary policy and effective supervision of financial institutions, the functional departments are complemented by five supporting departments, namely, the Research Bureau, the Bureau of Currency, Gold and Silver Administration, the Bureau of State Treasury, the Security Office, and the Training Center. The PBC maintains two operations offices, nine regional branches, 326 prefecture-level sub-branches and 1827 county-level sub-branches. Other affiliates of the PBC include the Bank Note Printing Company, the Clearing Center, China Foreign Exchange Trading Center and a number of representative offices in major international financial centers.

R (Reporter): It's very nice of you to meet me. Since your bank has scored an excellent performance, the general public is increasingly interested in your bank. Could you please say something of your organizational structure first?

V (Vice Governor): With pleasure. First of all, we are under the leadership of the Board of Directors. Parallel to the body of Top Management, there are five committees namely: the Asset-Liability Management and Budget Committee, the Risk Review Committee namely, the Auditing Committee, the Business Development and Co-ordination Committee and the Remuneration Committee.

We have three divisions at the operational level. The business division is the largest, since it is composed of nine departments. They are respectively Corporate Banking Department, Financial Institutions Department, Retail Banking Department, Credit Card Center, Settlement Department, Treasury Department, NPA Management Department and Workout Department and Banking Department.

The Management Division is headed by the Governor's Office, then the Asset-Liability Management Department, the Risk Management Department, the Accounting Department, the Investment Management Department and the Overseas Business Department.

The Supporting Division at the operational level includes the Human Resources Department, the IT Department, the Legal and Compliance Department, the Institute of International Finance, the Clearing Center and the General Affairs Department.

The Supervisory level is consisted of three departments, which are the Auditing Department, the Inspection Department and the Compliance Department.

R: Thank you very much. We now have a general picture of how your bank is organized.

## Vice-Governor, Bank of China

R: Mr. Vice Governor, I was told that your bank is said to be the oldest one in China. When was it founded?

V: Yes, our bank has been existed for 92 years since 1912. After the establishment of the Provisional Government of the Republic of China, Dr. Sun Yatsen, the Provisional President, sanctioned the change of the Da Qing Bank into the Bank of China, with functions as a central bank. On February 5, the Bank of China (BOC)

R: started operations at Number 3, Hankou Road, Shanghai, the premises of the former Da Qing Bank. Afterwards, the Bank of China issued bank notes.

R: Did BOC attach great importance to its reputation even in the early days?

V: Yes, I would like to tell you that in 1916 when the Government of the Northern Warlords wired to BOC the Order to Suspend Redemption of Bank Notes for Silver, to maintain the Bank's creditworthiness, BOC Shanghai Branch rejected the order and continued the redemption as usual,

which not only halted a run on the Bank, but also enormously enhanced the reputation and prestige of BOC.

R: When did BOC become a government chartered international exchange bank?

V: In 1928 BOC became a government chartered international exchange bank.

R: When was BOC's London office established?

V: BOC London Agency was established in 1929. It was also the first overseas branch of Chinese banks. From then on, BOC built up its global network with 34 overseas branches opening within two decades.

R: Your bank suspended its operation for sometime because of the civil war, as I understand it. But, when did you resume your business?

V: On 5 June 1949 BOC resumed normal business operations shortly after the new government took over the bank. The headquarters moved from Shanghai to Beijing in December, 1949.

R: Was the board of directors formed soon afterwards?

V: Yes, the first meeting of the new board of directors of BOC of New China was held in Beijing (on 9 April 1950). Mr. Nan Hanchen was appointed Chairman of the Board and Madam He Xiangning Chief Supervisor.

R: When BOC was authorized to handle foreign exchange for New China?

V: In October 1953 the State Council promulgated an act, which authorized the Bank of China to be the specialized foreign exchange bank.

R: When did your bank issue your first overseas bonds? Was it the first bond PR of China ever issued abroad?

V: On 6 November 1984, BOC successfully issued 20 billion yen of Samurai bonds in Japan, which was the first overseas bond issued by modern China. By the end of 2001, BOC had issued bonds in the international capital market 27 times, raising funds in excess of US $ 5 billion. BOC is now an established issuer.

R: Did you start the incorporation of foreign-funded enterprises into the foreign exchanges sales system in 1993?

V: In 1993 China initiated a process of foreign exchange system reform and hence captured the world's interest. BOC played a critical role in the unification of exchange rates, foreign exchange purchases and sales, the incorporation of foreign-funded enterprises into the foreign exchange sales system, etc.. In 1994, BOC embarked on a transformation from a specialized bank to a wider based state-owned commercial bank.

R: And you became a note-issuing bank in Hong Kong shortly afterwards.

V: Yes, on 1 May 1994, BOC became the third note-issuing bank in Hong Kong by issuing its first BOC Hong Kong Dollar notes. In October 1995, BOC similarly issued Macao Pataca notes. The issuing of both Hong Kong Dollar and Macao Pataca notes helped stabilize the financial markets of Hong Kong and Macao; it also reflected BOC's substantial financial strength.

R: I understand that in 1998 your Hong Kong branch merged with 10 other banks and became an investment bank.

V: No, it was later. In 1998 BOC International Holdings Ltd., the wholly owned subsidiary of BOC specializing in investment banking, was located and incorporated in Hong Kong. This is the most internationalized investment bank established overseas by the Chinese banking industry, Hence, it has the strongest professional team, the largest international distribution and retail network, and the most assets under management. It was on 1 October 2001 that the Bank of China (Hong Kong) Ltd. was incorporated as a result of the merging of 10 member banks of the former BOC Group, marking a new level of BOC's operations in Hong Kong, and a critical move forward for the restructuring of BOC.

R: It was your 90th birthday in 2002.

## Commercial Banking 商业银行

V: Yeh, on 4 February 2002, BOC celebrated solemnly its 90th anniversary. In July 2002, BOC Hong Kong (Holdings) was successfully listed on the Hong Kong Stock Exchange. The USD 2.8 billion offering was over-subscribed by 7.5 times. The deal was a landmark in the development of the Bank of China and a significant move in the reform of China's banking industry.

R: I am really impressed. Thank you very much for your introduction and your time. I wish your bank a second successful 90 years.

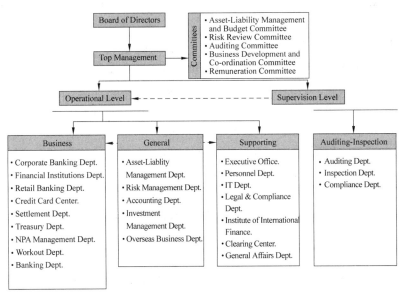

## Ken Lewis, Chairman and Chief Executive Officer, Bank of America (Asia)

Hong Kong has been our home for 90 years. Our story started in February 1912 when the Bank of America (Asia) was founded by prominent Chinese businessmen as the Bank of Canton-the first Chinese-owned bank in the territory. Its growth parallelled Hong Kong's development and we thrived until the Great Depression in the 1930s and the Second World War in the 40s disrupted our operations. Former staff rebuilt the Bank when Hong Kong was liberated in 1945, and soon we were back in business.

Over the next four decades, we continued to expand, establishing a network of branches, building a stable customer base and offering an increasing number of consumer and commercial banking products. Following the acquisition by Security Pacific National Bank in 1988, Bank of Canton was renamed as Security Pacific Asian Bank.

In 1992, we became part of Bank of America upon Security Pacific Corporation's merger with Bank of America Corporation. We changed its name to Bank of America (Asia) Ltd.. in 1993. In 1998, Bank of America Corporation merged with Nations Bank Corporation to form the new Bank of America. In terms of net assets, having 15 branches in Hong Kong and Macao, Bank of America (Asia) is the most profitable and the largest subsidiary of Bank of America outside of the US.

The bank offers a wide range of consumer and commercial banking products and services. These include a full array of deposit and loan products, trade finance, foreign exchange, factoring, leasing, insurance, investment, online and wireless banking services. The affiliated companies of the Bank in Hong Kong are QBE Hongkong & Shanghai Insurance Limited and Inchroy Credit Corporation. QBE Hong Kong & Shanghai Insurance Limited, a joint venture between Bank of America (Asia) Ltd. And QBE Insurance, offers a comprehensive range of personal and commercial insurance services. Inchroy is a joint venture of our parent bank with Inchcape Pacific plc that offers motor vehicle and equipment finance, and consumer loans.

You can depend on us because we are well regarded in the industry. Moody's Investors Service has also rated our long-term Hong Kong dollar deposits as Aa3. Bank of America (Asia)'s parent company, Bank of America, is one of the world's leading financial services companies. The bank is committed to making banking work for customers like it never has before. It has full-service consumer and commercial operations in 21 states and the District of Columbia, serving 30 million households and two million businesses. Internationally, it operates in 30 countries around the world.

## The spokesman for Bank of America (Asia) continues

So, what is happening in our market is precisely what should be happening: Regulatory, technology and market forces are working together to achieve the elimination of excess capacity and inefficiency and the increase of competition where needed. To that point, the industry has been adding more than 150 new banks a year over the past decade.

Expansion of choice and access at the local level is the result of new and growing delivery channels, as well as the growth of non-bank financial service competitors. The ability of banks to expand into new markets through de novo branching or interstate merger has had a very positive effect on access to financial services.

While the number of commercial banks dropped by almost half over the past 70 years, the number of bank offices has increased more than five-fold, to more than 74,000, an all-time high. Obviously, the proliferation of other channels, such as ATMs, telephone banking and online banking amplify this effect.

As our industry consolidates nationally and expands locally, the dual banking system has been a key factor underlying the innovation and strength of the US banking system. Both federal and state charters have their advantages. The critical element of the system for those banks that have chosen a national charter is the opportunity to do business in multiple states under a single, uniform set of laws, rules and regulations. That uniform regulatory standard provides tremendous benefits to national banking companies, their customers and shareholders, including certainty and predictability of rules across multiple jurisdictions, greatly reduced execution risk, compliance risk and, ultimately, cost.

Support of uniform national standards must not be confused with the desire for lower standards. We support strong federal banking regulation and strong consumer protections. We require our own associates to uphold the highest standards of business conduct at all times. And we take swift, decisive action when individuals fall short of those standards.

# Sample Examination Questions 模拟试题

## Vocabulary

1. Use the following words or phrases in a sentence.

    a. fiscal

    b. reserves

    c. circulate

    d. workout

    e. domestic

    f. gold

2. Define the following words and phrases and provide a Chinese translation.

    a. department

    b. monetary policy

    c. circulation

    d. issue

    e. reserve requirements

    f. discount rate

    g. open market operations

    h. settlement

## Understanding

1. What is the People's Bank of China?
2. What is the role of the People's Bank of China?
3. What is the Federal Reserve System?
4. Why do governments use central banks as part of their economic management strategy?
5. What tools do central banks have to manage the economy?
6. What is the difference between fiscal and monetary policy and what are the

advantages and disadvantages of each?

7. How do actions by the central bank affect commercial banks?

8. By acting as the "bankers' bank", what do central banks ensure will happen?

9. What is the mission of the Federal Reserve System?

10. What are the differences between corporate banking and retail banking?

11. What is the function of the board of directors?

12. Why is it important for a bank to have a good reputation and what steps can it take to ensure that it maintains a good reputation?

Answer to the questions

#A2

I

- Governor's Office
- Legal Department
- Monetary Policy Department
- Banking Supervision Department I
- Banking Supervision Department II
- Department of Non-Bank Financial Institutions
- Department of Cooperative Finance, Statistics Department
- Accounting and Treasury Department
- Payment System and Technology Development Department, International Department
- Internal Auditing Department
- Personnel and Education Department

II

There are five supporting departments, namely, the Research Bureau, the Bureau of Currency, Gold and Silver Administration, the Bureau of State Treasury, the Security Office, and the Training Center.

III

The PBC maintains two operations offices, nine regional branches, 326 prefecture-level sub-branches and 1827 county-level sub-branches. Other affiliates of the PBC include the Bank

Note Printing Company, the Clearing Center, China Foreign Exchange Trading Center and a number of representative offices in major international financial centers.

#C2

1. exactly what are happening: regulatory, technology and market forces will work together

2. no more than 20 new banks over the last few years

3. the new banking competitors

4. a bad effect on the entering into financial service

5. no less than three-fold, to over 63,000, an all-time high

6. affected this change

7. reason for reforming the American banking system

8. certain rules across jurisdictions, great reduction of risk and cost

9. a wish for better standard

10. professional behavior at all times

Commercial Banking 商业银行

# Part II

## Retail Banking: Bank Accounts
## 私人业务：银行账户

Don't leave your money in a piggy bank or under your mattress. Put it in a bank account and watch it grow!

### Commercial banks

Provide a wide range of services to individuals and their families.

We can save our money in bank accounts, get cash when we need it from automated teller machines (ATM) and borrow money to pay for important purchases.

Part II—Retail Banking: Bank Accounts  私人业务：银行账户

## Introduction  导语

This chapter explains various ways in which the individuals can save money in a bank. It describes the advantages of each type of deposit.

We see how we can use our bank accounts to help manage our financial affairs, pay our bills and save money for achieving our goals.

While we hope that we never run into a problem, the section explains the procedures should our passbook, debit card or certificate of deposit get lost or stolen.

Foreign currency deposits, an important service by commercial banks, is also covered.

## Section A—Deposit Accounts  存款账户

### Skill-building exercise #A1—Listening and speaking

Listen twice to a dialogue between a customer and a bank teller on savings deposit, and then have a role-play with your partner in reproducing the dialogue.

### Skill-building exercise #A2—Speaking

Give definition in English to the following words:

1. savings deposit
2. lump-sum deposit
3. lump-sum withdrawal
4. time deposit
5. passbook
6. small savings
7. principal receiving
8. debit card
9. certificate
10. maturity

### Skill-building exercise #A3—Speaking

Listen twice to a dialogue between a customer and a teller on time deposit, and then have a role-play with your partner in reproducing the dialogue.

### Skill-building exercise #A4—Vocabulary

Give definition in English to the following words:

1. installment
2. principal
3. certificate of deposit

4. default
5. maturity
6. sub-division
7. consumption
8. telephone banking

## Section B—Foreign Currency Deposits  外汇存款

### Skill-building exercise #B1—Listening comprehension

You are going to hear Richard King, the Director of Deposit Department, Who is giving an outline of foreign currency deposits. As you listen, look at these headings. Then discuss among yourselves and see if you can retell each heading.

- Types of foreign currency deposits the bank provides
- Types of accounts the bank operates
- Kinds of foreign currency the bank accepts
- Kinds of foreign currency deposit the bank offers

### Skill-building exercise #B2—Understanding

Look through the following list of currency codes. Then write the appropriate currency code next to the country or region to which it relates in the grid below.

HKD  DEM  SEK  CHF  BEF  CAD  USD  GBP  ITL  NLG  NOK  DKK  FRF  JPY  AUD  ESP

| Currency code | Country or region | Currency code | Country or region |
|---|---|---|---|
|  | Holland |  | Norway |
|  | Belgium |  | Sweden |
|  | Great Britain |  | Denmark |
|  | Australia |  | Switzerland |
|  | Italy |  | Germany |
|  | United State of America |  | France |
|  | Japan |  | Hong Kong |
|  | Canada |  | Spain |

## Section C—Deposits by Correspondence  邮寄存款

### Skill-building exercise #C1—Listening comprehension

Listen to Alan King who explains the function of **Deposits by Correspondence** and tick those items which he talks about.

- Deposits by correspondence refer to any Chinese who wishes to do so.
- They refer to overseas Chinese, Hong Kong, Macao and Taiwan compatriots, Chinese of foreign nationality and Chinese from mainland China who have settled down or been studying in foreign countries.
- The above listed people authorize domestic banks to handle savings deposit for their funds abroad.
- They have to apply for an Account of Deposits by Correspondence.
- They will choose the types of services.
- The deposit can only be withdrawn against depository certificate.

## Section D—Deposit Collections in Different Places  异地存款

### Skill-building exercise #D1—Listening comprehension

Listen to Helen Davidson who is telling you how to collect your deposit in other cities than where you got your passbook. As you listen, write in the missing words. Then compare your answers with those of a partner.

1. In case of _____ of job, or registration of _____ or other circumstances, clients may against their certificates of deposit or passbook ask the bank to collect their deposits in _____ and draw the deposits or continue to keep the deposits at _____.

2. The clients may ask a savings outlet to handle _____ in different places by presenting their own certificates of _____ and the certificates of deposit or the passbook.

3. _____ in different places cover: current deposits, time deposits and current-time optional deposits in local and foreign currencies. Only full amount of collections of the above-mentioned certificates of deposit or the passbook are _____. The collections apply to none of unregistered _____.

## Skill-building exercise #D2—Speaking

1. Please explain verbally the table below:

### RMB Deposit Rates

| | | Date: Feb. 21, 2002 |
|---|---|---|
| Types | | Interest Rate (% per annum) |
| 1. Demand | | 0.72 |
| 2. Term | | |
| Lump-sum Deposit for Lump-sum Withdrawal | | |
| | 3 Months | 1.71 |
| | 6 Months | 1.89 |
| | 12 Months | 1.98 |
| | 24 Months | 2.25 |
| | 36 Months | 2.52 |
| | 60 Months | 2.79 |
| Small Deposit for Lump-sum Withdrawal, Lump-sum Deposit for Small Withdrawals, Principal Deposit for Interest Withdrawals | | |
| | 12 Months | 1.71 |
| | 36 Months | 1.89 |
| | 60 Months | 1.98 |
| Time or Demand Optional Deposit | | 60% discount of the interest rate at which lump-sum time deposit for of lump-sum withdrawal are made for one year or less |

2. Please explain verbally the table below:

### Forex Deposit Rates

| | Date: Jan. 19, 2004 | Unit: Interest rate (% per annum) | | |
|---|---|---|---|---|
| | USD | EUR | JPY | HKD |
| Demand | 0.0750 | 0.1000 | 0.0001 | 0.0001 |
| 7 Days-notice Deposit | 0.1250 | 0.3750 | 0.0005 | 0.0010 |
| 1 Month | 0.2500 | 0.7500 | 0.0100 | 0.0025 |
| 3 Months | 0.4375 | 1.0000 | 0.0100 | 0.0050 |
| 6 Months | 0.5000 | 1.1250 | 0.0100 | 0.0200 |
| 12 Months | 0.5625 | 1.2500 | 0.0100 | 0.1000 |
| 24 Months | 0.6875 | 1.3125 | 0.0100 | 0.1625 |

Commercial Banking 商业银行

## Section E—Loss Reporting 报失

### Skill-building exercise #E1—Speaking

Read the text on **Deposit Certificate Loss Reporting** and have a role play with your partner.

### E1. Loss Reporting Procedures

If a certificate of deposit, a bank passbook or a seal of a client is lost or stolen, or the password is forgotten, loss reporting may be handled at the bank according to the following procedures:

1. The client shall immediately initiate the loss-reporting procedures in writing at the original depository bank. The client shall present personal credentials (I. D. card, residence permit, passport, etc.) and also provide related deposit contents such as account No., account holder's name, account opening time, amount, type of currency and maturity. The loss reporting procedures may be handled after the bank certifies and finds them correct. If the client is unable to be present at the bank to handle loss-reporting, he or she may authorize another person to act on his / her behalf. At the same time, the credentials of the agent shall be presented. Loss reporting of password may not be handled by an agent.

**Attention**: If the deposit had already been falsely claimed prior to loss-reporting, the bank would not handle the above procedure.

2. If an overseas Chinese or a Hong Kong, Macao or Taiwan compatriot is to handle loss reporting of a domestic certificate of deposit, and he or she is unable to return to the mainland to handle the procedures by himself or herself, he or she may authorize a relative or a friend in the mainland to handle on agency and shall also issue a letter of authorization for handling the loss reporting on agency (the letter of authorization shall be notarized by the Chinese embassy in that country). The proxy shall present credentials in handling the procedures.

3. In handling the loss reporting procedures, the client shall fill in the application for loss reporting, with an extra copy of the application kept by the client, and shall apply for a new certificate of deposit through handling redepositing or cashing procedures at the

depository bank seven days later by presenting the application and his or her credentials.

4. If, for an objective reason, the client is unable to handle loss reporting at the bank in time or in person, he or she may first request for interim loss reporting orally, by mail or by telephone, and then handle the formal loss reporting procedures at the depository bank within five days. Otherwise, the loss reporting would become invalid.

5. For a current account passbook opened with a savings branch connected with the computer network, interim loss reporting procedures may be handled at any savings outlet. But the loss reporting procedures for many written shall be handled at the depository bank.

6. If, after formal loss reporting procedures are handled, the original lost certificate of deposit is found, the client may cancel the loss reporting status at the bank by presenting his or her credentials, and also return the extra copy of the application. The original certificate of deposit is still valid. Cancellation of loss reporting may not be handled through mail or in any form of telecommunications, such as: telephone, fax, telex, etc. Loss reporting does not apply to certificates of deposit (passbooks) on which deposit certification and certificate of deposit (CD) (CD-pledged or passbook-pledged) have been handled.

### E2. Loss Reporting for Personal Cheques

The client shall fill in an application for loss reporting and stop-payment by presenting his or her valid credentials and submit it to the bank where a checking account is kept. The said bank is to confirm that the lost cheque has not been cashed up till the point of loss-reporting. According to provisions of the law on Negotiable Instruments, the person reporting loss shall also handle related procedures with the people's court at the place of the paying bank of loss reporting. Once the loss-reporting procedure has started, no cancellation is allowed.

## Commercial Banking 商业银行

### Dialogue—Savings Deposit

C (Customer): Could you please tell me what should be done if I want to deposit some money?

S (Counter Staff): Sure. First of all you should know that there are five ways to deposit your local money: savings (current) deposit(活期储蓄存款), time deposit of lump-sum deposit and withdrawal(整存整取定期储蓄存款), time deposit of small savings for lump-sum withdrawal(零存整取定期储蓄存款), time deposit of principal receiving and interest withdrawal(存本取息定期储蓄存款) and time or savings optional deposit(定活两便储蓄存款).

C: My goodness, it's so complicated. Could you please explain to me one by one, the savings deposit first, please?

S: Savings deposit is a method of deposit that sets no limit on length of maturity, time and amount of deposit and withdrawal. It is the most basic and conventional method of deposit of a bank. A client may deposit and withdraw such deposit at any time. For free and flexible use of funds, such deposit is taken as the basis of a client's financial asset management.

C: O.K. How do I open such an account?

S: You should get a passbook and a debit card, if you wish, at any branch of a major bank if a deposit slip is filled in and a certain amount of cash (￥1.00 at least) is deposited. When opening an account, you may choose the method of withdrawal by password or by the passbook. If the method of withdrawal password is chosen, you should put on the spot a six-digit password into the said savings account. The password is put in through the password device on the counter and is unknown to any other person including the clerk of the bank. The password is the key with which to withdraw and must be kept in mind firmly and not leaked to others. Please be very careful: keep the passbook and the password separately so as to avoid false claim by others in case the passbook is lost.

C: Thank you very much for what you have told me. But how about the other kinds of deposit?

S: Well, apart from savings deposit, all others are referred to as time deposit. It is a kind of deposit with a definite length of maturity, deposited and, withdrawn together with the interest in a lump sum or by installment. The longer the length of maturity of a time deposit is, the higher its interest rate will be. Time deposits operated by local banks mainly include the following types:

The first is Time Deposit of Lump-sum Deposit and Withdrawal.

C: I see. What is the lowest amount required for this type of deposit?

S: The minimum amount for this type of time deposit is set at RMB ￥ 50.00, without any upper limit. The maturities range from three months, half a year, one year, two years and three to five years. At the time of account opening, you will be asked to fill in a deposit slip, and the savings outlet will give you a certificate of deposit against which the principal and interest may be withdrawn at time of malurily. Withdrawal in advance and collection from other places are permitted. Such deposit has the characteristics of long maturity and high interest rate, suitable for depositing savings that will not be used within quite a long period of time. Partial or full amount withdrawal in advance is permitted. For withdrawal in advance, the interest is computed at the current deposit rate quoted for the day of withdrawal.

C: It sounds very promising. Thank you for the detailed introduction.

S: You are most welcome.

## Dialogue—Time Deposits

S: Would you like to know a little bit about other types?

C: Certainly, please.

S: The next category we operate is Time Deposit of Small Savings for Lump-sum Withdrawal. The minimum amount for this type of time deposit is set at RMB ￥ 5.00. The length of maturity and a fixed amount of deposit are agreed at the time of account opening, and money is deposited by month. If there is any omission of deposit within the agreed period, it should be made up in the following month. Failure to make up the amount agreed is deemed default and for the portion deposited after default, the interest is computed at the rate for savings deposit at the time of withdrawal. The maturities for this type of time deposit vary in three grades: one year, three years and five years. Such deposit is deposited monthly, and suitable for depositors with fixed income.

C: That is a very interesting type.

S: The next type I will tell you might be more interesting. It is called Principal-receiving and Interest Withdrawing Time Deposit. It refers to savings deposit whose principal is deposited by lump sum, whose interest is withdrawn by installment and whose principal is repaid when on due date. The minimum amount for such a deposit is RMB ¥5,000, and maturities extend from one year, three years to five years. You can cash interest at the bank at the agreed time by presenting the certificate of deposit. If you want to withdraw the principal in advance, the bank will default back the excessive interest already paid.

C: Fair enough.

S: The other deposit service we provide is Time or Savings Optional Deposit. It is a kind of deposit with indefinite length of maturity whose interest rate varies in line with the length of maturity. The minimum amount of such a deposit is RMB ¥50.00; the length of maturity is not set at the time of deposit, and the savings outlet issues a certificate of deposit against which the client withdraws the deposit. If the actual length of maturity is less than three months, the interest is computed at the interest rate for savings deposit; if the actual length of maturity is three months or more but less than half a year, the interest for the whole length of maturity is computed at a rate equal to 60% of that for three-month time deposit of lump-sum deposit and withdrawal at the date of withdrawal; if the actual length of maturity is half a year or more but less than one year, the interest for the whole length of maturity is computed at a rate equal to 60% of that for six-month time deposit of lump-sum deposit and withdrawal at the date of withdrawal; if the length of maturity is one year or more, regardless of the actual length, the interest for the whole length of maturity is computed at a rate equal to 60% of that for one-year time deposit of lump-sum deposit and withdrawal at the date of withdrawal. Such deposit boasts the flexibility of withdrawal at any time as a savings deposit, and also enjoys a preferential interest rate approaching that for time deposit.

C: Very impressive. I didn't know you provide such a complete line of services. As I come and go quite often, I think I shall start with a savings deposit account. I would like to know more about it, if possible.

S: By all means. I would like to say that savings deposit is convenient and flexible. You can withdraw or transfer money with no time limit. It may also transfer funds swiftly through telephone banking or ATM service. The passbook can also function as a principal account. A savings deposit account may serve as a principal account of a client. It may be connected through the computer network with such accounts as credit card account, telephone banking account, electronic debit card account, checking account and time and current account passbooks so that fund flows between the current and time accounts and other accounts are realized. Please remember that interest on a savings deposit is computed once on June 30 of every year at the interest rate for current deposits quoted for the date of interest settlement. If the account is closed prior to the date of interest settlement, the interest is computed up to the day prior to the account closing date at the interest rate for current deposits quoted for the closing date. In case of interest rate adjustment within the maturity, the interest amounts are computed without sub-division.

C: What else can I do with the savings deposit?

S: Aside from the functions of deposit and withdrawal, a savings deposit account also has the following functions: Firstly, you can apply for supportive electronic debit card with which to handle such banking services as withdrawal and transfer on an ATM, and consumption at designated shops; Secondly, you can use it for salary payment service on agency; Thirdly, you can use it to apply for telephone banking service; Fourthly, it can also be used for automatic banking. A client with a savings deposit account at any operational unit of the branches and sub-branches of the Bank you have deposited your money in may handle deposit and withdrawal at all local operating units of the Bank connected with the computer network by presenting the passbook.

C: O.K. I am determined to apply for a savings deposit account.

S: All right. Please fill in this slip of paper. ... Now, please type a six-digit number as your password. ... Excellent. This is your passbook.

C: It is a pleasure to do business with your bank. Thank you very much for your time and assistance.

S: The pleasure is mine. We are ready at any time to render our service.

### Richard King, Director of Deposit Department

I am Richard King, Director of Deposit Department. I am pleased to have the opportunity to explain to you our foreign currency deposit services. We divide such services into B-type foreign currency deposits and C-type foreign currency deposits.

B-type Foreign Currency Deposit serves foreigners, Chinese of foreign nationalities and overseas Chinese living in and outside the Chinese territory, Hong Kong, Macao and Taiwan regions. Compatriots in Hong Kong, Macao and Taiwan are permitted to open accounts of such deposits in their own names so well.

C-type Foreign Currency Deposit is for all prospective Chinese residents customers holding foreign currencies.

The account for B-type is referred to in our Bank as accounts of deposit in foreign exchange; and for C-type as accounts of deposit in foreign bank notes, i. e. accounts of foreign exchange and accounts of foreign bank notes. They are managed in our bank separately. Let me give you some details to each of them.

Let me talk about Accounts of Foreign Exchange (or Foreign Exchange Accounts) first.

All convertible foreign exchange remitted, brought or mailed into the mainland of China from abroad may be deposited in the foreign exchange accounts. For foreign currency bills for which prompt payment may not be made, they have to be collected by the Bank first and then deposited in the Bank.

As far as Accounts of Foreign Bank-notes (or Foreign Bank-notes Accounts) are concerned, I would like to say that all convertible foreign bank notes brought into the mainland of China from abroad may be deposited in the foreign bank-notes accounts.

I would like to draw your attention to the following: in opening an account for B-type foreign currency deposits, the depositor shall present his or her passport or other valid credentials. Starting from November 1, 2000, the "form for foreign residents applying to enjoy the treatment under the double taxation treaty" must be filled in respect to the above taxation treatment enjoyed by foreign residents.

You may ask what currencies our bank accepts. The types of currency that may directly be deposited in foreign bank-notes accounts include: US dollar, Pound sterling, French Franc, Deutschmark, Japanese yen, and Hong Kong dollar; the types of currency that may directly be deposited in foreign exchange accounts, aside from the above-mentioned six types, also include: Canadian dollar, Euro, Australian dollar, Swiss Franc, Belgian Franc Dutch Guilder, etc. For other convertible foreign currencies, the depositor may choose any of the above-mentioned types and deposit after conversion according to the foreign exchange quotations on the very day.

I guess you would like to know what varieties of deposit are available to you. Well, the first one I wish to mention is Savings Deposits. Foreign currency savings deposits may be kept in a passbook or a checking account. They may be deposited and withdrawn at any time. The minimum amount for opening an account for such deposit is foreign currencies with a value not less than the equivalent of RMB ￥100.00 for a B-type account of deposit, or foreign currencies with a value not less than the equivalent of RMB ￥20.00 for a C-type account of deposit.

The second deposit service available is Time Deposits. Or to be exact: Time Deposits of Lump-sum Depositing and Lump-sum Withdrawal. Time deposits of lump-sum depositing and lump-sum withdrawal are fixed deposits that are deposited by lump-sum and whose principal and interest are paid by lump-sum upon maturity. Their terms of deposit are divided into the five grades: one month, three months, six months, one year and two years. The Bank issues registered certificates of deposit for such deposits. The minimum amount for such a deposit: foreign currencies with a value not less than the equivalent of RMB ￥500.00 for a B-type deposit, or foreign currencies with a value not less than the equivalent of RMB ￥50.00 for a C-type deposit. Such deposit may be withdrawn fully or partly prior to maturity for once. The bank can, upon authorization in advance by the depositor, handle on agency renewal of the deposit upon its maturity.

The other tool you can use is what we call Savings / Time Optional Deposits. This type, which opens to time or current deposits in foreign currency, is a registered deposit without fixed amount, without definite maturity, whose interest rate varies in line with the length of maturity. The minimum amount of deposit is foreign currencies with a value not less than the equivalent of RMB ￥50.00. The longest maturity is one year, and interest amounts are calculated at a discount rate relevant to the corresponding grade of interest rate for time deposits of lump-sum depositing and lump-sum withdrawal according to the actual number of days deposited. The interest amounts are calculated with reference to interest rate of the Renminbi time / current optional deposits.

Seven-day Notice Deposits are also a service we provide. In this type, the principal is deposited in a lump-sum for a maturity of not less than seven days. The minimum amount of deposit is foreign currencies with a value not less than the equivalent RMB ￥5,000. For withdrawal of such a deposit, the Bank should be informed in writing seven days in advance.

### Alan King—Deposits by Correspondence

Deposits by correspondence refer to the way in which overseas Chinese, Hong Kong, Macao and Taiwan compatriots, Chinese of foreign nationality and domestic residents approved to settle down or study abroad or in Hong Kong, Macao or Taiwan, authorize domestic banks to handle savings deposits for their funds abroad.

A client sending a letter authorizing the bank to handle deposits by correspondence may go through the account opening procedures by attaching duplicates of his or her I.D. card, passport, exit pass or other valid credentials, filling in the Application for Opening Account of Deposits by correspondence, choosing the type of deposit according to the types of services already transacted by the bank (say, current, time and current-time optional deposits, etc.), and also arranging for the way of withdrawal later.

After an account is opened, the bank, as an agent, will keep the certificate of deposit, and mail or issue the Depository Certificate by Agency. The deposit can be withdrawn only against the Depository Certificate, and such depository certificate is open to loss reporting and may be brought out of the country.

### Helen Davidson

In case of change of job, or registration of residence or other circumstances, clients may ask the bank against their certificates of deposit or passbook to collect their deposits in different places and draw the deposits or continue to keep the deposits at the local bank.

The clients may ask a savings outlet to handle deposit collections in different places by presenting their own certificates of identification and the certificates of deposit or the passbook.

Services of deposit collections in different places cover: current deposits, time deposits and current-time optional deposits in local and foreign currencies. Only full amount collections of the above-mentioned certificates of deposit or the passbook are handled. The collections apply to none of unregistered deposits.

# Sample Examination Questions 模拟试题

## Vocabulary

1. Use the following words or phrases in a sentence.
   a. minimum
   b. deposit slip
   c. lump sum
   d. installment
   e. certificate of deposit
   f. principal
   g. banknote(s)

2. Define the following words and phrases and provide a Chinese translation.
   a. time deposit
   b. demand deposit
   c. withdrawal
   d. account
   e. passbook
   f. maturity

## Understanding

1. Why might a customer want to have a foreign currency bank account?

2. What types of bank accounts are provided by commercial banks in China and what are their advantages?

3. What are currency codes?

4. What is meant by 'authorized officer'?

5. What kinds of bank clients can use the deposits-by-correspondence service? What benefits does it provide to them? What do they have to provide to the bank to use the service?

6. Explain the loss-reporting procedures for a bank passbook.

7. What is standard bank policy if a certificate of deposit has been fraudulently cashed and the rightful owner later makes a claim? Explain to a client the reason for this policy.

Commercial Banking  商业银行

# Part III
## Retail Banking: Loans  私人业务：贷款

*Commercial banks can help individuals and families realize their financial goals by making money available for houses, education and automobiles.*

## Introduction  导语

This chapter explains the types of loans that banks make available to individuals and families. Excellent programs are available for borrowing money to pay for the education of your children, to buy homes and cars.

Part Ⅲ—Retail Banking: Loans  私人业务：贷款

## Section A—Housing Loans for Individuals  私人住房贷款

### Skill-building exercise #A1—Listening comprehension

You are going to hear Claire Seal, Deputy Director of Retail Department in charge of Housing Loans for Individuals, giving some information about housing loans to a group of customers. Before you listen to her presentation, look at these questions. Then listen and answer the questions.

1. What is a housing loan?
2. How many categories are there in housing loans?
3. Explain what Housing Loans for Personal Possession are.
4. Who can be potential borrowers of this type of loan?
5. What is the length of maturity for this type of loan?
6. What is the lending rate for this type of loan?
7. What are the lending currencies for this type of loan?
8. What are the ways of guarantee for this type of loan?

### Skill-building exercise #A2—Listening comprehension

You are going to listen again to Claire Seal who continues with her presentation. While you do so, look at the headings below. Which ones does she talk about and in which order?

- Procedures of applying for Housing Loans on Authorization
- Ways of guarantee for this type of loan
- The combined loan
- What currencies can be used for this type of loan
- The lending rate
- Length of maturity

## Section B—Auto Loans  购车贷款

### Skill-building exercise #B1—Translation

Before you listen to Lucy John, Claire Seal's assistant, look at the following expressions in Chinese and try to find out their equivalent in English while you listen.

代偿   质物   首期付款   保证人   法人代码证   财务报告   分期付款

## Section C—Education Loans  教育贷款

### Skill-building exercise #C1—Listening comprehension

Listen to the talk given by Diane Hope and try to grasp the meaning of words given below:

1. commercial educational loans
2. state educational loans with fiscal interest discount
3. tuition
4. miscellaneous fees
5. guardianship
6. higher learning institute

## C1 Commercial Educational Loans

### Skill-building exercise #C2—Reading and listening comprehension

You are going to listen to Diane Hope, who is speaking to a group of high school graduating students. Read the following text first, and then fill in the blanks, while you listen.

1. It is a pleasure for me to speak to our _____. All of you may become our customers. We shall be ready to provide our services to you. Before you choose our products, you should know what _____. Since you are entering into universities, the most immediate product you may wish to consider is _____. Any natural person with _____ can apply for such a loan with documents like a permanent residence or a valid residence permit, and holder's own passport or border pass if studying at a college abroad, _____ from the school for study, student's identity card, and the materials of certification on necessary tuition and miscellaneous fees during the period of study provided by the school for study. The applicant should also provide asset mortgage or pledge accepted by the lender or a guarantee provided by a third party guarantor that has _____ and also holds joint and several liability.

2. The borrower should also have a certain proportion of the money needed by the prospective student in question. In other words, our loan can only _____ of the entire expenses for the student, and the rest has to be provided by the student himself or his family.

3. The length of maturity of an educational loan is usually _____, with the longest not exceeding ten years inclusive. The specific length of maturity depends on the study conditions of the borrower and the nature of guarantee.

4. The interest rate for loans of the same grade stipulated by the People's Bank of China applies to the lending rate for educational loans. If the length of maturity is one year or shorter, interest shall be computed in accordance with the _____, and the contracted interest rate shall remain unchanged in case of _____; if the length of maturity is over one year, in case of adjustment of the legal interest rate, the interest rate shall be _____ by the People's Bank of China.

5. I would like to draw your attention to the fact that this type of loan is only available in _____ .

6. As I said earlier that the ceiling of an educational loan should in principle not _____ of the total amount of tuition and miscellaneous fees.

7. I am sure you all understand that there must be a guarantee in place before we give out any loans. For a loan of this nature, there are three guarantee modes, namely, _____ .

8. If a loan is applied by mortgaging _____ , the rate of mortgage is 70% of the evaluated value, but the loan may not exceed _____ of the total amount of tuition and miscellaneous fees.

9. If a loan is applied by pledging _____ , the rate of pledge for certificates of deposit or registered treasury bonds is 90%, and for certificates of deposit issued by other banks or other pledged security, _____ , but the loan may not exceed _____ of the total amount of tuition and miscellaneous fees.

10. If a loan is applied in the mode of third party guarantee, the ceiling of borrowing may not exceed _____ of the total amount of tuition and miscellaneous fees. But it may be raised to _____ in case of joint and several liability guarantees provided by a bank or an insurance company.

11. In applying for an educational loan, the borrower shall file a written borrowing application to the lender, fill in related application forms and also present the following documents and certification materials: I. D. card of the borrower, the original of valid residence certificates, or an original of the passport or a border pass of the applying student and its duplicate for file keeping in case of _____ ; the notarized guardianship between _____ and the latter's certificate of birth; the Enrollment Notification of the school for study or student's identity card, and materials of certification drawn by the school for study on the total amount of tuition and miscellaneous fees needed by the applying student during the period of study.

12. If property is used for mortgage or pledge, it is necessary to provide a detailed list of _____ and the commitment or statement agreeing to the mortgage or pledge by the person entitled to the disposal (including co-owner of property) with his/her signature

thereon. For mortgaged property, an evaluation report issued by the competent department and the _____ issued by the insurance company shall be provided, and for pledged property, a document of ownership or entitlement certification shall be provided. If a guarantee is provided by a third party, a written document _____ and the related credit certification materials shall be provided.

### C2 State Educational Loans

### Skill-building exercise #C3—Listening comprehension

Answer the following questions after you listen to the continued talk by Diane Hope.

1. Who can apply for the State Educational Loans?

2. In terms of qualification, what is different from that of the Commercial Educational Loans?

3. Could a default be publicized if the applicant failed to repay the loan?

4. What is the maximum amount if one apply for such a loan?

5. Is the application procedure different from that of the Commercial Educational Loans?

## Section D—Secured Personal Loans　以定期存款/国库券做担保的私人贷款

### Skill-building exercise #D1—Vocabulary

Read the following passage and pay special attention to the words below:

- CD
- treasury bonds
- hypothecation
- personal loan
- pledged by
- undue certificate
- automatic renewal
- working capital

## Commercial Banking  商业银行

Personal loan pledged by certificates of deposit (CD) /treasury bonds is a kind of business combining deposit and loan in which the client gets a certain amount of Renminbi loan from the bank by pledging undue certificate(s) of time deposit and also repays the principal and interest accrued on schedule. CDs used for hypothecation are limited to certificates of time deposits issued by the savings outlets in the local administrated area of the grade-one branches or branches directly under the headquarters of our bank.

Any resident in China with full capacity for civil conduct, holder of undue certificates of time deposit in local or foreign currencies issued by our bank or treasury bonds may apply for a personal loan pledged by CDs/treasure bonds to the Bank. A borrower applying for personal loan pledged by CDs/treasury bonds must also meet the following conditions:

- Being a natural person with full capacity of civil conduct;
- Having a locally registered permanent residence or valid credentials;
- Being a holder of undue certificate(s) of time deposit or treasury bonds issued by the Bank;
- Other conditions provided for by the lender.

The length of maturity of a personal loan pledged by CDs/treasury bonds may not exceed the due date of the pledged CD. Besides, the longest maturity shall be one year. If multiple certificates of personal deposit are pledged, the length of maturity shall be set according to the nearest due date. For automatic renewal certificates of deposit, the length of maturity shall be set according to the length of automatic renewal.

The interest rate for loans of the same grade announced by the People's Bank of China applies to the interest rate for personal loans pledged by CDs/treasury bonds. The interest rate shall not float beyond the ceiling rate specified by the People's Bank of China. If the length of maturity is less than six months, the interest rate shall be that for the six-month loan. For repayment before maturity date, the interest shall be calculated according to the originally set interest rate and the actual number of days of borrowing. In case the People's Bank of China adjusts the interest rate, the contracted interest rate is still adopted within the length of maturity.

Borrowers may use the loans for purchases of houses, cars and expensive consumer durables, for house refurbishing, vacation and travel, education and other consumer demands, as well as for working capital demand in normal operations.

The minimum amount of a personal loan pledged by CDs/treasury bonds is RMB ¥1,000. The amount of the loan shall in principle not exceed 90% of the face value of the pledged CD (for deposits in foreign currencies, calculated in Renminbi translated at the current day buying rate of foreign exchange [bank note]). The maximum borrowing limit of a single loan shall in principle not exceed RMB ¥3,000,000.

The following materials shall support the application for a personal loan pledged by CDs/treasury bonds:

- An application for personal loan pledged by CDs/treasury bonds;
- Presentation of valid original credentials of the borrower, personal documents (referring to I.D. card, residence registration and other valid residence certificates), and also provision of their duplicates;
- Valid original certificate(s) of personal time deposit issued by the Bank;
- Signature or password for the certificate(s) of deposit held by the borrower;
- Other documents of certification or materials required by the lender.

The borrowers may use cash or deposits with the Bank for debt service. With the consent of the lender, the borrowers may repay the principal and interest of the loans ahead of schedule.

## Section E—Other Type of Loans 其他私人贷款

### E1 Small Consumer Credit (Loan)

### Skill-building exercise #E1—Listening comprehension

Before you listen to John Morley's speech on small consumer credit loan, look at the following statements. Put a tick by the ones you might expect to hear in the talk and a cross by those you would not expect to hear. Then, compare your answers with those of a partner and discuss any differences.

1. Small consumer credit loan can help the borrower to purchase houses and cars.
2. The borrower must be over 18 but under 60 years of age.
3. It's necessary to evaluate the credit standing of a customer holding a credit card for over two years.

4. Interest rate for the same grade set by the People's Bank of China is adopted for this type of loan.

## Skill-building exercise #E2—Understanding

Based on what you have learned about personal loans, try to complete the table below after discussing with your partner and then check it against similar kinds of loans provided by your bank or other banks.

| Type of Loans | Applicant's Qualification | Modes of Guarantee | Maximum Amount | Interest Rate | Ways of Application |
|---|---|---|---|---|---|
| Loan for Housing Refurbishing | | | | | |
| Loan for Vocation & Travel | | | | | |
| Loan for Durable Commodities | | | | | |

# Listening Material 听力材料

### Claire Seal, Deputy Director, Housing Loans for Individuals

Welcome to my office. I am very pleased to speak to you about services this office offers. Perhaps we could begin by explaining to you what a housing loan is. To put it simply, they are loans granted by our bank to borrowers to facilitate their housing purchases. Housing loans are divided into housing loans for personal possession and housing loans on authorization and combined loans.

Now, let me talk about Housing Loans for Personal Possession first. They refer to loans granted to individual housing buyers to facilitate housing purchases by taking credit funds from the bank as the source of payment. You may ask who can be potential borrowers of this type of loan. Well, any natural person with full capacity for civil conduct can be a borrower. For loans in Renminbi, the maximum length of maturity can be 30 years; while for loans in foreign currency, the maximum length of maturity is five years. The lending rate set by the People's Bank of China applies to the interest rate for housing loans for personal possession. For housing loans in foreign currencies, the corresponding lending rate announced by Bank of China is adopted. Housing loans for personal possession are made in Renminbi and foreign currencies. Prospective borrowers of loans in foreign currencies shall be overseas Chinese, Hong Kong and Macao compatriots, employees of enterprises invested with foreign currency and others who have higher economic incomes, sources of repayment and reliable guarantee. As far as the borrowing limit is concerned, the amount of a single loan shall exceed neither 80% of the evaluated value of the house to be purchased, nor in the meantime the borrowing ceiling as provided by the lender. Guarantee has to be arranged for a loan. Our bank can accept the following guarantees:

1. Pledging the property of the borrower or a third party (including both a legal person or a natural person);

2. Mortgaging the property of the borrower or a third party (including both a legal person or a natural person), including mortgaging the house to be purchased with the loan in question;

3. Guarantee by a third party with joint and several liability;

4. Combined guarantee. If the value of the mortgaged property and house or pledged property provided by the borrower is inadequate to cover the amount of the loan, guarantee by

a third party with joint and several liability may be added to the shortfall;

5. The borrower can also buy general credit insurance.

I believe any potential borrower would feel at ease since there are so many choices of guarantee are available. Having learned the above, you would certainly like to know how one could apply for such a loan. I wish to stress that the application for a housing loan will have to be supported by the following documents:

1. Credentials (referring to I. D. card, residence registration or other valid residence certificate);

2. Testimonial to prove steady family income of the borrower;

3. Housing purchase contract, letter of intent, agreement or other document of approval that comply with the provisions;

4. A detailed list of mortgaged or pledged property, certificate of ownership (title deed for a house or other titles), and the certificate certifying the consent to mortgage or pledge given by the person entitled to disposal.

5. An evaluation certificate for the mortgaged property issued by a competent department;

6. A written document stating the consent given by the guarantor to the guarantee, and a credit standing certificate about the guarantor;

7. Other materials required by the lender.

I wish what I told you would be useful. Now, it's time for a coffee break. We shall start again 15 minutes later.

### Claire Seal Continues Her Presentation

Now, I would like to say a few words about Housing Loans on Authorization. They refer to loans to individuals who buy ordinary houses granted by the bank on the authorization of the public reserve fund management department, according to the prescribed requirements, and with the public reserve deposits as the source of funding. Identically, any natural person who has full capacity for civil conduct can be a potential borrower. Yet, the person must have deposited housing reserve funds at the funds management center, or the person has to be one of the retired veteran cadres, retired workers and staff members of collective housing reserve deposit units. The maximum length of maturity of this type of loan is 30 years. The interest rate for housing reserve loans set by the People's Bank of China will apply to the lending rate. Obviously only Renminbi is used in this type of loan. The amount of a single loan shall not exceed 80% of the evaluated value of the house to be purchased, and shall not exceed RMB ￥390,000. We accept the following ways of guarantee:

1. Mortgage plus general guarantee;
2. Mortgage plus all-risks insurance for housing purchase;
3. Pledge guarantee;
4. Guarantee with joint and several liability.

The application for a housing loan has to be supported by the following documents:

5. Valid credentials, residence registration and marriage certificate;
6. Borrowing application that is filled in and sealed by the employer which the borrower works;
7. Housing purchase contract or letter of intent;
8. If involving the provision of guarantee, a letter of guarantee stating the consent given by the guarantor to the guarantee;
9. Other materials the presentation of which is required by the handling person of the funds management center.

This bank also offers combined Housing Loans. A combined housing loan refers to a loan granted by the bank to the same borrower to facilitate the purchase of an ordinary house for his or her own use that takes the public reserve deposit and the credit fund as the sources of funding. It is a combination of a housing loan on authorization and a housing loan of personal possession from the bank.

### Lucy John, Auto Loans

Good morning. I am Lucy John in charge of auto loans. They are Renminbi consumer-loans granted to individuals or legal persons to finance the purchases of cars. These loans are available to individuals with full capacity for civil conduct, with stable occupation and capacity of debt service and good credit standing; the individuals should be able to provide valid property for mortgage or pledge, or have individual or institutional guarantor with full repayment capacity by subrogation and be able to afford the down payment for the car purchase.

We also provide such loans to legal persons with a legal person status, loan repayment capacity, proceeds for the down payment for the car purchase that are not less than the prescribed amount placed at the designated bank and a guarantee approved by the lender. Length of maturity is usually one to three years, and five years maximum. This type of loan is limited to Renminbi for now. The applicant will have to pay the down payment, which is

20% of the car price, the amount of borrowing should not exceed 80% of the car price; Lending rate is adopted according to the corresponding lending rate announced by the People's Bank of China. Following documents will be required of an individual for a car loan application: an application for borrowing; valid credentials; certificate of occupation and income, certificate of debt service ability approved by the creditor; car purchase contract or agreement signed with the designated dealers; documents of certification required for guarantee. In case of a legal person of an enterprise or an undertaking an application for borrowing, legal person license, certificate of legal person code, and documents of certification of the legal representative, financial statements for the previous year and recent period, borrowing card or borrowing permit granted by the People's Bank of China, car purchase contract or agreement signed with the designated dealer; and all documents of certification required in the guarantee would be required.

As far as loan repayment is concerned, the borrower and the lender may choose a repayment pattern by consultation, the monthly installment to be repaid can include either an amount, which is equal to the principal or to both the principal and interest. The borrower shall deposit prior to monthly repayment date provided for in the loan contract sufficient monthly installment in its account so that the bank can directly deduct the repayment of the loan principal and interest. With the consent of the lender, the borrower is permitted to effect an early payment in part or in full.

### Diane Hope, Commercial Education Loans

It is a pleasure for me to speak to our potential customers. You can all become our customers. We shall be ready to provide our services to you. Before you choose our products, you should know what services are available to you. Today I shall concentrate on educational loans. They include commercial educational loans and state educational loans with fiscal interest discounts. Commercial educational loans refer to consumer loans granted by the lender to borrowers to finance the tuition and miscellaneous fees (including the traveling expenses for going abroad) of the borrowers or the persons under their legal guardianship in studying at domestic secondary schools or ordinary higher learning institutes or for master's or doctor's degree, or studying at universities or for master's or doctor's degree outside China with approval. State educational loans refer to educational loans granted by the lender to borrowers that are given fiscal interest discounts by the central financial authorities or local financial sectors, and are used for the tuition and miscellaneous fees, lodging and living expenses of the borrowers in studying at domestic higher learning institutes for full-time undergraduate, professional, or graduate courses.

State educational loans belong to credit loans and enjoy a 50% fiscal interest discount. The applicants must meet the condition that the involved schools have access to state educational loans. Loans for studying abroad are currently limited to commercial loans.

### Diane Hope Continues

Since you are entering into universities, the most immediate product you wish to consider is Commercial Educational Loans. Any natural person with full capacity for civil conduct can apply for such a loan with documents like a permanent residence or a valid residence permit, and holder's own passport or border pass if studying at a college abroad, the enrollment notification or letter of offer from the school of study, student's identity card, and the materials of certification on necessary tuition and miscellaneous fees during the period of study provided by the school of study. The applicant should also provide asset mortgage or pledge that is accepted by the lender or a guarantee provided by a third party guarantor that has the capacity of repayment by subrogation and also holds joint and several liability.

The borrower should also have a certain proportion of the money needed by the prospective student in question. In other words, our loan can only cover a greater part of the entire expenses for the student, and the rest has to be provided by the student himself or his family.

The length of maturity of an educational loan is usually one to six years, maximum not exceeding ten years inclusive. The specific length of maturity depends on the study conditions of the borrower and the nature of guarantee.

The interest rate for loans of the same grade stipulated by the People's Bank of China applies to the lending rate for educational loans. If the length of maturity is one year or shorter, interest shall be computed in accordance with the contracted interest rate, and the contracted interest rate shall remain unchanged in case of adjustment of the legal interest rate; if the length of maturity is over one year, in case of adjustment of the legal interest rate, the interest rate shall be subject to the adjustment by the People's Bank of China.

I would like to draw your attention to the fact that this type of loan is only available in the Chinese local currency—Renminbi.

As I said earlier that the ceiling of an educational loan should in principle not exceed 80% of the total amount of tuition and miscellaneous fees.

## Commercial Banking  商业银行

I am sure you all understand that there must be a guarantee before we give out any loans. For a loan of this nature, there are three guarantee modes, namely, mortgage, pledge and guarantee.

If a loan is applied for mortgaging a house or other real estate, the rate of mortgage is 70% of the evaluated value, but the loan may not exceed 80% of the total amount of tuition and miscellaneous fees.

If a loan is applied by pledging certificates of deposit or registered treasury bonds, the rate of pledge for certificates of deposit or registered treasury bonds is 90%, and for certificates of deposit issued by other banks or other pledged security, the rate of pledge depends on the value of the pledge security, but the loan may not exceed 80% of the total amount of tuition and miscellaneous fees.

If a loan is applied in the mode of third party guarantee, the ceiling of borrowing may not exceed 70% of the total amount of tuition and miscellaneous fees. But it may be raised to 80% in case of joint and several liability guarantees provided by a bank or an insurance company.

In applying for an educational loan, the borrower shall file a written borrowing application to the lender, fill in related application forms and also present the following documents and certification materials: I.D. cards of the borrower, the original of valid residence certificates, or an original of the passport or a border pass of the applying student and its duplicate for file keeping in case of studying abroad; the notarized guardianship between the borrower and the student in question and the latter's certificate of birth; the Enrollment Notification of the school for study or student's identity card, and materials of certification drawn by the school for study on the total amount of tuition and miscellaneous fees needed by the applying student during the period of study.

If property is used for mortgage or pledge, it is necessary to provide a detailed list of the mortgaged or pledged property and the commitment or statement agreeing to the mortgage or pledge by the person entitled to the disposal (including co-owner of property) with his/her signature thereon. For mortgaged property, an evaluation report issued by the competent department and the insurance document issued by the insurance company shall be provided, and for pledged property, a document of ownership or entitlement certification shall be provided. If a guarantee is provided by a third party, a written document of the guarantor agreeing to guarantee and the related credit certification materials shall be provided.

## Diane Hope—State Educational Loans

I would like to give you now a general picture of **State Educational Loans.** I mentioned at the start what it is and its functions. I shall add that a person having full capacity for civil conduct (for a minor, a written letter of consent provided by his or her legal guardian is necessary) can apply for it. Besides, the person must have a valid residence permit, qualification report on study and conduct required by the lender, without any act of bad credit; most importantly, the school for study should have signed a bank-school cooperation agreement with our Bank; the person must also have a recommendation by a person of reference and also with a witness to provide a written certificate of his or her identity; the person should also agree that if the loan is overdue for one year and an extension is not approved, the lender is to make public his or her name, the number of his or her I.D. card and the act of default at the higher learning institute where he or she studies or on related media.

The length of maturity of a state educational loan usually does not generally exceed eight years. If a student granted a loan for further studies for a graduate or a second bachelor's degree after the undergraduate course ends, the length of maturity during the period of study is extended accordingly, and the principal and interest of the loan shall be repaid up within four years after graduation from the graduate or the second bachelor's degree.

The interest rate for loans of the same grade stipulated by the People's Bank of China applies to the lending rate for state educational loans.

The amount of a state educational loan shall in principle not exceed RMB ¥6,000 per person for one year.

In applying for a state educational loan, the borrower shall file a written borrowing application to the lender, fill in related application forms and also present the following documents, certificates and materials:

- Original and duplicate of valid personal certificates of residence permit and identity;
- Enrollment Notification of the school for study and its duplicate, or student's identity card and duplicate;
- Certificate of tuition and miscellaneous fees and living expenses of the student during the period of study drawn by the school for study;
- Letter of recommendation and a certificate agreeing to the borrower's access to 50% interest discount of state educational loan drawn by the school for study.

I hope I have made myself clear. I am sure some of you will apply for one of the two types of loans I just described. If you have no further questions, I shall see those of you who wish to apply the loans in my office. Thank you for your attention.

### John Morley—Small Consumer Credit Loan

Small consumer credit loans of our Bank are consumer credit loans granted by the lender to borrowers with good credit standing to facilitate normal consumption, labor service and other fee payments.

A borrower (natural person) applying for small consumer credit loans of the Bank must meet the following conditions:

- Being a natural person aged 18~60 with full capacity of civil conduct;
- Having city/town registered permanent residence or a valid residence permit;
- Having a legitimate occupation and a stable income, and having the capacity of repaying the loan principal and interest accrued on schedule;
- Having opened a demand account or credit card account with the Bank;

The personal credit standing has to be evaluated and accepted by the lender. For a holder of the golden credit card of the Bank or a holder of ordinary card for two years or more, separate evaluation of personal credit is unnecessary; and other conditions set by the lender must also be met.

The longest maturity of a small consumer credit is one year.

The maximum borrowing limit of a small consumer credit is temporarily set at RMB ¥100,000.

For the interest rate for small consumer credit loans, the interest rate for loans of the same grade set by the People's Bank of China applies. Upward fluctuation of the interest rate shall not surpass the range provided for by the People's Bank of China.

The application by the borrower to the lender for a loan, shall be supported by the following materials:

- An application for borrowing;
- Valid credentials of the borrower (referring to an I.D. card, a residence registration and other valid residence certificates);
- Testimonials of occupation and income (an employee's card and a pay sheet, or a passbook for salary payment through an agency or other valid certificates);
- For a credit card holder, his credit card to be produced; and other documents or materials required by the lender.

# Sample Examination Questions 模拟试题

## Vocabulary

1. Use the following words or phrases in a sentence.
   a. capacity
   b. mortgage
   c. value
   d. evaluation certificate
   e. personal loan
   f. borrowing limit

2. Define the following words and phrases and provide a Chinese translation.
   a. joint and several liability
   b. fiscal interest discount
   c. hypothecation
   d. automatic renewal
   e. treasury bond

## Understanding

1. What are the categories of housing loans?
2. What is the purpose of housing loans?
3. What are the criteria for qualifying for a housing loan?
4. What documents should a client provide to the bank in support of an application for a housing loan?
5. What kind of security is generally required for a housing loan?
6. What does a client have to demonstrate to the bank when applying for an auto loan?
7. What criteria should a client meet in order to qualify for a consumer loan?

Commercial Banking 商业银行

## Part IV Retail Banking: Foreign Currency
## 私人银行业务：外汇

With international travel and business becoming such an important part of our daily lives, the foreign currency services offered by banks are especially valuable.

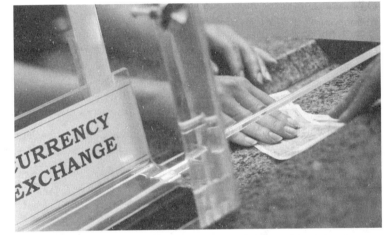

Part IV—Retail Banking: Foreign Currency 私人银行业务：外汇

## Introduction 导语

This section talks about foreign currency and how commercial banks facilitate transactions in a wide variety of currencies from all over the world. Also covered is the safety deposit service offered by banks. It is an important way of keeping our valuables secure.

## Section A—Currency Conversion 汇兑

### Skill-building exercise #A1—Listening comprehension

Allen Slattery, Director of Human Resources, is giving a training course to a bunch of new employees of the bank. You will listen to him talking about service of currency conversion. While you do so, try to memorize answers to the following questions.

1. How many currencies can be converted in China? What are they?
2. What is the procedure in converting them?
3. Can one cash a traveler's cheque in China? If so, what kinds of cheques can be cashed?

## Section B—Collection from Abroad 托收

### Skill-building exercise #B1—Listening and speaking

Listen again to Allen Slattery who talks about **Collection from Abroad** and then try to retell what he says in class.

### Skill-building exercise #B2—Translation

Listen to Allen Slattery again and look at the words in the left-hand column, and then match them with the Chinese words from the right-hand column.

| | |
|---|---|
| personal cheque | 追索权 |
| postal order | 手续费 |
| fiscal cheque | 公证处 |
| draft | 收款人 |
| corporate cheque | 本人 |

| | |
|---|---|
| bank cheque | 付款责任 |
| paying liability | 银行本票 |
| the principal | 公司支票 |
| beneficiary | 汇票 |
| notary office | 财政支票 |
| commission | 邮政支票 |
| recourse | 私人支票 |

## Section C—International Remittance of Foreign Currency  国外汇款

### Skill-building exercise #C1—Listening comprehension

Look at the questions below, and try to answer them after listening to Allen Slattery who talks about international remittance of foreign currency.

1. How many ways are there in remitting out foreign currency?
2. What are the charges for them?
3. What are the related state stipulations for remitting foreign currency?

### Skill-building exercise #C2—Understanding

Listen to Allen Slattery and then try to advise your client on:

1. How can he receive a remittance sent from abroad in a timely manner?
2. What should be done if the remitted currency is different from that of his account?
3. Why the received amount is less than the original?

## Section D—Foreign Exchange Dealings for Individuals  私人外汇交易

### Skill-building exercise #D1—Translation

Before listening to Allen Slattery who talks about **foreign exchange dealings for accounts of individuals**, read the following Chinese words and find out the meaning after listening.

外汇买卖　　柜面　　国际金融市场　　汇价　　剧烈的波动
自助交易　　异地操作　　技术分析　　市价交易　　委托交易

市价交易　　挂盘交易

### Skill-building exercise #D2—Vocabulary

Listen to Allen Slattery who continues to talk about **foreign exchange dealings for accounts of individuals** and write down the words that he actually uses in place of the words printed in *italics*.

1. Residents or individuals within mainland China who, with full capacity for civil conduct, bear valid *driver's license can conduct commodity dealings.*

2. ... he should go to the designated branch of this Bank to fill in the relevant *documents and give these papers to the clerks upstairs.*

3. For dealings by telephone, the client should get *a current passbook* and a credit card issued by this Bank and deposit *some cash.*

4. The client should now insert the password *of seven digits* for the account and then the account for dealings by telephone is open.

5. He can now start his business by dialing the number for dealings and inserting *the password.*

6. The client can now conduct the dealings by inserting the correct password into the device provided especially for *foreign currency dealings.*

## Section E—Automatic Banking of Savings Deposits　自动储蓄存款业务

### Skill-building exercise #E1—Writing

Listen to Clive Bond, Assistant Director of Retail Banking, who is talking about other services this bank provides and complete his note for him in the box below.

---

One thing this bank is proud of is that we have realized automatic banking of local and foreign currency current and time deposits _____. That is to say a client who has a deposit account in any operational unit of the branches and sub-branches of the Bank in the local province may _____ in all operational units of the Bank in the local province that are connected by the computer network. In the meantime, the NIC-NAP network of the Bank enables clients to realize _____ by using electronic debit cards through the ATMs and DECs of our bank in the whole country.

## Section F—Multifunctional Debit Card　多功能借记卡

### Skill-building exercise #F1—Speaking

After listening to Clive for the 2nd time, discuss with your partner what the features of the debit card of the bank are.

### Skill-building exercise #F2—Speaking

After listening to Clive again, instruct your partner who has just got his/her debit card on what to do. Then, switch roles with your partner.

## Section G—Personal Cheque Deposits　私人支票存款

### Skill-building exercise #G1—Listening comprehension

Christine Stannard talks about **Personal Cheque Deposits.** Listen to her and then answer the following questions:
1. What is a personal cheque deposit?
2. What customers are most suitable for such a service?
3. How does a cheque issuer inquire about the conditions of a certified cheque?

## Section H—Safety Deposit Box　保险箱

### Skill-building exercise #H1—Writing

Look at the questions below before you listen to Christine again and put your answers on paper after listening.
1. What is a safety deposit box?
2. How to apply for such a box?

## Section I—Fee-based Business　收费业务

### Skill-building exercise #I1—Speaking

Look at the following questions before you listen to Christine again and discuss your answers with your partner after listening.

1. What does fee-based business include?
2. What does bill payment service include?
3. How is bill payment service rendered?

## Section J—Automatic Deposit Service   自动存款服务

### Skill-building exercise #J1—Speaking

After listening to Christine, try to describe to the accountant from the nearby department store on how **automatic deposit service** is provided.

## Section K—Transfer Service for Security Firm   为证券公司提供转账服务

### Skill-building exercise #K1—Translation

After reading the passages below, discuss with your partner what the following Chinese expressions mean in English:

代理股票交易业务    银证转账服务    代理股票交易委托服务
证券保证金账户    相互转账    股民    认购

Currently, the bank's main agency services for stock trading include banking-securities transfer service and stock trading settlement service on commission.

Banking-securities transfer service: it refers to service of mutual transfers between accounts of bank deposits and accounts of securities margins provided to clients through such methods as savings counters, telephone banking service and POS system of the bank.

Stock trading settlement service on commission refers to receipt, payment, transfer and settlement of stock trading funds through the current account of a stock investor that is handled by the bank as agent of the securities company when a stock transaction takes place. This is aimed to facilitate share subscription and trading of stock investors.

## Listening Material 听力材料

### Allen Slattery, Director of Human Resources-Currency Conversion

Dear colleagues, this is your first week of training. I am pleased to close this week by telling you something about our foreign currency dealings for individual customers, an important part of the services this bank provides. Perhaps I should begin with Conversion of Foreign Bank Notes. This first question any one may ask is naturally what currencies can be converted at our bank. Well, they are Pound Sterling, US Dollar, Swiss Franc, Deutsche Mark, French Franc, Singapore Dollar, Dutch Guilder, Swedish Krona, Danish Krone, Norwegian Krone, Austrian Schilling, Belgian Franc, Italian Lira, Japanese Yen, Canadian Dollar, Australian Dollar, Finnish Markka, Philippine Peso and Thai Baht, and the currencies of Hong Kong Dollar, New Taiwan Dollar, and Macao Pataca. Besides, cheques in denomination of Euro and Spanish Peseta are also convertible.

The client shall go through the procedures by producing any of the following valid credentials: his/her own I.D. card (Chinese citizens), residence booklet (Chinese citizens aged under 16), identification credentials for army man (the Chinese People's Liberation Army), identification credentials for armed policeman (the Chinese People's Armed Police), pass for Hong Kong and Macao residents for travel between the mainland and Hong Kong and Macao (Hong Kong and Macao residents), pass for Taiwan residents for travel between the Mainland and Taiwan (Taiwan residents), passport (foreign citizens or Chinese citizens with passport), and other valid credentials provided by relevant laws and administrative regulations.

Any one who wishes to convert currency has to fill in an exchange memo.

Now I would like to describe to you what re-exchange procedures are. Those who have brought in foreign currency when coming into China will convert back the amount that has not been spent. Foreign clients and Hong Kong, Macao and Taiwan compatriots may handle re-exchange procedures at the time of exit within six months against the original exchange memo issued by the Bank and the passport.

One can also cash traveler's cheques. Traveler's cheques issued by Thomas Cook and

Barclays of the U. K. , American Express and City bank of the United States, and traveler's cheques issued by such Japanese banks as Sumitomo Bank, the Bank of Tokyo-Mitsubishi, Ltd. and Fuji Bank can be cashed at our bank.

In cashing a traveler's cheque, the client shall produce his or her own valid passport or pass for travel between the Mainland and Hong Kong, Macao and Taiwan, and the purchase agreement.

The client needs to countersign the traveler's cheque in the presence of the paying cashier immediately and the countersignature shall be consistent with the initial signature.

The client will be asked to fill in the exchange memo; the contents filled in should be identical to that for the exchange memo of foreign currencies in cash.

Having to pay advances in cashing a traveler's cheque, our bank will, when converting the traveler's cheque into cash or deposit, deduct a discount interest at the rate of 7.5 per thousand of the face value and make the payment in the currency of the face of cheque.

## Allen Slattery—Collection from Abroad

Our bank may, entrusted by the client, collect from the relevant payer abroad such bills as personal cheque, postal order, fiscal cheque, draft, corporate cheque and bank cheque for which our Bank does not bear paying liability.

Such business is handled in this way: the client has to present valid credentials of the principal; if the principal is absent, presenting valid credentials of his own / her own and the agent. The name of the beneficiary on the bill must be consistent with the name on the valid credentials of the beneficiary. If the name of the beneficiary on the bill is written in Chinese phonetic alphabet, it must conform to the name of the credentials; if not, in view of the interest protection of the beneficiary, a certificate issued by the working unit or the executive office of the neighborhood community under the district, or a law firm or notary office is necessary so as to confirm the real name of the beneficiary.

When collection is handled, a collection application in duplicate shall be filled in, with one copy returned to the client to serve as a certificate for obtaining proceeds.

Our bank charges a commission on an one thousandth basis for the amount of the bill and the paying region with the minimum at RMB ￥10 and the maximum at RMB ￥250. If what is collected is foreign currency in cash, then our commission is five thousandth of the amount and the paying region is the same as the foregoing. If postage is involved in the collection, we charge RMB ￥5 for the Hong Kong and Macao regions, and RMB ￥10 for other regions.

How much time is needed for bill collection?

In accordance with geographical locations from where the bill is to be collected and different places for currency clearing, bill collection usually needs about 40 days. It needs a longer time for some places, say, about 60 days from Canada for collection of USD bills as they need to be cleared in the United States.

There are bills that can be directly paid into account. A bill that is less than US $ 1,000 (including non-personal cheque of US $ 1,000), and a bank in the United States bears the paying liability, the beneficiary may directly handle bill deposit with a minimum maturity of three months by presenting its own credentials.

You have to know that since the paying bank abroad has the right of recourse, no withdrawal in advance is permitted. As our bank pays advances for the deposit, a 7.5% discount thus needs to be deducted, which is paid in the denomination currency of the bill.

For a personal cheque in foreign currency, regardless of different amounts, the actual proceeds should be collected from the paying bank abroad according to the trust of the client before related deposit and withdrawal procedures can be handled at the requests of the client.

## Allen Slattery—International Remittance of Foreign Currency

Now it's time to tell you how to help your customers remitting their foreign currency out of China. Such service means that the client gives the remittance to a bank and authorizes the bank to remit the money to the payee abroad. Outward remittance is divided into T/T and D/D.

T/T is a method of remittance in which the remitting bank, upon application by the remitter, informs the branch or correspondent bank at the place where the payee is located, i.e. the paying bank, by test key telegraph, telex or SWIFT (mostly via SWIFT currently), instructing it to pay a prescribed amount of money to the payee.

Requirements in handling T/T: If a client chooses the method of T/T, you should ask the client to provide the name of the payee, the name of the depository bank, its address, the account number and SWIFT CODE or Routing number.

D/D is a method of remittance in which the remitting bank, upon application by the remitter, issues in favor of the remitter a demand draft that takes its branch or one of its correspondent banks as the paying bank, and the remitter can either mail it to the payee or bring it out of China, and the designated paying bank should effect payment of a prescribed amount of money to the payee upon presentation of the draft.

If the client chooses the method of D/D, only the name of the payee and the names of the country and city where the payee is located shall be provided.

It is a matter of course that this bank shall charge for Personal Outward Remittance by collecting a commission. For both ways of remittance, we charge one thousandth of the amount remitted, with the highest at RMB ¥250 and the lowest at RMB ¥20. We also collect a spread charge, which is about 3% of the amount remitted for cash foreign banknotes (no such charge for spot exchange). If there is telegraphic charge involved, we collect RMB ¥150 (RMB ¥80 for remittance to Hong Kong and Macao).

As a staff of this bank, you are supposed to be familiar with relevant provisions of the State Administration of Exchange Control, i.e. Personal Outward Remittances of Foreign Exchange Used as Expenditures under Current Account:

If spot exchange less than USD $ 10,000 or equivalent is remitted outward in a lump sum from an account of personal spot exchange deposit, or cash foreign banknotes less than USD $ 2,000 or equivalent are remitted outward in a lump sum from foreign banknote holding or from an account of personal foreign banknote deposit, the outward remittance procedures may be followed directly at the bank.

If spot exchange of more than USD $ 10,000 (USD $ 10,000 inclusive) but less than USD $ 50,000 is remitted outward in a lump sum, or foreign banknotes valued at more than USD $ 2,000 (USD $ 2,000 inclusive) but less than USD $ 10,000 or equivalent are remitted outward in a lump sum, an application shall be filed with the local state administration of exchange control by presenting the certificate materials for current account expenditures and related customs declaration for inward foreign exchange or bank documents or bank certificate. After examination of truthfulness by the state administration of exchange control, outward remittance procedures may be followed at the bank against the certificate of approval issued by the state administration exchange control.

If spot exchange valued at USD $ 50,000 (USD $ 50,000 inclusive) or more is remitted outward in a lump sum or equivalent, or foreign banknotes valued at USD ＄ 10,000 (USD ＄ 10,000 inclusive) or more are remitted outward in a lump sum, the local administration exchange control shall report it to the State Administration of Exchange control for examination and approval, and the outward remittance procedures may be followed at the bank against the certificate of approval issued by the local state administration of exchange control.

## Allen Slattery Continues on the Subject of International Remittance

Our customers often ask how to receive their proceeds of remittance from abroad very quickly. Well, the only answer is to ask the client to open a current account in foreign exchange with our bank or our subsidiaries, and then inform the remitter abroad of the account number, the name of the account holder (in standard Chinese phonetic alphabet), and the name of the depository bank, its address, and the SWIFT CODE.

What to do if the remitted currency is different from that of his account? If the currency of inward remittance is different from the currency of the inward remittance account your client designates, say, an inward remittance is in Canadian dollars while your account is a US dollar account, it will be entered into the account after the proceeds are converted into the US dollars according to the exchange rate for the current day. If the inward remittance is in Renminbi, it cannot be converted into a foreign currency but entered direct into the account; if the inward remittance is in a foreign currency, it can be entered into a Renminbi account after conversion.

Why is the amount of a T/T remittance received sometimes less than the original amount of remittance?

If the remitting bank and our bank mutually open nostro/vostro accounts, a remittance may usually reach our bank in full. However, as most remitting banks do not have any account relationship with our bank, a remittance may have to be transferred to our bank via one or several correspondent banks. Each correspondent bank deducts a service charge when handling the transfer service. Therefore, the amount of the T/T remittance you receive is probably less than the original amount of remittance.

## Allen Slattery—Foreign Exchange Dealings for Individuals

We also provide service to our customers in foreign exchange dealings for accounts of individuals. It refers to firm foreign exchange dealings conducted by individuals through the service personnel behind the counter or through electronic banking service methods within the dialing time set by the Bank.

This service is marked with such characteristics: firstly, we provide longer service time for dealings. To be specific, business hours of each branch vary with different conditions. The longest dealing hours can last 18 hours each day, covering business hours of the main international financial markets. Secondly, fluctuations of exchange rates are quite frequent. Banks make offers according to the quotations of the international foreign exchange market and in line with international practices. Affected by various kinds of political and economic factors in the world and by contingencies, the exchange rates often show radical fluctuations. As a result, risks and opportunities co-exist in foreign exchange dealings for accounts of individuals. This leaves room for individual investors to conduct deals. Thirdly, this bank provides varied methods for dealings. Dealings can be carried out through the service personnel behind the counter, by telephone or self-service devices, etc. Each of the aforesaid three methods has its advantages:

In dealings at the counter, good services offered can be felt in a human atmosphere. It is particularly suitable for the investors who have just begun to be involved in foreign exchange dealings for accounts of individuals.

Dealings by telephone can make prompt conclusions and can be operated in other places than the investor's home city. It is particularly suitable for the white-collar investors who are occupied with their work.

Self-service dealings can provide substantial information and can provide various charts for technical analysis. It is particularly suitable for the investors who are experienced in foreign exchange dealings.

Dealings can both be made either according to market prices or on an agent basis. A dealing made as per the market price is otherwise called a real-time dealing, which is concluded as per the current prices offered by the Bank. A dealing made on an agent basis is otherwise called a dealing as per offered prices, which means an investor can leave the order for a dealing to the Bank first, and when the Bank offers reach the level expected by the investor, the computer system of the bank will conclude the business immediately according to the order of the investor. A dealing made through telephone is an operating method that saves both time and energy to the fullest extent.

Fund settlement for foreign exchange dealings can be done very quickly at this bank; therefore counter-offers can be conducted many times within the same day, thus providing more opportunities for investment.

## Allen Slattery Continues—Foreign Exchange Dealings for Individuals

Having said the above, you might wish to know to whom this product is provided. Residents or individuals within mainland China who, with full capacity for civil conduct, bear valid identification certificates can conduct firm foreign exchange dealings.

Now, let me describe procedures for handling the dealings. For dealings at the counter, the customer must have certain amount of foreign currency deposits and he should go to the designated branch of this Bank to fill in relevant forms and documents and then give them to the clerks across the counter. For dealings by telephone, the client should get a one-for-all current passbook (一本通) and a credit card issued by this Bank and deposit certain amount of foreign currencies.

The client should then file an application at any spot of this bank's networks with his valid identification card, fill out relevant application form and sign an agreement and then give them to the clerks across the counter together with the one-for-all demand passbook and the credit card. The client should now insert the password of six digits for the account and then the account for dealings by telephone is open. The client can use an (touch-tone) phone. He can now start his business by dialing the number for dealings and inserting the correct account number and password.

We mentioned about dealings by self-service. How is that done? Well, like the first step for dealings by telephone, the client should get a one-for-all demand passbook and a credit card and deposit certain amount of foreign currencies. The client should then file an application at a spot in the networks of this Bank with his valid identification card, fill out the relevant application form and sign an agreement and then give them to the clerks across the counter together with the one-for-all demand passbook and the credit card.

The client should then insert the password of six digits for the account and then the account for self-service dealings is open. The client can now conduct the dealings by inserting the correct password into the device provided especially for self-service dealings.

### Clive Bond, Assistant Director of Retail Banking

One thing this bank is proud of is that we have realized automatic banking of local and foreign currency current and time deposits through out the country. That is to say a client who has a deposit account in any operational unit of the branches and sub-branches of the Bank in the local province may deposit and cash money against a debit card or the passbook in all operational units of the Bank in the local province that are connected by the computer network. In the meantime, the NIC-NAP network of the Bank enables clients to realize consumption and cash withdrawal by using electronic debit cards through the ATMs and DECs of our bank through the country.

### Clive Bond—Multifunctional Debit Card

As a member of this bank, you have to be very familiar with our service of multifunctional debit card. It provides convenience to cardholders. A cardholder can cash or consume without the need to bring his or her certificate of deposit passbook or I.D. card. It can serve many purposes including withdrawal, transfer, inquiry, consumption, settlement and deposit. What is more, with a laser anti-fake mark and a personal password, the card is incomparably safe. The card is connected with a computer network of international standard. It is currently usable in the ATM network of host regions in China and will gradually be usable in the whole country or even in the whole world. The application procedures are fairly simple. Card account opening service is available at all operational outlets of branches and sub-branches of the Bank that have already opened the electronic debit card service, and there is no need for guarantee.

### Clive Bond Continues—Multifunctional Debit Card

When a client has successfully applied for a debit card, it is your duty to advise the person of how to use the card. The first thing you should tell the client is to change the password. That is to say after a client has got a card, the person may change the password of the card at his or her will at the banking outlets and ATMs connected with the computer network. A password is composed of six digits, the cardholder should choose six numbers that are easy for him/her to remember. The next thing the client should know is that the cardholder may use the debit card to inquire the balance of the card account at an ATM. You should also tell the client that if the balance of the card account is ample, the maximum amount the person may withdraw in a single day is RMB ¥5,000. Lastly, you should tell your client that he or she can transfer the funds in the card account to other accounts.

You must inform your client in case he or she failed to operate properly or typed in a wrong password, the ATM would swallow the card. If that happened, the client should go to the outlet where the card was issued with his or her I.D. card and the debit card account to get it back three days later.

In order to avoid such a hassle, you should advise the client the following:

1. After a single operation on an ATM is completed, the card shall be taken out fully before a second deal is to be made. Otherwise the ATM may confiscate the card.

2. The daily ceiling for encashment of ATM is RMB ¥5,000. Multiple withdrawals are permitted, with the minimum amount being RMB ¥50. The daily ceiling for transfer is RMB ¥50,000, amounts involving jiao and fen digits are permitted.

3. The client should keep the "notice to clients" for future reference.

4. Advise the client not to put password and card together lest loss should be incurred in case of theft.

### Christine Stannard—Personal Cheque Deposits

Personal cheque deposits this bank provides are current deposits guaranteed by personal credit worthiness and such a cheque can serve as a payment settlement certificate. A personal cheque may be used for transfer, cashing and shopping.

Such deposits are suitable for clients with big-amount or frequent receipts and payments. The cheque validity is 10 days.

A cheque issuer already applying for telephone banking service may certify a cheque issued through the telephone banking service, and the drawee may inquire the condition of certification the said cheque through the special telephone line of the bank.

### Christine Stannard—Safety Deposit Boxes

A safe deposit box is a kind of service rendered by the bank that keeps valuables for the renter who rents a safe deposit box.

A renter aged 18 or above may apply for renting a safe deposit box against his or her valid credentials (for a unit renter, with the seal of the unit and signet of its legal representative affixed); the applicant should fill in the Application for Renting Safe Deposit Box, and sign a Box Renting Contract with the bank on a voluntary basis.

### Christine Stannard—Fee-Based Business

Our bank, acting as agent, currently provides such fee-based business as payment of fees, giving pay packets, handling stock fund transfer, handling securities trading settlement and handling insurance service. All these are intermediary services of the bank.

Let me talk about Bill Payment Service first. Bill payment service is a kind of transfer settlement service in which the bank collects fees from their users as an agent of fee collectors (such as postal, power, gas and water supply departments).

All the fee collectors and their users should open current accounts with the agent bank. On the days of fee collection provided in the agreements, the bank regularly debits the accounts of the users with the amounts listed in the fee collection sheets issued by the collectors and brings them to the credit of the accounts of the collectors, and also takes commissions according to the number of times payments are made by the users. The clients may also pay such fees, say, fixed telephone charges, mobile phone charges, traffic violation fines, insurance premiums, etc., in cash across the bank counters.

### Christine Stannard—Automatic Deposit Service

Automatic deposit service is a kind of service provided by the bank, which is entrusted by state organs, public institutions and enterprises to allocate pays directly to their staff members and workers through their current accounts opened with the bank.

To do so, the paying party, after consultations with the bank, shall fill in and address a letter of authorization to the bank for allocating salaries on its behalf, each staff member of the paying party shall open a current account with the bank who in turn issues to them passbooks or ATM cards with which they may withdraw their deposits. This kind of business departs from the traditional practice of clients, as it is more convenient for the clients and it changes the behavior of "use before depositing" to "use after depositing".

# Sample Examination Questions

## Vocabulary

1. Use the following words or phrases in a sentence.
   - a. traveler's cheque
   - b. commission
   - c. recourse
   - d. certified cheque
   - e. password
   - f. T/T remittance
2. List the names of ten foreign currencies.
3. Define the following words and phrases and provide a Chinese translation.
   - a. spot exchange rate
   - b. remitting bank
   - c. beneficiary
   - d. credit card

## Understanding

1. What credentials must be presented in order for a bank customer to convert one currency into another?
2. What is an exchange memo used for?
3. Who is Thomas Cook?
4. What would a bank client use a safety deposit box for?
5. What are the advantages to a client of a debit card?
6. What is the first thing a client should do after receiving a debit card from your bank?
7. What are the three ways of dealing in foreign currencies with a bank and what are the advantages of each method?
8. What does a bank customer need to do in order to cash a traveler's cheque?
9. Explain why a bank client may receive less than the face amount of a bill or draft that has been sent for collection.
10. How is a debit card protected against fraudulent use?
11. What are some of the ways in which a bank can earn fees or commissions?
12. Explain the procedure to a client if a remittance is in a currency different from the currency of his or her account.
13. Customers can pay certain bills at commercial banks. What must an organization that wants the bank to collect its bills for it do in order to use this service?

# Part V

## Corporate Banking: Loans
## 公司业务：贷款

*Building a factory, a pipeline, oil refinery, operating an airline, developing a mine—banks can provide a large part of the financing you need.*

Large projects like offshore oil-drilling rigs require large amounts of capital to set up. International commercial banks have teams of specialists who are experts at analyzing project requirements and developing the best financing package. The cash flow of the project is used to pay interest and principal on the loan. In many cases, no outside guarantee or security needs to be provided by the project sponsors.

Commercial Banking  商业银行

## Introduction  导语

One of the most important functions of commercial banks is providing loans for businesses to operate and grow. As businesses expand, they need more workers so that jobs are created and the well being of the country increases.

This section explains ways in which banks make money available to businesses.

Working capital loans provide businesses with the financing that they need to buy raw materials and to pay operating costs like wages, fuel and utilities until they collect cash from their customers.

Part Ⅴ—Corporate Banking: Loans　公司业务: 贷款

Government departments and businesses use fixed asset loans from banks to help finance the cost of constructing new plants and infrastructure facilities such as this waste water treatment plant being built in southern China.

Some project loans such as the one to build a 4,000 kilometer pipeline are just too large for one bank to handle alone. In these cases, banks compete to win the mandate to arrange and manage the financing. When an agreement has been reached between the project sponsor and the bank, the bank will invite other banks to join in the financing. This process is called syndication and will be described later in this section.

## Section A—RMB Working Capital Loan　人民币流动资金贷款

### Skill—building exercise #A1—Translation

Peter Baker, Assistant Director of Corporate Banking, is having a meeting with Roy Meadow, Chief Accountant of Packaging Equipment Company. Peter is explaining RMB Working Capital Loan to Roy. Before listening to their conversation, look at the Chinese expressions below and then discuss their meaning in English with your partner after listening.

流动资金　　融资　　工商行政管理局　　企业法人　　营业执照
公司章程　　审计　　财务报表

### Skill-building exercise #A2—Understanding

Listen to the conversation between Peter Baker and Roy Meadow again and then answer these two questions.

1. What is a RMB Working Capital Loan?
2. How can one apply for this type of loan?

### Skill-building exercise #A3—Speaking

Play the role of Peter Baker and ask your partner to play the role of Roy Meadow, and then switch roles.

## Section B—Fixed Asset Loan  固定资产贷款

### Skill-building exercise #B1—Translation

Dora Walker, an accountant of a real estate developer, is talking to Peter Baker about getting a loan for fixed asset. Look at the Chinese expressions below and discuss their meaning in English with your partner after listening.

| | | | | |
|---|---|---|---|---|
| 基本建设 | 技术改造 | 工程建设 | 周转性贷款 | 事业法人 |
| 贷款证 | 信用状况 | 基本账户 | 产业政策 | |

### Skill-building exercise #B2—Listening comprehension

Listen to the dialogue again and answer the following questions:

1. What is a Fixed Asset Loan?
2. Who can apply for it?
3. What are the procedures for application?

### Skill-building exercise #B3—Speaking

Play the role of Peter Baker and ask your partner to play the role of Dora Walker. And then switch roles.

# Section C—Foreign Currency Loans  外汇贷款

### Skill-building exercise #C1—Listening comprehension

Peter now talks to Jennifer Kent, Chief Financial Officer of Anna Steel Works. As you listen to their conversation, look at these headings. Which ones do they talk about and in which order?

- What can Foreign Currency Loan do
- Procedures for applying
- Qualification of the applicant
- Documents needed for application

### Skill-building exercise #C2—Vocabulary

Look at the terms in the left-hand column. Match each one with its correct definition in the right-hand column.

| | |
|---|---|
| Fixed interest rate | money lent by a bank for export |
| Floating interest rate | an economic organization |
| LIBOR | something required as a condition |
| Comprehensive cost | give something in exchange for something else |
| Swap | a cost in every aspect |
| Export credit | the freely varying amount of payment made by the borrower expressed as a percentage of capital |
| Economic entity | London inter-bank offer rate |
| Precondition | the set amount of payment made by the borrower expressed as a percentage of capital |

### Skill-building exercise #C3—Listening comprehension

Look at the questions below and try to answer them after listening to the dialogue again.
1. What is a Foreign Currency Loan?
2. How is the interest rate calculated for that loan?
3. Who can apply for such a loan?
4. What is the procedure for application?

### Skill-building exercise #C4—Speaking

Reproduce the dialogue by playing the roles of Peter Baker and Jennifer Kent with your partner.

## Section D—Project Financing  项目融资

### Skill-building exercise #D1—Understanding

Janet Edmund, Chief Accountant of Dayang Road and Bridge Construction Corporation, comes to Peter Baker for financing a bridge project. As you listen to their conversation, look at these headings. Which ones do they talk about and in which order?

- Documents to be provided for application
- Forms of financing
- What project financing
- Applying procedures

### Skill-building exercise #D2—Translation

Look at the Chinese expressions below and discuss their meaning in English with your partner:

项目融资    追索权    还本付息    物权担保    第三方    可行性研究报告
专利    完工担保    超支    合同和章程    税务登记

### Skill-building exercise #D3—Understanding

Look at the questions below and try to answer them after listening to the dialogue again:
1. What is project financing?
2. How many forms in rendering them? Describe each of them.
3. What does the bank have to check on the borrowing party?
4. Is there any difference in the procedure of application from other loans?

### Skill-building exercise #D4—Speaking

Reproduce the dialogue by playing the roles of Peter Baker and Janet Edmund with your partner.

## Section E—Bill Discount 票据贴现

### Skill-building exercise #E1—Translation

Look at the Chinese expressions below and discuss their meaning in English after reading the following text.

票据　　未到期　　承兑汇票　　商业承兑汇票　　贴现　　变现　　票面金额
银行垫付的款项　　诚实守信　　承兑人

This bank can extend credit to companies by purchasing undue bank acceptance bills and trade acceptance bills. Bill discount is a credit service. A recipient or a bill holder may apply to the bank for discount of an undue bank acceptance bill or a trade acceptance bill, and the bank, after deducting discount interest from the face value of the bill, pays remaining sum to the applicant. After discount, the bill belongs to the discounting bank, which may collect the sum under the bill from the acceptor when the bill becomes due.

As an efficient financing method, bill discount has the following characteristics: first of all, a client would be able to encash his commercial bills quickly. The formality is simple and the cost of financing is low. Secondly, with the fund advanced by the bank, a client is able to speed up the turnover of his working fund and improve the efficiency of fund utilization.

To enjoy this service, the draft to be discounted must be a valid one under the *Law of Commercial Instruments of the People's Republic of China and Methods of Payment and Settlement of the People's Bank of China*, and all necessary factors should be on the draft. The face value of a single draft cannot exceed RMB 10 million. The draft is issued and acquired in good faith and based on true and lawful transaction and liability relations.

The following documents have to be provided to the bank for review: the immature acceptance bill and the certificate for the applicant's status as an enterprise legal person and related legal documents, the business license (copy) of the enterprise (legal person), which has been verified in the annual check, the legal representative's certificate or power of attorney, resolution of the board and articles of association of the applying company, the applicant's recent financial statements, a letter of application for discount and a copy of the transaction contract between the Discount Applicant and the issuer of the bill and a copy of the value added invoice under the contract.

To apply for this service, the applicant should go to a branch of the bank with the undue bank acceptance bill or trade acceptance bill, and fills up the Application Form for Discount of Bank Acceptance Bills or the Application Form for Discount of Trade Acceptance Bills.

The applicant should provide the materials mentioned in the foregoing paragraph to the bank. The bank will then check the authenticity and validity of the draft and the trade background according to prescribed procedures. The bank will also calculate the discount interest and the discounted amount. Discount Interest is equal to the face value of the draft multiplied by the number of actual discount days times monthly discount rate divided by 30 days. Actually Discounted Amount is face value of the draft minus discount interest. The bank would then extend the loan, which is the actually discounted amount.

### Skill-building exercise #E2—Understanding

The text contains five paragraphs. Match the ideas below with the appropriate paragraph.
- Required materials
- Application qualifications
- Characteristics of the service
- Application procedures
- Summary of the service

### Skill-building exercise #E3—Speaking

Discuss the following questions with your partner and then present to the class:
1. What is Bill Discount?
2. Why do people apply for it?
3. Who can apply for it?

## Section F—Syndicated Loan  银团贷款

### Skill-building exercise #F1—Translation

Look at the Chinese expressions below and discuss their meaning in English after reading the following text.

| 银团贷款 | 双边贷款 | 分散风险 | 贷款通则 | 重点工程 | 备忘录 |
| 验资报告 | 承建商 | 贷款额度 | 融资招标书 | 牵头行 | 主承销行 |

The syndicated loan is a financing method evolved from bilateral loans. Under the arrangement of syndicated loan, one bank or several banks (as the arrangers) organize other banks to grant loans to the same borrower under one loan agreement according to agreed terms.

With rapid development of international trade and investment, the international demand for credit funds also increases sharply. But an individual bank is often unable or reluctant to extend credit in huge amount. To diversify risks, several banks can provide a loan together under strict rules and agreement. The syndicated loan thus came into being.

Syndicated loans have the following features: to compare to government loans and export credit, syndicated loans can offer a much larger amount of funds with a longer term and less restriction on purposes of loan; it is easier to manage (compared with loans borrowed separately from different banks); and lessens pressure on banks; and its risks are more dispersed. As far as the borrower is concerned, syndicated loans can satisfy its need for much larger amount of funds with a longer term and easier operation and management (only need to contact with the agent bank).

According to the national industrial policies and economic development plans of the local government, syndicated loans are focused on energy, transportation, hi-tech industries and regional key projects. Eligible applicants include corporations incorporated inside China or other economic organizations approved by the banks (referred to as the borrower) that comply with *General Rules on Loans and Interim Regulation on Syndicated Loans*.

Documents needed for application are the following: information on the borrower, its Chinese and foreign shareholders and its guarantors should be provided to the lead bank. The borrower should also provide to the bank copies of government approval on project recommendation, feasibility studies and the overall estimate on the cost of construction. Other documents the bank needs to check on are the verifying report or certificate on the injection of registered capital by the borrower, the articles of association of the company, contract of joint venture or cooperation between the borrower and foreign investment or native enterprises, commercial contracts and other related contracts of equipment purchase and technology, the engineering and construction contract and information on the contractor, contract of supply of raw materials, secondary material and fuel, letter of intent or sales contract of products of the project, government approval of domestic sales for purpose of substituting products of import, contracts of water and power supply, documents to show the scale of examination of the project at the end of year and the size of borrowing foreign loan issued by government planning department, paper of approval on borrowing from abroad by state administration of foreign exchange, approvals by the administration of industry and commerce, tax bureaus, environment authorities and the customs, certificate on ownership of properties mortgaged, a list of and report on these properties and other documents and information required by the bank.

When the bank is informed of the needs of a loan or bidding documents for financing by the client, the bank will discuss the loan provisions and financing structure with the client, and drafts the related documents. The bank should then be duly designated as the lead bank/underwriter for the syndicated loan. The bank then confirms the amount of credit, defines the syndicate timetable, strategy and composition of the syndicate. The bank should then prepare the loan memorandum and invitation to the syndicate and invite all the related financial institutions. The next thing to do is for the participating banks to make commitment on their subscription. The credit lines of the participating banks should be finalized. All parties should then reach consensus on the loan agreement and guarantee agreement. Lastly, all members of the syndicate should sign the agreement. When this is done, all routine work is left to the agent bank.

### Skill-building exercise #F2—Understanding

The text contains six paragraphs. Match the ideas below with the appropriate paragraph.
- Required materials
- Application qualifications
- Characteristics of the service
- Application procedures
- Summary of the service
- Eligible applicant

### Skill-building exercise #F3—Speaking

Discuss the following questions with your partner and then present to the class:
1. What is a Syndicated loan?
2. What is special about it?
3. Who can apply for it?

## Dialogue—Working Capital Loan

P (Peter Baker): Hi, Roy! So nice to see you again.

R (Roy): Hi. You may know our company is a bit short recently, because of more incoming orders. So, I am sent by our director to see if we can get some kind of a working capital loan.

P: I am pleased you come to us. Because we do have the right thing for you.

R: How nice! Now, please tell me about your product.

P: Well, what we can provide to you is RMB Working Capital Facility. It is a kind of loan used to meet short-term demands of customers in the course of production and operation. The RMB Working Capital Facility has become an efficient and practical financing means and has been widely used among customers because of its shorter term, simple procedures, high revolving nature and lower cost.

R: Excellent. We are the right people to use it. How long do we have to pay it back?

P: In terms of the length of maturity, RMB Working Capital Loans can be divided into the short-term loan with its maturity of less than one year and the medium-term loan with its maturity ranging from one to three years.

R: I see. What kind of guarantee do you want from us?

P: This is something we can discuss. Generally speaking, based on the means of supporting the loan, RMB Working Capital Loans can be divided into a guaranteed loan, which can be supported by a guarantee, mortgage, or pledge and a credit loan.

R: You see we have received several letters of credit from our customers abroad. Can we use them as a pledge?

P: I shall come back to that question. Considering the using procedure, RMB Working Capital Loans can be arranged in two ways, one is to be applied and approved every time; the other is a revolving loan, which is subject to a certain amount and period set by the bank.

R: The revolving one is very attractive.

P: As a procedure, we have to check the qualification of your company.

R: By all means. We have been on the up beat for almost a decade.

P: Good. Generally we would request that the borrower should be an enterprise or institutional legal person, or other economic organization or a private industrial and commercial company registered after verification and ratification by the industrial and commercial administrative organs (or other competent authorities), and should bear a "Business License for the Enterprise Legal Person" issued by the industrial and commercial administrative departments.

R: We see no difficulties in providing such documents.

P: What's more, the usage of loan should result in good economic effect and the borrower should be able to pay principal and interest in due time; the borrower should also satisfy other requirements for the loan set by related regulations of the Bank.

R: Oh, you can be assured of that. Our internal return rate is somewhere around 10%.

P: I am impressed. How long does it take you to finish an order?

R: For an order of normal size, it usually takes us 45 days.

P: I see. You can apply for a loan for 45 days. You know what, since you are new to this product, for the first loan why not mortgage the equipment you produce in the same value as the loan you are asking. Then, from the second loan onwards, we can use the revolving pattern. Next year, if both of us are satisfied and you still need this vehicle, we can think of a pledge.

R: Fair enough. Please tell me what documents I should bring to you.

P: A written application of course, a Certificate of the representative of the enterprise legal person, or a letter of authorization from the representative if you are going to sign agreements with us, related resolutions of the Board of Directors and the charter of your company; Business License for the Enterprise Legal Person verified in the annual check. (Copy files accepted); the audited financial statements for last three years and the recent financial statements, a Loan Card if you have got one and other documents and certificates required by Bank.

R: All right. I have taken note of all the documents. How do I go about it?

P: You should submit the written application as well as supplementary documents to this department, i. e. the Corporate Banking Department; the Bank will then examine and verify the application materials of the potential borrower; when the application is accepted by the Bank, your company will sign a RMB Working Capital Loan Agreement and other agreements (such as a guarantee letter, a mortgage agreement, or a pledge agreement) if necessary with us. You have to open a RMB loan account in this Bank for purpose of drawing. Well, that's about it.

R: Thank you so much for the detailed introduction and discussion. I shall report to our director and the board and come back to you very soon.

P: We certainly look forward to that. Thank you for coming.

## Dialogue—Fixed Asset Loan

W(Dora Walker): Hello, Pete. How are you doing?

P: Hello, Dora. Long time no see. You must be here for business.

W: Yes, I am.

P: So, what is your problem?

W: I would like to know a little bit about your Fixed Asset Loan.

P: I see. I can explain it to you. The purpose of providing this loan is to resolve fund demands of enterprises in their investments in fixed assets. You certainly know that investments by enterprises in fixed assets including capital construction, technical innovation, developing and manufacturing new products as well as related house purchase, civil engineering, purchase and installation of the technical equipment and so on.

W: Yes, I know. I also know that there are three categories in this loan: long-term loan, temporary circulating loan and foreign exchange loan.

P: You are right. Almost every bank divides such a loan into these three kinds. It can be used in capital construction, which includes infrastructure, municipal works, service facilities, new or enlarged productive projects ratified and approved by the authorities concerned.

W: Can it be used in projects of technical innovation?

P: Even though it is called fixed asset loan, it can be used in technical innovation items aimed at expanding reproduction by existing enterprises.

W: There is a research and development department in our company. Could this department apply for this loan?

P: Well, research projects aiming at upgrading technology and applying it in production can enjoy services of this loan. If enterprises do not build houses or facilities themselves, they can use it to purchase them directly for production, storage and office work. The department you mentioned cannot apply for it, because it is not a legal person.

W: Do you mean the applicant must be a legal person?

P: Yes, the applicant must be a legal person. That is to say an enterprise legal person, a legal person of an undertaking and other economic organizations that have registered upon verification and ratification by the industrial and commercial administrative bureau (or other competent authorities) and conducted an independent accounting can apply for this loan.

W: But I am sure not all legal persons are qualified for application.

P: Smart! Aside from being a legal person, the applicant must bear a Business License that has passed the annual examination by the industrial and commercial administrative departments and the legal person of an undertaking must bear documents certifying its legal status.

W: Is that all what is needed?

P: Of course not, there are other things needed, things like the Permit or Card for Loan verified and issued by the People's Bank of China. The applicant should have good economic returns, a sound creditability, a strong capability to repay debt and a complete and excellent management system. It should fulfill guarantees acknowledged by the Bank; the applicant should also open a basic account or an ordinary deposit account with the Bank; most importantly, the items for which a fixed asset loan is applied for should comply with the State industrial policies and credit policies. At the same time, the applicant must possess a certain amount of capital, and the proportion of which conforms to the stipulation of the government. The project should have been examined and approved by the governmental departments concerned, with complete auxiliary conditions and ready sources of supply of equipment and materials from abroad. Last but not least, the applicant must have in its hands an import instrument or import registration documents if a foreign exchange fixed asset loan is to be applied.

W: That's quite complicated. But I have noted all of them down. Now, what are the procedures of application?

P: The borrower should first of all submit a written application to us. The applying party should then hand in the demanded relevant documents, including the Business License, Charter of the Company, financial reports for the recent three years, documents about establishment of the project and documents of approval, analysis of the project economic benefits and plans for use and repayment of the loans, etc..

W: You will then check on the documents.

P: Yes, we shall make pre-loan investigations and evaluations, look into the credit standing of the borrower as well as into the legitimacy, safety and profitability of the borrowing, verify and examine the pledges, properties and guarantors and come up with a conclusion on evaluations.

W: Agreements will be signed if evaluations ended in a positive way, I suppose.

P: Upon confirmation after review and examination in the bank, both parties will agree on terms and conditions stipulated in the borrowing contract, the mortgage contract and the guarantee contract and all sides concerned will sign the contracts. After signing, the borrower will go through relevant formalities such as registration of the contracted mortgage, etc.. The borrower will file an application for drawing money. When all these are done, the funds will then be transferred into the bank account for the borrower.

W: I learned a lot from our conversation. I shall discuss with my boss and see what he will decide to do, and come back to you.

P: Terrific.

## Dialogue—Foreign Currency Loan

J (Jennifer Kent): Welcome, Mr. Baker. You are on time for our regular meeting.

P: It's a pleasure to be here. Every time I come, I can find something new.

J: Nice to here that. As you may have noticed, we are expanding our production. For this purpose, we plan to import some milling machines from Luxemburg. Before we strike any deals with the foreign side, I have to be sure what loan vehicles we shall use.

P: I think our Foreign Currency Loan will serve your purpose. It is granted to enterprises, our bank raises foreign currencies used in this loan by itself.

J: What currency do you think is better for this loan?

P: We render this loan only in five currencies: they are US dollar, Euro, pound sterling, Japanese yen and Hong Kong dollar. Personally, Euro can be your first choice. It is depreciating a little bit.

J: We shall think about that. How about interest rate?

P: Both fixed interest rate and floating interest rate can be used for this type of loan. Yet, the floating rate is decided with reference to LIBOR plus comprehensive cost of the bank's financing and relevant profits. We can swap the floating rate into a fixed one if our customers do request so. Compared with foreign government loans and Export Credit offered by foreign banks, Foreign Currency Loans can serve more diversified purposes, and can be used in equipment and material purchase from any country or regions.

J: We will most probably ask you to swap. Do you think you can arrange a medium term for this loan?

P: As it can be rendered in a short-term, a long-term and a medium-term as well, we can certainly arrange it.

J: Since you know us so well. I am sure you will take us as a qualified applicant for this loan.

P: The Foreign Currency Loan of this bank is only extended to enterprises. Your company has an enterprise legal person status, you have an account opened in this bank and I believe you also have the ability to repay the loan. So you are basically all right.

J: What do you mean?

P: Aside from the application you are going to file, our legal department and my department will have to double check on your registration at the industrial and commercial administrative bureau, your business license, your purpose of borrowing, the perspective of return rate and your source of foreign currency (If the borrowers have no foreign exchange income, they shall be authorized by the foreign exchange administrative organ to purchase foreign exchange for the repayment). You have to conform to other loan related regulations of this bank. Of course, you will be asked to provide necessary documents, and this is something you are so familiar with.

J: Yes, I know. Every thing will be ready for you, like business license, audited financial statements for the last three years and recent financial statements, the Certificate of Loan and so on.

P: Exactly. I would like to repeat to you that after an internal approval has been obtained, we should sign a loan contract with you. I should stress that before you can draw money according to the loan contract, you should first fulfill preconditions for the withdrawal and register with the foreign exchange administration.

J: I really appreciate your patience in explaining all this to me. I am totally clear about the possibilities and related procedures. I shall call you as when I would come with all necessary documents to conclude the contract.

P: Fine. I look forward to that. Thank you very much for your time and coffee.

## Dialogue—Project Financing

J: How are you, Pete?

P: Fine, thank you. And you?

J: As you can see, I am terribly tired.

P: Sorry to hear that. What can I do to help you?

J: That's what I am here for. We have just won the bid for the bridge between Chongming and Qidong. We need money for this project.

P: Congratulations! Our product of **project financing** will suit you perfectly. It refers to the practice that the sponsor (i.e. shareholder) of a project, which establishes a project company to borrow loans in the name of the company, uses cash flows and revenues of the company to pay back the loans and leaves the assets of the company as the guarantee. This financing mode is commonly applied to large-scale infrastructure projects, which generate steady cash flows, such as power generation, roads, railways, airports, bridges, etc. The scope of application is expanding to some

## Commercial Banking 商业银行

other areas such as big petrol chemical projects. That's why I say it's perfect for you.

J: Thank you for saying so. I was told this product is delivered in two forms. Can you tell me more about it?

P: I shall be pleased to do so. You are right. One form is project financing without recourse. It is also referred to as pure project financing. In this form of financing, repayment of the interest and principal of the loans solely depends on performance of the project operation. At the same time, the lending bank acquires property right of the project assets as collateral for the loan. If the project fails to be completed or suffers operational losses, and if its assets or proceeds are inadequate to repay all the loans, the lending bank will have no recourse to the sponsor of the project.

J: That sounds very inviting. We shall try this one.

P: Well, you never know. We may be able to offer it to you. But you have to wait until we go through our checking procedures. Given the record you have created, the likelihood is quite high. Do you want to know about the other form?

J: Yes, I certainly do. Please.

P: The other form is what we call **project financing with limited recourse.** In this form of financing, our bank will require a third party to provide guarantee to the loan, even though you will use operational revenue stream of the project as the source of repayment and your property right as a guarantee. By doing so, our bank has recourse to the third party guarantor. Please note that the guarantor is only liable to the amount of guarantee. So it is referred to as project financing with limited recourse.

J: Honestly, it is not difficult for us to find a third party guarantor. You mentioned just now about your checking procedures. What are they?

P: We have to check if competent government authorities have formally approved the project. Secondly we shall look at the feasibility study report of the project and see if it has been reviewed and approved by related government departments. We would then make sure if any introduction of foreign technology, equipment, and patents has been rectified by the economic and foreign trade authorities. The next thing we should do is to check if you have secured raw material supple for the project. This can be proved by your supply contract or a letter of intent with your supplier. You should also provide us with a guarantee for the completion of the project, and a financial arrangement for over-expenditure of capital construction cost. You should not only agree to transfer the insurance interests to our bank, but also agree to mortgage your fixed assets both being and already built and pledge the proceeds made from the project to us. The shareholders of the project should also agree to pledge their equity rights to us.

J: Well, there are shareholders in our company. They are all state owned enterprises.

P: This applied to any shareholders.

J: You are really demanding. Your checking list is quite long.

P: Wait a minute. I haven't finished yet.

J: My goodness.

P: We have to be convinced that the project has a good marketing channel, preferably if you have secured "take or pay" purchases and sales contracts. Products of the project should have sound market prospects and good potential of development and profitability. In your specific case, we must know if the bridge, when it is completed, can generate good income. I would like to add that the land use right of the project must also be secured. If water and power supply, communications and other support facilities are involved, you must proved that they will be available.

J: I don't see any difficulties in passing through your cheques. I suppose we have to provide all necessary documents.

P: This is what I was going to emphasize to you. You have to provide with the following documents: approval of the feasibility study report issued by related government authorities, approval by the environment authorities (a foreign invested enterprise must provide the official written approval of the joint venture contract and articles of association issued by the Ministry of Foreign Trade and Economic Cooperation), a copy of the business license, the tax registration license of both "national tax and local tax", a copy of the institution reference code certificate of the People's Republic of China, a copy of the foreign currency registration certificate (foreign-invested enterprise), land planning permit for construction, construction project planning permit, identity certificate of the representative of the legal person and your loan card. We have to keep copies of "take or pay" purchase and sale contract if you have one, material supply contracts, completion guarantee, plan for overspent costs, transfer of insurance interests, mortgage of construction in progress or already built fixed assets, pledge of the project's proceeds and shareholders' equity right.

J: There is one thing I have to make clear to you. The government does not allow us to charge a toll on passing the bridge. To compensate us, the government will give us some subsidies.

P: In this case, we must have a copy of the government decision on that, which should state clearly the amount of subsidy and for how long you will enjoy it.

J: No problem. I gather the applying procedure is not different from other loans.

P: It's more or less the same. Except the normal procedures, we have to negotiate and reach agreements on the arrangements of "take or pay" purchase and sale contracts (I know this does not fit your case), material supply contracts, completion guarantee, arrangements for overspent costs, transfer of insurance interests, mortgage of fixed assets already built or being built, pledge of the project's proceeds and shareholders' equity right, and other financing arrangements. This bank will review the application according to the credit approval procedures. Upon approval, your company will negotiate on the text of financing contract with us. When the contract is signed, it can then be executed and the loan is available for withdrawal.

J: Thank you very much for the detailed description. I shall be back with all necessary documents and our written application sometime next week.

P: You are most welcome. We would be ready at any time to render our services.

# Sample Examination Questions 模拟试题

## Vocabulary

1. Use the following words or phrases in a sentence.
   a. pledge
   b. loan
   c. written application
   d. encash
2. Define the following words and phrases and provide a Chinese translation.
   a. non-recourse
   b. bill discount
   c. banker's acceptance
   d. syndicated loan

## Understanding

1. What is the difference between a short term loan and a medium term loan?
2. What is a working capital loan used for?
3. Explain what is meant by the revolving nature of a working capital loan.
4. In order to qualify for a working capital loan, what does a client need to prove to the bank?
5. What documents does a client need to produce in order to obtain a working capital loan?
6. What kinds of bank customers might use a fixed asset loan and for what purposes?
7. Explain the difference between a fixed interest rate and a floating interest rate.
8. Why might a client want a foreign currency loan?
9. What documents must be provided to the bank in order to support an application for a project loan?
10. Explain how a bank can extend credit to a client by discounting bills.
11. What are the advantages of bill discounting to a bank client?
12. What kinds of loans are suitable for syndication and why do banks syndicate loans?
13. What does 'LIBOR' stand for, what does it mean and how is it used?
14. What are the three categories of fixed asset loan?
15. What are the advantages to a client of a non-recourse or limited recourse project loan?

Commercial Banking 商业银行

# Part VI

## Corporate Banking: Credit Lines; Trade Finance  公司业务：信用额度；商业信贷

*International trade contributes much to the economic growth of a country. Without banks, trading among businesses in many countries would be very difficult.*

Many of the products of our farms and factories would not reach overseas markets without the help of commercial banks.

# Part Ⅵ—Corporate Banking: Credit Lines; Trade Finance  公司业务：信用额度；商业信贷

## Introduction  导语

In order to get the raw materials for businesses manufacturing products for export to overseas markets, businesses need money. Banks provide revolving credit lines to manufacturers for this purpose. This section explains how it works. And when it comes to

getting paid by the foreign buyer, banks are there to help out. Letters of credit which are described more fully in this section are such an important part of international trading that it is difficult to imagine business without them.

## Section A—Credit Line　信用额度

### Skill-building exercise #A1—Translation

Ralph Edward, Chief Accountant of Electrical Appliance Limited, is talking to Kitty Homes, Assistant Manager of Corporate Banking Department on filing an application for a Credit Line. Look at the Chinese expressions below and discuss their meaning in English with your partner.

授信额度　　存量管理指标　　余额　　　快捷性　　便利性　　　开证　　保函
押汇　　　　投标保函　　　　履约保函　预付款保函　关税付款保函　海事保函

### Skill-building exercise #A2—Understanding

What have Ralph and Kitty discussed? And in what order?
1. How to apply for a Credit Line?
2. What business can a Credit Line cover?

### Skill-building exercise #A3—Understanding

Listen to the dialogue again and answer the following questions:
1. What is a Credit Line?
2. Who can apply for a Credit Line?
3. What documents are needed for the application?
4. What is the procedure for applying?

### Skill-building exercise #A4—Speaking

Work in pairs. One will play the part of Ralph Edward and the other Kitty Homes, and then switch roles.

## Section B—Worldwide Credit　统一授信

### Skill-building exercise #B1—Translation

Gary Wu, Deputy Director of Jiangsu Branch, Bank of China is calling on Lucy Menzis, Chief Representative of General Appliances Co., a world famous international

## Part Ⅵ—Corporate Banking: Credit Lines; Trade Finance  公司业务：信用额度；商业信贷

company in production and sales of electrical appliances. Gary is trying to sell the product of Worldwide Credit to the GA Company.

Look at the Chinese expressions below and discuss their meaning in English with your partner after listening to the dialogue.

统一大授信　　　整体性　　　海外跨国企业集团　　　统一授信
整体授信　　　　综合服务　　　总部　　　节省

### Skill-building exercise #B2—Listening comprehension

Listen to the dialogue again and answer the following questions：
1. Who is Lucy Menzis? Who is Gary Wu?
2. Why is Gary Wu calling on Lucy Menzis?
3. Can Lucy's office apply directly for a Worldwide Credit? If not, who can?
4. What is a Worldwide Credit?

### Skill-building exercise #B3—Speaking

Tell your partner what are needed in the application for the Worldwide Credit and how to apply.

### Skill-building exercise #B4—Speaking

Work in pairs, One plays the part of Gary Wu and the other Lucy Menzis, and then switch parts.

## Section C—Export Buyer's Credit  出口买方信贷

### Skill-building exercise #C1—Translation

Hugh Small, a manager of Sunrise Fishing Company, and Douglas Chen, manager of export of Fangzhou Shipyard are talking to Sophia Huang, assistant director of Dalian Branch of Industrial and Commercial Bank of China about a possible Export Buyer's Credit. Look at the Chinese expressions below and discuss their meaning in English with your partner after listening to their conversation：

成套设备　　船舶　　机电产品　　国际惯例　　承担费　　法定主权级借款部门
出口信用保险　　损益表　　现金流量表　　草本

## Commercial Banking 商业银行

### Skill-building exercise #C2—Listening comprehension

Listen to the conversation again and answer the following questions:

1. What is an Export Buyer's Credit?
2. Who can apply for it?
3. How much value can such a loan cover in the total value of the export contract?
4. What documents are needed in the application of such a loan?

### Skill-building exercise #C3—Speaking

Work with other two students. One plays the part of Gary, one Sophia and one Hugh, and then change roles.

### Skill-building exercise #C4—Reading comprehension

Read this letter which concerns a documentary credit issued by Sunrise Fishing Co.'s bank in Birmingham.

---

Letter head

Dalian Branch, Industrial and Commercial Bank of China

128, People's Road
Dalian, Liaoning, PRC

June 5, 2004
Fangzhou Shipyard
1069, Chuanchang Road
Dalian, Liaoning

Dear Sirs,

We have been requested by Metropolitan and Provincial Bank, Birmingham, to advise you of the issue of their irrevocable credit number ST2023 in your favor for account of Sunrise Fishing Co Ltd., 167 Corporation Street Birmingham B1 2PS, for GBP 7,086,000 (say pounds sterling seven million and eighty six thousand) available for your drafts on Dalian Branch, Industrial and Commercial Bank of China at 60 days sight accompanied by the documents specified below:

1. Invoice in quadruplicate, indicating LC No. PWH77YL.

2. Full set clean on board bills of lading, marked "Freight Prepaid" and "Notify Sunrise Fishing Co Ltd., 167 Corporation Street Birmingham B1 2PS".

3. Packing list in triplicate.

4. Insurance certificate in duplicate.

Covering:

"2 FISHING VESSELS MODEL RK-69 AS PER PURCHASE ORDER NO. 233/QL8 DATED MAY 15, 2004" (All of which must be stated on your invoice.)

Shipment from Dalian to Birmingham C.I.F. not later than July 15, 2004.

Partial shipment not permitted.

Transshipment not permitted.

Drafts drawn under this Credit must be presented not later than July 15, 2004.

We are requested by our principals to add our confirmation to this Credit. Accordingly, we undertake to honor all drafts drawn under and in strict conformity with the terms of the Credit, provided that such drafts bear the date and number of the credit, and that the credit and any amendments thereto are attached.

We are instructed to claim our charges in connection with this credit from your goodselves.

Yours Faithfully,

K. Johnson

Manager

Now look through the extract from a blank documentary credit form below. What information did this part of the form contain when the Dalian Branch, Industrial and Commercial Bank of China received it from Birmingham? Look through the above letter again and then write in the relevant information on the form.

| NAME OF ISSUING BANK | IRREVOCABLE DOCUMENTARY CREDIT NUMBER: <br> DATE: |
|---|---|
| APPLICANT | BENEFICIARY |
| ADVISING BANK | AMOUNT |
|  | Partial shipments <br> Allowed ☐   not allowed ☐ |
| Shipment/dispatch from <br><br> For transportation to | Transshipment <br> Allowed ☐   not allowed ☐ |
|  | Date of expiry |

We have issued the documentary credit as detailed below. We request you to notify the said credit to the beneficiary

☐ without adding your confirmation          ☐ adding your confirmation

## Section D—Export Seller's Credit   出口卖方信贷

### Skill-building exercise #D1—Translation

Charlie Peng, Deputy Manager, Shanghai Branch, Bank of China, is talking to Arnold Liu, Director, Shanghai Transformer Factory, and Joan Adams, Assistant General Manager of Robert Network, about an Export Seller's Credit. Look at the Chinese expressions below and discuss their meaning in English with your partner after listening to the conversation.

出口卖方信贷    资产负债比例    定金    宽限期    经营管理正常
财务信用状况    配套条件    还款保证    不可撤销信用证    赔付款

### Skill-building exercise #D2—Listening comprehension

Listen to the conversation again and try to answer the following questions:

1. What is an Export Seller's Credit?
2. Who can apply for it?
3. How should one apply for it?

### Skill-building exercise #D3—Speaking

Work in a group of three. One takes the part of Charlie, one Arnold and the last one Joan, and then switch parts among you three.

## Dialogue—Credit Line

K (Kitty Homes): Good morning, Ralph. It's so nice to see you again.

R (Ralph): Good morning, Kitty. It's a lovely day. On such a lovely day, I wish to have a lovely conversation with you.

K: You certainly will.

R: We have got short-term loans from you since two years ago. As things are happening at a much quicker space, I wonder if we can apply for a Credit Line from you. I understand it works much faster.

K: You are right. Our Credit Line is a sort of stock control indicator for the short-term credit business verified and determined for clients by this bank, on the condition that so long as the credit balance does not exceed the corresponding business assortment indicator, the Corporate Banking Department of this bank can swiftly offer short-term credit to the clients no matter how much or how many times the accumulated amount has been granted. That is to say, enterprises can conveniently use the bank's short-term credit funds revolvingly so as to meet the demands of the clients for rapidness and convenience in financial service.

R: Rapidness and convenience are just what we need. What can your Credit Line cover? Could we use it for a tender guarantee if we are bidding for a project?

K: By all means. What this product can cover include loans, opening of a letter of credit, a letter of guarantee and bill of exchange within a period of one year (including one year) etc., of which tender guarantee, performance guarantee, advanced payment guarantee, customs duty payment guarantee and maritime guarantee can last more than one year.

R: Excellent. I suppose we can apply.

K: As long as you are an independent enterprise legal person, because only an independent enterprise legal person can apply to this bank for the Credit Line Facility. We do not offer this service to clients such as organizations of undertakings and government departments, which are not legal persons, neither do we offer it to economic organizations without legal status (such as branch companies), which are subordinates to a legal person.

R: You know we are an independent enterprise legal person. O. K. What documents do I have to bring to you?

K: Fairly simple. I need your Business License, your Permit for Loans and your Financial Statement and other documents demanded by the bank.

R: I gather we have to write an application.

K: Yes, you do. After our bank examines and ratifies your application, we have to agree on terms and conditions, and then sign a Credit Line Agreement. After all these the Credit Line can be commissioned.

R: Well, as I said we did have a lovely talk on a lovely day. I am encouraged and impressed. Thank you very much for your advice.

K: You are most welcome.

## Dialogue—Worldwide Credit

L (Lucy Menzis): Hello, Mr. Wu, welcome to my office.

W (Gary Wu): Hello, Lucy. Thank you very much for receiving me. I am here to discuss one of our new products with you.

L: What is it? I am curious to learn.

W: It is a service we provide to international enterprise groups like yours.

L: That's interesting.

W: It is Worldwide Credit, a business mode with which all branches, under the co-ordination of the Head Office of Bank of China, that provides unified group credit in an integrative way to international group enterprises to meet their demand for the global business development, especially their business development in China.

L: It is really new. It is the first time for me to hear about it. Judging from the way you were describing, it could give us more convenience in getting an integrative and packaged loan.

W: Exactly. Integrated credit and a massive amount of service are the main features of this product, which is based on the evaluation of the overall situation and business prospects of a given overseas international enterprise group. The Head Office of Bank of China will work out credit policies and a comprehensive service plan for the group.

L: You mean we have to talk to your head office in Beijing.

W: It is so at the beginning. The Head Office will co-ordinate and accumulate experience from a few spots in order to expand it much wider. The Head Office of Bank of China will directly establish integrative co-operative relations with the headquarters of overseas international enterprise groups (inside or outside China). The co-operation may cover the credit demands of the subsidiaries all over the world (where Bank of China has branches) of these groups and their other business demands.

L: If our headquarters established cooperation relations with your head office, could your office in London, New York or Paris respond to our requests very quickly?

W: Yes, I can assure you of that. What's more, our service will be as standardized as other major banks all over the world. This product can save your cost quite considerably. I think it can also strengthen the financing capability and the integrated management of your group.

L: That sounds very attractive. What is your minimum requirements?

W: The applicant should be a world-famous international enterprise. The mother company should be an independent enterprise legal person incorporated overseas where Bank of China has branches or sub-branches. The applicant should also have subsidiaries inside or outside China and the mother company should have close controlling relations with its subordinate subsidiaries.

L: Well, we seem to be a very suitable applicant. I shall write to our headquarters about this new product of yours. But I have to inform them the application procedures.

W: The procedures are fairly simple. We need a letter of application, which should include your specific business demands (what kind of loans you wish to get) and the co-operative partners (which subsidiaries will be involved). The letter should be with the effective authorization of the authoritative departments of your headquarters.

L: I suppose you need some documents, which verifies the legal status of our enterprise group.

W: You are right. Besides, we also need a detailed statement of the correlation between members of your enterprise group, which are to be involved in Worldwide Credit in terms of stockholding right, management, production and sales as well as profit distribution. We must have a copy of your Business License and the recent audited financial report of your group. That's all I know about documents to be provided, if there are other documents demanded by Bank of China, you should also provide.

L: I understand. We should submit the application and the above-mentioned documents to the Corporate Banking Department of the Head Office of Bank of China, shouldn't we?

W: Yes, you should. Your headquarters and our head office should tailor up a preliminary cooperative plan and agree on major aspects and conditions of cooperation. Then, upon approval of the plan through internal procedures of the Head Office of Bank of China, the head office will sign a framework agreement of cooperation with your headquarters. Finally, branches or sub-branches of Bank of China at home and abroad will start specific cooperations with your company according to the General Agreement.

L: That is quite simple. I gather you will also charge a fee for your service.

W: Yes, we will collect a service charge for providing the Worldwide Credit, the amount of which will be determined by the agreement.

L: I appreciate very much of your visit and description of Worldwide Credit. I am sure our headquarters will be interested in it. I shall inform you of their decisions as soon as I know. It's a pleasure to do business with you.

W: The pleasure is mine. Thank you very much for your time and patience.

L: No sweat. I certainly look for a very fruitful cooperation in this new product. I'll see you to the door.

## Dialogue—Export Buyer's Credit

C: Good morning, Sophia. This is Sophia. This is Hugh Small from Sunrise Fishing Co.

H: Nice to see both of you. You are building more vessels, if I am right.

C: Yes, we are. We shall enter into a contract for three fishing vessels with Mr. Small's company.

S(Sophia): I am here to see if we can get an Export Buyer's Credit from you.

C: Could you please describe your Export Buyer's Credit to Mr. Small, Sophia? His company is a new customer.

H: I would be most pleased to do so. Export Buyer's Credit refers to the loans offered by Chinese domestic banks to borrowers outside China to support export of Chinese complete sets of equipment, vessels and other machinery and electrical products.

S: I am delighted to learn that this service is available for foreign companies.

H: Well, not precisely so. A Chinese company registered outside China can also use this vehicle.

S: That company can be considered a foreign company, I am afraid. In any case, what currencies can you offer with such a loan?

H: US Dollars and 16 other currencies can be accepted in China. This is a list of all of them. Please have a look.

S: That's very useful, thank you. Does your loan cover the total value of the contract, if I may ask?

H: No, I don't think any bank will do that. For export of vessels the value of the loan generally does not exceed 80% of the total value of the commercial contract. For your information, value for complete sets of equipment and other machinery and electrical products does not exceed 85% of the total value of the commercial contract.

S: Why is the vessel category lower than the other one? No, you don't have to worry. It is already good enough. How long do we honor the debts?

H: Ten years the maximum, not exceeding ten years, I hope. We shall calculate the length from the date of the borrowing contract becoming effective to the last repayment date.

S: I understand. But how do you calculate the interest rate?

H: Loan interest rate will be determined through negotiations. But it is based on the level of commercial loan rate.

S: That's perfectly acceptable. What do you charge for your service? What are they?

H: We shall collect two fees according to international practice. They are management fees and commitment fees.

S: I see. How do you verify our commercial standing? I mean you don't give out loans to anybody. You have to make sure you know the borrower.

H: You are right. They have to be acknowledged by our bank. They can be a foreign importer or an importer's bank, a statutory sovereign department such as the Ministry of Finance or the Central Bank of a country would be most preferable.

S: Is that all?

H: No. We have requirements on the projects that intend to use Export Buyer's Credit. First of all, the total value of the commercial contract should be no less than one million US dollars. Secondly, the value of the export commodities made in China should usually account for no less than 70% of the total value of the commercial contract for complete sets of equipment and should account for no less than 50% of the total value of the commercial contract for vessels or for aircraft, otherwise the proportion of the loan value in the total value of the commercial contract will be reduced accordingly.

S: Douglas, I wonder if you have calculated the value of what you are going to produce and the proportion of it?

C: Yes, we have. The sophisticated equipment you will bring in only takes up one third of the total value. So, you don't have to worry about that.

S: Good for you. Any other requirements, Sophia?

H: The Advance Payment for vessels should not be lower than 20% of the total value of the commercial contract and not be lower than 15% of the total value of the commercial contract for complete sets of equipment.

S: You know I have a bit of a grudge against the way you classify equipment. Isn't vessel making a complete set of equipment?

H: There is something in your question. The definition of a complete set is that every thing in it should be manufactured in China. Did you say you would import some sophisticated equipment just now?

S: You are very sharp. Yes, we do. Now I understand. What else do I have to know?

H: Commercial contracts under Export Buyer's Credit must comply with the relevant laws and regulations laid down by the governments of both trading parties. The export enterprises under Export Buyer's Credit should insure itself against export credit at export credit insurance institutions according to requirements of this bank.

S: Will do that Douglas?

C: Oh, yes. We are familiar with that practice.

H: In case there are some new requirements by the bank, I shall let you know and you are expected to satisfy them.

S: Terrific. Could you please advise me of the procedures of application?

H: The export enterprise, the shipyard in your case, should approach this bank as soon as possible before making tenders abroad or signing commercial contracts and provide relevant materials about the project in question and its specific needs for finance.

C: My office is preparing some documents for you, which, I hope, will bring you up to date of what we have been doing.

H: That's good to know. The borrower, the fishing company in your case, Mr. Small, who intends to adopt the Export Buyer's Credit should file a formal application to this bank in the course of the negotiation for financing and should supply the following documents and materials: legal address and name of the borrower, recent balance sheet, profit and loss account, cash-flow statement and other documents describing your operational status, draft commercial contract and other relevant documents, usage of the loans and the plan for repayment and other documents we may demand.

S: O.K. I don't see any problem in doing that.

H: Our bank will process the application for loans right after receipt of all the above-mentioned documents and will conduct an assessment procedure of the project. Upon approval through examination of the project on loan, my bank will sign an agreement on Export Buyer's Credit Loan with your company. Then you may draw the loans as prescribed after satisfying all the prerequisites to the funds stipulated in the loan agreement.

S: I think I have all the information needed for the application from you. I shall talk to our president tonight and may come back to you tomorrow for specific arrangement.

H: Excellent. We shall process your application as soon as it is formally filed.

C: Thank you, Sophia, for your valuable support.

H: You are most welcome. Good-bye for now.

S & C: Good-bye. We'll see you tomorrow.

## Commercial Banking  商业银行

### Dialogue—Export Seller's Credit

P: Hello, Liu. What a surprise! Where have you been hiding yourself?

L(Liu): I was on internship in Guangzhou. That's why you couldn't see me. Let me introduce Miss Adams. Joan, this is Charlie Peng, Deputy Manager of Shanghai Branch of Bank of China. Joan is the Assistant General Manager of Robert Network of New Zealand. Joan has placed an order of transformers of various sizes with us. We are about to reach an agreement. Before we do that, we would like to ask you to enlighten us on a possible Export Seller's Credit.

J: Liu said I'd better come here, because we shall be involved in the arrangement.

P: That's correct. Honestly, this vehicle is set up to support China's export, especially the export of machinery and electrical products. To be specific, it supports China's import and export corporations and manufacturing enterprises that export their products. It is designed on the basis of the economic guidelines and monetary policies of the State. It will be executed in accordance with the requirements on equity-debt ratio and in compliance with the principle of "safety, liquidity and effectiveness".

J: I am impressed. So, your loan will mainly be in local currency, I take.

P: We can also provide loans in US dollars, if there is such a need.

J: How much of the total value does your loan cover?

P: The maximum credit amount usually does not exceed the total export cost minus deposit and funds raised by the enterprise itself.

J: So, you don't have a set percentage.

P: No, we don't. The length of maturity does not exceed ten years the longest from the date of signature of the borrowing contract to the date of payoff of the loan principal and interest (including the grace period).

J: That's much longer than our banks do. What is your normal interest rate? I am asking too many questions, Liu. Maybe you should speak.

L: Just go ahead. Charlie speaks English so fluently. It is a pleasure to listen to both of you.

P: The loan interest rate will be carried out in accordance with relevant regulations of the People's Bank of China and the Bank of China.

J: That's a very vague reply. Can you indicate a rough number?

P: I prefer to wait until we come to the details of the contract.

J: Fair enough. I suppose Shanghai Transformer Factory is a qualified borrower.

P: Generally speaking, the applicant for Export Seller's Credit should be an import and export enterprise or a production enterprise who has assumed an enterprise legal person status and who has the right after approval of the State to conduct export of the machinery and electrical products.

J: Do you think you can fit very well into this category?

L: Oh, yes. My factory has been performing very well.

P: Let me add that applications can be made for Export Seller's Credit Loan for export contracts for a complete plant, vessels and other machinery and electrical products with the contractual amount no less than US $500 thousand and with the deferred payment being adopted for no less than one year.

L: Fortunately, our contract value is close to a million.

J: You are right.

P: The borrowing enterprise should be engaged in normal operation and management, should have a favorable financial position and credit standing, should be in a position to execute export contracts, should be able to ascertain reliable guarantees for repayment and should open an account with Bank of China.

J: Do you have an account here, Liu?

L: Charlie can answer that question.

P: Yeh, Liu's factory does have an account with us. I am not quite sure about their performance in the last six months, but judging from their records before it shouldn't be too bad, if nothing wrong had happened. Please note that the export project should comply with the relevant policies of the State and with the legal business scope of the enterprise and should be approved through examination by the departments concerned, and have valid contracts to be executed.

L: I don't see any problems in that.

P: The export project should bear good economic benefits, the associated costs in foreign exchange are within reasonable bounds and all complimentary conditions should be successfully secured.

L: There will be no foreign exchange involved this time. Every thing is home made.

P: You should know that, Bank of China, before the signature of the contract, should acknowledge the commercial terms and conditions of the contract.

L: Here is a draft contract between us. Let us know if you have any comments.

P: Thank you very much. I shall do that. The credit status of the importer, in your case, the Robert Network, should be reliable and the importer should provide payment guarantees of foreign banks or other payment guarantees acceptable to Bank of China.

J: I don't see any difficulties in doing that. When do you need guarantee from our bank?

P: As soon as possible.

J: I'll see what I can do.

P: Export credit insurance should be covered for export contracts in principle.

L: We shall do that when the contract is finalized.

P: The borrowing enterprise should provide in principle repayment guarantees acceptable to Bank of China. If the borrower applies for a foreign exchange loan, then he must ascertain relevant sources of paying back the foreign exchange.

L: I would like to discuss with you regarding the ways of guarantee later.

P: We shall surely do that. After the export contract has become effective, then the borrowing enterprise can put forward an application for loan to Bank of China and meanwhile submit following documents to us: a written application for loan (including loan amount demanded by the enterprise, currency type, length of maturity, usage, repayment source, repayment guarantee and use / repayment plan, etc.), a resolution applying for the loan approved by the Board of Directors, if the applicant is a joint-stock enterprise and a borrowing letter of authorization. For a first timer of application, the company charter and a certificate certifying the allocation of funds for the export project should be presented. Business license of your factory, which should have undergone the annual examination, financial statements upon annual examination for the recent three years and the loan card should also be handed in. Instrument of ratification of the project issued by competent authorities concerned (including documents of ratification needed for the import by using foreign exchange loans) will also be expected. Copy of the relevant commercial contract (including export contract, domestic procurement contract and the import contract using foreign exchange loans) should be presented to us. An introduction to the basic conditions of the project and an analytical report on economic effect, a guarantee by the importer's bank for deferred payment (namely, an irrevocable letter of credit or a letter of guarantee) should be provided. Besides, we also need the following documents: a letter of intent by the insurance institution committing to deal with export credit insurance, a certificate testifying that the borrower agrees to give priority to the use of reparations under export credit insurance as the repayment, relevant documents under guarantee (including instruments for property on security or on pledge and the evaluation report, as well as the guarantor's business license, copy of the financial statement and the letter of intent on guarantee, etc.) and other relevant documents Bank of China may demand later.

J: My goodness. This is a very long list. I only remembered what you will expect from us. Liu, I wish you have noted down everything.

L: I am quite familiar with all these requirements.

J: Good for you. What are the charges for the service, if I may ask?

P: All fees to be collected by this bank shall be determined in the contract, so I don't have a specific number now.

L: I suppose we have been fully informed. Do you have any more questions, Joan?

J: No, I don't think so. Maybe we should take our leave. Charlie, I am really impressed with your English.

P: Thank you for your compliment. My English is only functional.

J: You are being modest. Well, thank you for your time and advice.

P: Good-bye for now. I hope to see both of you soon.

Commercial Banking 商业银行

## Vocabulary

1. Use the following words or phrases in a sentence.
   a. credit balance
   b. verified
   c. granted
   d. amount
   e. commercial contract

2. Define the following words and phrases and provide a Chinese translation.
   a. corresponding business assortment indicator
   b. preliminary
   c. export buyer's credit
   d. beneficiary
   e. advising bank
   f. confirming bank
   g. irrevocable
   h. letter of credit
   i. financial statement
   j. export credit insurance

## Understanding

1. What can a credit line be used for?
2. What is a "worldwide credit" program and what are its advantages to a bank client?
3. What criteria must a client meet in order to qualify for the worldwide credit program?
4. What should the client's application for the worldwide credit program include?
5. Explain to a client how the interest rate on an export buyer's credit is determined.
6. How does a bank verify a client's commercial standing?
7. What are the criteria for projects to qualify for the export buyer's credit program?
8. If a letter of credit provides for partial shipments, what is the advantage to the client?
9. What is the purpose of the export seller's program?
10. How is the maximum credit amount determined?
11. What is the advantage to a client of having its own bank confirm a letter of credit received from a foreign bank?
12. What types of businesses would generally qualify for an export buyer's credit?

# Part VII

## Corporate Banking: Other Services
## 公司业务：其他服务

Commercial banks use their worldwide networks and expertise to act as agents and advisors to corporations, individuals and governments.

## Introduction  导语

In addition to lending and maintaining the bank accounts we use for saving and paying bills, banks also provide valuable advice and agent services. This section explains how we can benefit from their knowledge and experience.

## Commercial Banking  商业银行

Loans for houses and apartments require sophisticated computer systems and a lot of time and effort to administer.

Many small principal, interest and tax payments come in every day. Keeping track of them accurately is a big job. Banks greatly increase the amount of money available for would-be homeowners by packaging large numbers of residential mortgage loans together and selling them to investors. This frees up money for the banks to make more mortgage loans.

Since the investors are not set up to administer large numbers of loans, the banks do the administration for them, charging a small fee for the service.

Banks provide their clients with in-depth analysis of world financial and economic events. They help us manage our money effectively.

Part Ⅶ—Corporate Banking: Other Services  公司业务：其他服务

## Section A—Agent Bank Business  委托行业务

### Skill-building exercise #A1—Translation

Charlie Peng, Deputy Manager, Shanghai Branch, Bank of China, is introducing a new business to a group of newly enrolled staff. Look at the Chinese expression below and discuss their meaning in English with your partner after listening to the talk.

政策性银行　　　委托行　　　进出口银行　　　国家开发银行
内部费用　　　　凭证　　　　托管账户　　　　共管账户

### Skill-building exercise #A2—Listening comprehension

Listen to Charlie Peng again and tick those items he talks about.
1. Welcome remarks
2. What a policy bank is?
3. What China Import and Export Bank does?
4. What State Development Bank does?
5. Policy banks entrust management of their loan to an agent bank.
6. How to conclude such a consignment agreement?
7. Documents to be supplied for such a service
8. Procedures for applying for Agent Bank service

### Skill-building exercise #A3—Listening comprehension

Answer the following questions:
1. What is the *Agent Bank* business?
2. How many parties are involved in such a business?
3. What are policy banks in China?
4. What terms and conditions does a consignment agreement contain?
5. What documents are needed for the application for *Agent Bank* service?
6. What are the procedures of the application for *Agent Bank* service?

### Skill-building exercise #A4—Speaking

Try to retell to the class what Charlie Peng has told you.

## Section B—Trust Loan 委托贷款

### Skill-building exercise #B1—Translation

Charlie Peng, Deputy Manager, Shanghai Branch, Bank of China, is introducing a new business to a group of newly enrolled staff. Look at the Chinese expression below and discuss their meaning in English with your partner after listening to the talk.

委托贷款　　委托人　　受托人　　中间业务　　确定　　修改
变动　　　　结算往来　授权书　　印鉴　　　　有权签字样本

### Skill-building exercise #B2—Vocabulary

Listen to Charlie again and write down the words that he actually uses in place of the words printed in *italics*.

1. It is a loan given by a *government department* through a *bank* to an *enterprise*, and the *bank* will get the repayment back for the *department* from the *enterprise*.

2. The Trust Loan is an *interesting* business.

3. BOC will not accept trust loans for *pound sterling* for the time being.

4. ... contact and consult with the consignor if *revisions* of any clause in the trust loan contract are to be made.

5. We should check ... contract and *charter* of the consignor.

6. This is how this business is handled: first of all, the *borrower* shall apply to BOC for a Trust Loan.

7. Then the bank will examine the sources of funds, *purpose* of the borrowing and source of repayment provided in the application form.

8. At the later stage of management of the Trust Loan, the bank will assist the consignor in recovering the *funds* of the loan in the name of the consignee.

### Skill-building exercise #B3—Understanding

Answer the following questions:

1. What is a Trust Loan?
2. How many parties are involved in such a loan? Who are they?
3. Who should be the applicant?
4. With whom does the bank sign the Trust Loan contract?
5. Are materials provided to the bank by both the consignor and the borrower the same?

6. How to apply for a Trust Loan?

### Skill-building exercise #B4—Speaking

Try to retell what Charlie said to the class.

## Section C—Financial Advisory Service 财务顾问

### Skill-building exercise #C1—Translation

Charlie Peng, Deputy Manager, Shanghai Branch, Bank of China, is introducing a new business to a group of newly enrolled staff. Look at the Chinese expression below and discuss their meaning in English with your partner after listening to the talk.

| 财务顾问 | 大型建设项目 | 企业并购 | 融资结构 | 融资安排 |
| 专业性方案 | 结构调整 | 资本充实 | 重新核定 | 破产 | 资产重组 |
| 债务管理 | 企业改制上市 | 债券发行 | 票据发行 | 企业诊断 |

### Skill-building exercise #C2—Vocabulary

Listen to Charlie again and write down the words that he actually uses in place of the words printed in *Italics*.

1. Today I wish to introduce to you what a Financial Advisory Service (FAS) is. It is an intermediary business of *advising* provided by BOC to cater for the growing demand of the market and enterprises in recent years. FAS covers two fields, namely *big size* construction projects and corporate merger and acquisition (M&A).

2. With regards to FAS for large-scale construction projects, our bank can provide *professional* design of financing structure and financing execution plans for large-scale construction projects. The FAS for corporate M&A refers to financial consulting provided by our bank to both sides of M&A activity. The bank not only participates in the process of corporate M&A, but also as an advisor for sustainable development of enterprises, takes part in the corporate *restructuring*, asset *sufficiency* and *reassessment* as well as planning and operation of reorganization projects for the insolvent and impoverished companies.

3. The FAS of this bank can cover the following aspects: consulting in corporate investment and financing, project financing, M&A, asset reorganization/management, indebtedness management, arrangement of syndicate loans, advisory services of the restructuring and publication, bonds and bills *issuance*, management, research and analysis, training and diagnosing of enterprises.

4. Any enterprise legal person *requiring* such services can apply for the FAS according to the practical condition.

5. FAS can be extended to a substantial variety of projects and different documents are required for each type of them or even each single project. But the following materials are always included: an application form of FAS, business license (copy) of enterprises (legal persons) verified in the annual cheque; other related materials needed for financial advisory services.

6. Usually the following steps are included in the application *process*: to accept application by enterprises and institutions, to sign the Financial Advisory Agreement, to engage in market analysis, research and issuance of a financial advisory report, to *revise* and perfect financial advisory report according to customers' *response* and complete the services stipulated in the Financial Advisory Agreement. Fee of advice this bank will collect is to be decided through consultations between the two parties.

### Skill-building exercise #C3—Understanding

Answer the following questions:
1. What is a FAS?
2. What services does FAS cover?
3. What can FAS do for large-scale projects?
4. What can FAS do for merger and acquisition?
5. What is the procedure for the application of FAS?

### Skill-building exercise #C4—Speaking

Try to retell to the class what Charlie said.

### Skill-building exercise #C5—Reading comprehension

Read the telex offer sent out by Charlie Peng to several banks. Then answer the following questions.
1. Is the loan referred to medium-term or long-term?
2. Who is carrying out the contract in Northland?
3. What is the currency of the loan?
4. What is the interest rate on the loan?
5. Which country's laws govern the loan?

## Listening Material 听力材料

### Charlie Peng, Deputy Manager, Shanghai Branch, Bank of China

I am most delighted to see so many young and eager faces in the training class. I was told you are already half way on the course and that all of you have been learning very hard. I am here to tell you something about our new business. The Agent Bank program is one of them. BOC can now act as an agent for policy banks. In China there are two policy banks, namely, China Import and Export Bank and the State Development Bank. These two banks give out loans, but they don't manage the loans themselves, instead, they ask us to manage for them. When they decide to ask us to manage the loans for them, they give us an authorization. When that happens, they are consignment banks; we become their agent bank. The agreement is among three parties: the consignment bank, the agent bank and the borrower should define the specific management task.

This agent bank business has the following advantages. A policy bank may take advantage of BOC's extensive network and expertise to have its loans managed in an effective way while a borrower may take advantage of BOC's extensive network and expertise to enjoy convenient and quality financial services.

A policy bank should have approved the loan before approaching an agent bank. The policy bank should then choose and authorize an agent bank to manage its loan.

If BOC acts as an agent bank for the China Import & Export Bank, the borrower must provide: a copy of the lending contract between the borrower and the policy bank, a copy of the guaranty contract, the qualified export contract, associated purchase contract, service agreement and voucher of expenditure inside the borrower's company (may be provided by installment when the loans are used).

If BOC acts as an agent bank for the State Development Bank, the borrower must provide: a copy of the lending contract between the borrower and the policy bank, the related documents of project construction approved by competent authorities, documents relating to the use of construction funds approved by the State Development Bank, the purchase contract and service agreement financed by the loans or other documentary evidence (may be provided by installment when the loans are used) based on which loans are provided.

The three parties must sign a consignment agreement. A jointly monitored or a consignment bank account should be opened at a BOC branch. In case of a consignment account, the policy bank deposits the loans in the account and the borrower must apply for the use of funds in the account. Payment is made after the agent bank reviews and approves the application. In case of a jointly monitored account, the application is also subject to the approval of the policy bank.

Procedure charges are to be collected from the policy bank, and the amount should be determined in the agreement between the consignment bank and the agent bank.

So much for the Agent Bank Business. Thank you for your attention. If you don't have any questions, I shall talk about Trust Loan in the next session.

## Charlie Peng—Trust Loan

I shall now describe to you what a Trust Loan is. It is a loan given by a consignor through a consignee to a borrower, and the consignee will get the repayment back for the consignor from the borrower. Of course, banks always play the part of a consignee. Consignors can be government departments, enterprises or undertakings. At present, banks do not accept consignment from individuals. Consignors will decide on the type of prospective borrowers, purpose of loans, amount, credit period and interest rate. Consignees will act upon these decisions.

The Trust Loan is an intermediary business. The bank, contacts both consignors and borrowers. The proceeds belong to consignors and all risks are fully borne by consignors as well. BOC will not accept trust loans for foreign exchange for the time being. BOC shall reach agreement on terms and conditions of a trust loan contract with the consignor, and contact and consult with the consignor if amendment or change of any clause in the trust loan contract is to be made. BOC collects commissions based on the amount of loans.

You should be very clear about who can apply for it. Any corporate clients, who have opened deposit account, deposited a certain amount of fund with BOC and have business settlement with BOC, may file an application with us.

Before we process the application, we should check on such materials from the consignor as identity certificate of the consignor (legal identification of government departments, institutions and industrial and commercial enterprises), contract and articles of association of the consignor and relevant resolution of the board of directors and power of attorney, reserved seal of the consignor and sample of authorized signature and other materials BOC may require.

The borrowing party should provide us with loan applications (including description of loan purpose), identity certificate of the borrower, contract and articles of association of the borrower and relevant resolution of the board of directors and power of attorney and other materials the consignor may require.

This is how this business is handled: first of all, the consignor shall apply to BOC for a Trust Loan. The application form shall specify purpose of the loan, requirement, and types and business field of prospective borrower, terms and conditions, amount, credit period and method of interest calculation. Then the bank will examine the sources of funds, usage of the borrowing and source of repayment as provided in the application form. The consignor, the borrower and BOC, can now conclude a Trust Loan contract. BOC shall then release the loans on behalf of the consignor.

At the later stage of management of the Trust Loan, the bank will assist the consignor in recovering the principal and interest of the loan in the name of the consignee. The contract between the consignor and the consignee will determine the amount of commission for the latter.

That's all I have to say about the Trust Loan business. I wish what I just said could leave some impression on you. You may not fully comprehend my words, but later when you do it yourself with our help, you will find that it is not that difficult to grasp.

## Charlie Peng—Financial Advisory Service

Today I wish to introduce to you what a Financial Advisory Service (FAS) is. It is an intermediary business of consulting provided by BOC to cater for the growing demand of the market and enterprises in recent years. FAS covers two fields, namely large-scale construction projects and corporate merger and acquisition (M&A).

With regards to FAS for large-scale construction projects, our bank can provide specialized design of financing structure and financing arrangement for large-scale construction projects. The FAS for corporate M&A refers to financial consulting provided by our bank to both sides of M&A activity. The Bank not only participates in the process of corporate M&A, but also as an advisor for sustainable development of enterprises, takes part in the corporate reorganization, asset replenishment and reevaluation as well as planning and operation of reorganization projects for the insolvent and impoverished companies.

The FAS of this bank can cover the following aspects: consulting in corporate investment and financing, project financing, M&A, asset reorganization/management, indebtedness management, arrangement of syndicate loans, advisory services of the restructuring and publication, bonds and bills issuing, management, research and analysis, training and diagnosing of enterprises.

Any enterprise legal person demanding such services can apply for the FAS according to the practical condition.

FAS can be extended to a substantial variety of projects and different documents are required for each type of them or even each single project. But the following materials are always included: an application form of FAS, business license (copy) of enterprises (legal persons) verified in the annual check; other related materials needed for financial advisory services.

Usually the following steps are included in the application procedure: to accept application by enterprises and institutions, to sign the Financial Advisory Agreement, to engage in market analysis and research and issue financial advisory report, to amend and perfect financial advisory report according to customers' feedback and complete the services stipulated in the Financial Advisory Agreement. Consulting fee this bank will collect is to be decided through consultations between the two parties.

This brings to an end to my talks. I hope you have learned something from what I have said. I am sure some of you will be assigned to my department. I look forward to working with you. I sincerely wish each of you would find BOC an ideal place to work in. Thank you very much for your attention.

# Sample Examination Questions 模拟试题

## Vocabulary

1. Use the following words or phrases in a sentence.
    a. expertise
    b. network
2. Define the following words and phrases and provide a Chinese translation.
    a. agent
    b. consignment
    c. agreement
    d. prospective
    e. contract
    f. intermediary
    g. turnkey
    h. guarantor
    i. availability
    j. drawdown
    k. security

## Understanding

1. What are the two policy banks in China?
2. What are the advantages of the agent bank business to a commercial bank?
3. What documents must a borrower provide in order that a commercial bank can act as an agent bank?
4. What is a trust loan and how is it used?
5. What are the roles of the consignor and the consignee in a trust loan arrangement?
6. What does the borrower need to provide to the bank in order to support an application for a trust loan?
7. What should be specified in the application form for a trust loan?

8. What will the bank examine in considering whether or not to make a trust loan available to a client?

9. What is the "financial advisory service"; what types of bank clients can use it and how would they benefit from it?

10. What are the advantages to a commercial bank of offering a financial advisory service?

11. What is a "tombstone"? Why is it called that and why do banks want them?

12. Which party bears the risk in a trust loan arrangement?

# Investment Banking

# 投资银行

## Part I

### Introduction  导语

Just like the oil in your car's engine keeps it running smoothly, investment banking lubricates the economy. It is an essential part of a growing, vibrant society.

## Investment Banking  投资银行

Building a refinery, developing a mine, constructing a dam, pipeline or highway, saving for retirement or sending your children to a college, investment banking can provide you with the tools you need.

Investment banking is that part of the financial services sector of the economy which is involved with helping individuals, families, businesses and governments realize their goals by

A. arranging for getting the money they need,

B. helping them manage the money they have.

Part Ⅰ—Introduction 导语

## Section A—The Basics 基本定义

Investment banks are businesses that specialize in helping individuals, businesses and governments meet their financial needs. Their people are specialists in all matters relating to money. They advise their clients on the best way to manage their financial affairs. They help individuals, businesses, governments get the money they need. They find places for people with money that is surplus to current needs to put that money.

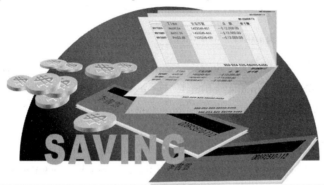

Investment banks are intermediaries (in the middle) between people who have money and people who need money. Investment banking is the process of getting and managing money. Investment bankers are the people, the experts, who work for investment banks and help individuals, businesses and governments to reach their financial goals.

# Investment Banking 投资银行

### A. What investment banking is

Investment banking can be divided into these main activities:
1. providing advice and guidance
    a. helping you set realistic and appropriate financial goals and
    b. developing strategies to reach them;
2. arranging for the money you need at the lowest possible cost;
3. helping you manage financial risk; and
4. buying and selling financial instruments like stocks and bonds.

### B. What investment bankers will do

A good investment banker will sit down with you whether you are a private individual, a corporate executive or a government official. He or she will analyze your needs, study your financial position, help you decide what is important for you to accomplish and then prepare a road map to guide you.

Not only will the road map show you how to reach your destination, but it can also be used to measure your progress—how far along you are towards reaching your goal. It is important to remember that your investment banker will be at your side every step of the way, guiding you, encouraging you, keeping you on track.

Once you have determined where you want to go—what you want to achieve financially—and how you are going to get there, your investment banker will implement your plan for you. Like the high quality oil that will keep your car's engine purring like a contented kitten, your investment banker will smooth your way toward financial success.

## Section B—Setting Goals  设立目标

Whether we are planning for our own future, the future of a business we are running or a government we are leading, we set goals, things we want to achieve in a certain time frame. This gives us something to work towards and a feeling of pride and accomplishment when we achieve them. Many of our goals involve with money and the management of money.

1. For example, in our personal lives our goals may be to
   - buy a house or apartment,
   - start a business,
   - send our children to university,
   - be able to travel around the world in style when we retire.

2. If we are managing a business, we may want to increase our company's profitability by

   - building a new factory,
   - buying the latest equipment,
   - developing a gold mining property,
   - doing advanced scientific research,
   - constructing a major oil pipeline,
   - buying out a competitor.

3. As a government leader, we probably want to see our region prosper and grow. We would like our people to have a higher standard of living. We believe that we can make that occur if we create an environment in which commerce flows smoothly, existing businesses are expanding rapidly and new industries are choosing to locate in our area.

We know we will succeed if we
   - fully develop our region's infrastructure
     - roads, highways and bridges,

- mass transit, (buses, subways, light rails),
- water treatment facilities,
- power generation,
- communications networks;

▮ build new schools so that we have a well educated work force; and

▮ provide tax and investment incentives.

## Section C—Needs and Money  需求与货币

What is similar about all of these goals whether they are personal, business or government, is that money is required to successfully reach them. If we want to send our son abroad to a prestigious university, we need money. If we need to build a new factory to achieve our profit target, we need money. If the only way we can attract a new industry to our city is by expanding its airport, we need money. In many cases the amount of money needed is more than we can earn from our wages, our company's profits or our city's taxes.

People have different needs at different times. Some people are earning more money than they need to spend to cover their daily living costs so they save the extra. Perhaps they are saving now so they will have money to travel when they retire.

Other people are buying houses now and in order to complete their purchases, they need more money than they have saved.

The government of a country might, for instance, need money to build a new expressway while certain companies are generating more cash than they can use effectively at that moment in their businesses.

These are examples of opposite needs that can be fulfilled them by matching them. The people and businesses that are saving money can make it available to those who need money. When needs are matched on a large scale, markets develop.

## Part I—Introduction  导语

## Section D—An Overview of Markets  市场概览

Markets are places where buyers go to satisfy their needs by finding suppliers of suitable products and services. Markets are places where suppliers (sellers) go to find people to buy their products and services.

There are different kinds of markets. For example, there is

1. the market for services such as restaurant meals, hotel rooms, airplane seats;

2. the market for products like books, food, clothing, automobiles, appliances; and

3. the financial market—the market for the use of money.

A market is not necessarily a physical place like a department store or a supermarket and goods traded are not necessarily physical goods. Trading might take place over the telephone or the Internet and goods traded might be something intangible like knowledge, for example.

### A. The financial marketplace

Financial markets such as the stock market work just the same way as, for example, the fruit and vegetable market where we shop for our daily provisions. The financial markets are simply places where people who have money—suppliers or sellers—meet people who need money—consumers or buyers.

An example of a buyer in the financial marketplace is a family which needs to borrow money to buy an apartment. An example of a seller is a life insurance company which is willing to lend the family the money it needs. Another example of a buyer is a government department which needs money to build new highway. Sellers (suppliers of money) in this case could be thousands of families which have money they want to save. The families can let the government use their money to build the highway. At some point in the future, a time agreed upon by the government and the families, the families will get their money back.

The market can be an actual place like a bank branch or a stock exchange or it can be "notional"—accessed by the telephone or the Internet. In the middle between buyers and sellers are firms called financial intermediaries which help buyers and sellers come together.

## Investment Banking  投资银行

### Dialogue—The Arrival

**Mr. Roberts:** Good morning. My name is James Roberts and this is Mr. Borden. We are here to see Mr. Brooks.

**Receptionist:** Yes, Mr. Roberts. Is Mr. Brooks expecting you?

**Mr. Roberts:** Yes. Our appointment is for 10 o'clock. We are a few minutes early.

**Receptionist:** I will let him know you are here.

Mr. Roberts and another gentleman are here to see Mr. Brooks.

**Secretary:** Mr. Brooks is on a conference call at the moment. I will let you know when he is free. It shouldn't be long.

**Receptionist:** Mr. Roberts, Mr. Brooks is tied up for a few moments. Would you mind taking a seat?

**Mr. Roberts:** Not at all. Thank you.

**Receptionist:** Can I get you some coffee or tea while you are waiting?

**Mr. Roberts:** Yes, coffee would be great, thank you.

**Receptionist:** How do you take it?

**Mr. Roberts:** Cream and two lumps of sugar, please.

**Receptionist:** And you sir?

**Mr. Borden:** Tea with lemon for me please.

**Receptionist:** Reception.

**Secretary:** Mr. Brooks is free now. Would you have them come up to the 11th floor, please?

**Receptionist:** Thank you.

Mr. Roberts, Mr. Brooks is available now. Would you take the elevator over there up to the 11th floor? His secretary will meet you there.

**Mr. Roberts:** Thank you very much.

### B. Supply and demand

Every market has buyers who want to buy products and services to satisfy their needs. We call this demand. Similarly every market has producers or suppliers who want to sell their products and services. This is called supply.

The market forces driving every market are therefore

a. the supply of an item or service where there is

b. a demand for that item or service.

---

**Important Note**

The market for money means the market for the **use of money**. The person who has extra money and wants to save it (the supplier), is temporarily giving someone else the right to use that money. The saver fully expects to get his or her money back at some point in the future.

---

The mechanism markets used to balance supply and demand and to have transactions (purchases and sales) take place is price. When buyer and seller agree on price for the product or service, a trade takes place.

The higher the price, the more of a particular product or service suppliers are willing to offer for sale. However, the higher the price, the fewer of that product, people will be willing to buy. On the other hand, if the price is low, more people will be willing to buy but fewer suppliers will be willing to sell. It is the price that exactly matches demand for a product or service with the supply of that product or service.

### C. Matching buyers and sellers

To match different financial needs such as the need to get money to use and the need to save money until it is needed, intermediaries are often used. Consider the following example.

1. An insurance company has collected money from its customers. Its managers want to place that money somewhere safe, a place where they know they can

 a. get it back when they need it to pay claims to policyholders and

 b. earn a profit on it until it is needed.

2. A manufacturing company needs to borrow some money to pay for the raw materials it has bought from its suppliers. It would repay the money from the sale of its product to its customers.

An intermediary tries to merge, to bring together, these different needs and demands of borrowers and lenders through negotiation and the use of different types of financial instruments. Once a deal is struck, a certificate is issued to the lender—in our example, the insurance company—entitling it the right to receive interest payments at an agreed upon rate and the repayment of the loan at a predetermined point in the future. These financial instruments are called securities and they come in a very wide variety of sizes, shapes and colours.

## Dialogue—The Investment Bankers

**Gerald:** All right. Let's go over the plans one more time just to be sure there is no misunderstanding.

**Roberta:** Good idea.

**Bradley** All right.

**Gerald:** Remember. Absolute secrecy is a must. If word gets out about our client's takeover plans for Sterling Chemical Company, the share price will rise, and other bidders will come into the market and the deal will probably get away from us.

**Roberta:** That's why we are staying at different hotels. If we happen to be seen together by a clever reporter, they might put two and two together and figure out why we are here.

**Bradley:** When our national oil company lost its bid to acquire Husky Oil to Li Ka Shin of Hong Kong, the market figured they would look elsewhere pretty soon.

**Gerald:** That's right. It wouldn't take too much imagination to figure out that the next target would be company here.

**Roberta:** The only reason for three high-powered investment bankers to be in this little city in the middle of nowhere would be to talk to Sterling about a takeover.

**Bradley:** No doubt about that! I can't imagine anyone coming here if they didn't absolutely have too!

**Gerald:** Now, now, it's not as bad as all that. The city has a few sights and some decent restaurants. However, this time I want you to keep a very low profile. Don't take a chance on being seen in any of the local watering holes. Order whatever you like from room service, but I do not want you to be seen. Walls have ears and you never know who may recognize you.

**Roberta:** Sounds fine to me. I'm tired after putting in a full day at the office, then a mad dash to the airport and finally a three-hour flight through some pretty turbulent weather.

**Bradley:** Me, too. I'm bushed. We have a big day tomorrow and I want to be well rested.

## D. Primary and secondary markets

The market for financial instruments, securities, issued for the first time is called the primary market. In the example above, a new security is created by the manufacturer and issued to the insurance company. This is the primary market at work.

Let us suppose that one month later the insurance company experiences an unusual large increase in the amount of money it has to pay out to its policyholders. It has the certificate evidencing the loan it made to the manufacturer. Unfortunately, for the insurance company, under the terms of the deal negotiated by the intermediary, the manufacturer is not required to repay the loan for another three months. The manufacturer has been making the interest payments to the insurance company as required, so it cannot be forced to repay the loan early.

> **Important Note**
>
> In order to enhance the marketability and tradability of these securities, these standards created for transactions are incorporated into financial instruments.

The insurance company, however, has another option. The instrument it bought (the loan it made) has standard terms and conditions. The insurance company's situation has changed so it needs to get its money back sooner than it expected. There are many other companies, individuals, organizations, governments, however, that need money or have surplus funds. It is most likely that one of these would have a need that is exactly fulfilled by the loan made by the insurance company to the manufacturer.

Enter the intermediary again. One month ago the intermediary found a safe place for the insurance company to place its money. Now the intermediary finds another company, a bank, for example, that has surplus funds in just the amount of and for the exact amount of time remaining on the insurance company's loan to the manufacturer. The intermediary negotiates a price between the insurance company and the bank and the loan and the security evidencing it passes from one to the other.

The insurance company gets the cash it needs today. Three months later when the loan matures, the manufacturer pays back the money it borrowed. The difference is that it pays it to the bank instead of the insurance company.

Part I—Introduction 导语

The needs of borrowers, lenders and investors are changing constantly. New needs develop so new players come into the market. In many cases these needs can be met by buying and selling securities that are already in existence. The market where instruments are traded subsequent to the first issue is called the secondary market.

## Section E—How Suppliers Make Their Money Available? 如何供款

People who have money that is surplus to their current needs and who make it available to those who need it are called suppliers. There are a variety of ways in which this money can be provided. Each way has its own particular advantages, disadvantages, rights and benefits. Loans and investments are the two most common ways.

### A. Loans

If we have money that is surplus to our current needs, we can lend it to someone else. We make a loan to them. They promise to pay us back at some later time. The person making a loan is called a lender and the person receiving the money is called a borrower. The time the borrower takes to repay the money is called the term of the loan. Loans can be a short period of time—short-term loan—or they can be long term. A bond is a long-term loan to a corporation or government.

## Dialogue—Day Is Done

**Greg:** Karen, you really ought to think about going to Barbados for your vacation. It's a great place!

**Karen:** I've been thinking of Hawaii. I just want to go someplace warm. I'm so tired of this cold weather. It seems like it will never end.

**Sam:** I know what you mean. I had to shovel out my driveway three times on the weekend! Then Monday morning before I came to work, the plow went by and pushed a bunch more snow back in.

**Karen:** I don't have a car so I don't have to worry about that. But I see my neighbours digging out and scraping ice off their windows. I sure don't envy them.

**Sam:** I don't drive to work either, but when it snows, everything gets backed up—subways, trains, buses. The switches froze on the Long Island Railroad this morning. It took an extra hour to get in. Good thing the boss is understanding.

**Karen:** I've got two weeks of vacation coming up at the end of the month and I really want a break. I just want to lie on the beach all day soaking up the sun and drinking pina coladas. I wouldn't mind if I didn't see a phone the whole time.

**Greg:** Barbados is the place. I know you'd love it. I took my fiancée there over Christmas. We had a fabulous time. Beautiful beaches, friendly people, good food, neat night life.

**Sam:** Sounds pretty nice all right. Where did you stay?

**Greg:** We stayed at Sandy Lane. It's one of those resorts that has everything. You really don't need to leave the grounds if you don't want to. We did something different every day. And you would love the duty free shops. I know you like nice things. The array of crystal, china, jewelry will just blow your mind.

**Karen:** That's a great suggestion, Greg. I'll start checking it out when I get home tonight.

## B. Investments

When we buy an asset such as real estate or put money into a business with the expectation of earning a profit, we are making an investment. A person making an investment is called an investor.

---

### Important Definitions

**Finance**

The management of money, banking, investment and credit.

**Financing**

The process of raising (obtaining) money for people, businesses, etc.. who need it to achieve their goals.

**Credit**

An agreement by which something of value—goods, services, money—is given in exchange for a promise to pay it back at some time in the future.

**Loan**

Money advanced to a borrower to be repaid at a later date.

**Lender**

A person or organization which lends money.

**Investment**

Money put into a business, used to buy real estate or placed with someone else all with the intent of earning a profit.

**Investor**

A person or organization which invests (makes investments).

**Share**

One of the parts into which the ownership of a company is divided.

**Profit**

A financial or monetary gain obtained from a loan or investment.

**Loss**

When the money we get back from a loan or investment is less than the amount we originally paid out.

The most common way of investing in a business is by purchasing shares in the company who is running it. The company does not promise to repay our money at some point in the future. Instead, we expect to get our money back out of the earnings of the business.

## Section F—What Suppliers of Money Expect—The Profit Motive 供款人的期望——盈利动机

People who have money that is surplus to their current needs and who make it available to those who need it are called suppliers. When we let someone else use our money for some period of time, we are giving up the opportunity to spend it today. For giving up this right, we expect something in return. We expect to get more money back from the user than we originally provided. We expect to earn a profit.

---

**Important Definitions**

**Rate of return**

The earnings or profit on money we lend or invest expressed as a percentage of the amount of money loaned or invested.

**Expected rate of return**

The rate of return that we expect to earn when we loan money to someone or invest in a business or in real estate.

---

This profit, expressed as a percentage of the money provided, is called the rate of return. As a supplier, we usually have a specific rate of return in mind when we put up the money. This number is called the *expected* rate of return.

Suppliers of money earn income in a variety of ways:
- When they make loans, they are generally paid interest.
- When they buy shares they may receive dividends.
- When they invest in real estate they may earn a profit.

## Section G—Buying and Selling The Right to Use Money  买卖货币使用权

When sellers meet buyers in a market and they want to transact business, they must agree on a price. When a price is agreed upon, a trade (sale) takes place. In markets for products and services, the price is usually expressed in terms of a currency.

The basic needs in the financial world are
    a. the need to find a place to save excess money (supply) and
    b. the need to borrow money (demand) where there is a shortage of money.

---

**Important Note**

Depending on the way in which the money is made available, the supplier earns interest (loans including bonds), dividends (shares) or profit (business or real estate).

---

In the financial market, the commodity being traded is money. To conclude a trade (purchase and sale), the buyer (the person who needs money) and the seller (the person who has money) must agree on a price. Remember, when we are talking about buying and selling money in this context, we are talking about buying and selling the right to use the money-not the ownership of the money itself. The price, therefore, paid for the use of money and on which buyer and seller must agree is called the interest rate.

## Section H—How Long Can The "Buyers" Use The Money?  货币"买家"可以使用货币多长时间呢?

The time a lender gives the borrower to repay the loan is called the term. Loans that have a term of one year or less are called short-term loans. Loans that are repayable after more than one year are called long-term loans.

> **Fundamental Principle of Finance #1**
>
> The longer the term related to a loan or investment, the higher will be the expected rate of return.

Generally speaking, the longer time a borrower takes repay a loan—the longer its term is—the higher will be the interest rate demanded by the lender. There are several reasons.

1. The lender is giving up the right to use his or her money for a longer period of time to others on the expectation of being paid more.

2. Provided the borrower is meeting its obligations relating to the loan, paying interest for example, the lender cannot get his or her money back earlier. The more time the borrower take to repay the loan, the more things will happen.

   a. The lender's financial situation may change such as it needs the money sooner than he or she expected.

   b. The lender may suddenly find that he or she has an opportunity to use the money in a way that will produce a higher expected rate of return.

   c. The borrower's financial condition may worsen so the lender becomes concerned about being able to get his or her money back.

   d. Economic conditions may change. The growth rate may fall. The rate of inflation may increase.

## Section I—Can Suppliers Always Be Sure of Getting Their Money Back? 货币使用权的归还

When someone makes his or her money available to someone else to use for a period of time, he or she expects to get all of his or her money back with a profit. However, in our world not everything is certain. There is always the possibility that

a. we will not earn as much profit as we expected,

b. we will not earn any profit—we will just get our money back,

> **Definition**
>
> **Risk**
>
> The possibility that a loan or investment will not produce the return we expect or that we will actually lose money.

c. we will get less money back than we originally loaned or invested,

d. we will not get any of our money back—we will lose the full amount of the loan or investment.

The possibility that we as a lender or investor will not get the return we expect or that we will lose all or part of our loan or investment is called risk. If there is a greater chance that we will lose money on an investment that we make, we want the possibility of earning a higher rate of return. If we believe that the risk is high on a loan or investment that we are about to make, we will expect to receive a high rate of return.

> **Fundamental Principle of Finance #2**
>
> The higher the risk related to a loan or investmentis, the higher will be the expected rate of return.

## Section J—Words and Expressions  术语及解释

**Credit**  信贷

An agreement by which something of value—goods, services, money—is given in exchange for a promise to pay it back at some time in the future.

**Dividend**  股息

The part of a company's profits which is distributed to shareholders.

**Expected rate of return**  预期收益率

The rate of return that we expect to earn when we loan money to someone or invest in a business or in real estate.

**Finance**  金融

The management of money, banking, investment and credit.

**Financing**  融资

The process of raising (obtaining) money for people, businesses, etc. who need it to achieve their goals.

**Interest**  利息

Money paid for the use of money.

**Interest rate**  利率

The rate charged for the use of money.

**Intermediary**  中介

A financial institution such as a bank that acts as a conduit between suppliers of funds (savers, investors) and users of funds (borrowers); a middleman.

By acting as a middleman between cash surplus units in the economy (savers) and deficit spending units (borrowers), a financial intermediary makes it possible for borrowers to tap into vast pools of capital to finance their projects.

**Investment**  投资

Money put into a business, used to buy real estate or placed with someone else all with the intent of earning a profit.

**Investor**  投资者

A person or an organization which invests (makes investments).

**Lender**  贷款人

A person or an organization which lends money.

**Loan**  贷款

Money advanced to a borrower to be repaid at a later date.

**Long-term loan**  长期贷款

A loan that is to be repaid at some distant point in the future, usually 10 years or more.

**Loss**  损失

The money we get back from a loan or investment is less than the amount we originally paid out.

**Market** 市场

A place where buyers meet sellers to transact business.

**Primary market** 初级市场

The market for new issues of securities.

**Profit** 利润

A financial or monetary gain obtained from a loan or investment.

**Rate of return** 收益率

The earnings or profit on money we lend or invest expressed as a percentage of the amount of money loaned or invested.

**Risk** 风险

The possibility that a loan or investment will not produce the return we expect or that we will actually lose money. Risk is the financial uncertainty that the actual return on an investment will be different from the expected return. Factors of risk that can affect an investment include inflation or deflation, currency exchange rates, liquidity, default by borrower and interest rate fluctuation.

**Secondary market** 二级市场

The market where existing financial instruments are traded.

**Share** 股份

One of the parts into which the ownership of a company is divided.

**Short-term loan** 短期贷款

A loan to be repaid within one year.

**Term** 定期

How fast a loan is to be repaid or an investment converted back into cash.

**Trade** 交易

The purchase and sale of a security in a financial market.

# Part II  The Financial Marketplace 金融市场

*Financial markets play a very important part in the well-being of every person. They interact with other markets and affect our country's wealth, growth and prosperity.*

## Section A—Introduction 导语

In Part I, we talked about the financial markets as a place where people who need money meet people who have money. The people who need money use it for various purposes: expanding their business, buying equipment, building a new factory, acquiring another company, paying operating expenses.

There are a variety of ways in which companies can get the money they need. In all cases, there is an exchange. The supplier (investor) gives the consumer a sum of money and in return the consumer (the company that needs the money) gives the investor a financial instrument evidenced by a piece of paper. These financial instruments can take various forms each with different terms, conditions, rights and benefits.

A sophisticated financial services sector has many different types of borrowers, lenders, investors, intermediaries (middlemen), places where trading takes place, financial instruments and financial services. So well-developed are many financial markets around the world that an almost unlimited variety of financial needs can be met.

Part II—The Financial Marketplace  金融市场

The trading floor of the New York Stock Exchange

## Section B—The Participants  入市者

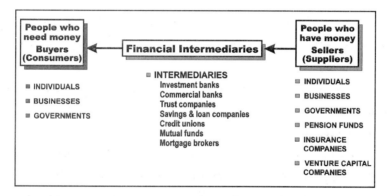

Notice that individuals, businesses and governments appear both as buyers and sellers. For example, when you get a mortgage loan to buy an apartment, you are a buyer (consumer). When you invest in stocks and bonds, you are a seller.

The financial intermediaries are in the middle. Their role is to bring buyers and sellers together.

## Section C—The Places  交易场所

The places where financial instruments are traded generally depend on the type of instruments and the type of participants. They can be actual places like stock exchanges and bank branches or they can be intangible-participants deal with each other and with intermediaries over the telephone, high speed data lines or through the Internet.

The Hong Kong Stock Exchange

Primary markets are usually the offices of intermediaries, borrowers, lenders and investors. Secondary markets can be either actual places where people interact face-to-face or they can exist only notionally.

■ **Physical markets**—the characteristics of these markets are determined by either the type of products or the type of participants.

■ Stock exchanges

Shares of many well-established companies are traded on stock exchanges. They all have a trading room or trading floor where transactions occur. In addition, some stock exchanges have introduced electronic trading where purchases and sales occur between individuals and computers over telephone or high speed data lines.

Examples are the stock exchanges in Shanghai, Shenzhen, New York, Hong Kong. Shares that are traded on stock exchanges are called listed shares.

■ Branches and offices of financial intermediaries

- Investment banks
- Commercial banks
- Trust companies, credit unions and savings and loan associations
- Mortgage brokers

## Part II—The Financial Marketplace  金融市场

- Your home
- Commodity exchanges

  Commodities such as crude oil, soybeans, wheat, gold, silver, pork bellies are traded on these exchanges.
- Futures exchanges

**Intangible or notional markets**—type of product
- Shares
  - Nasdaq

    Shares of companies such as Microsoft and Intel are traded in this market. There is no actual trading room. Purchases and sales take place between individuals or computers communicating over the telephone.
  - Over-the-counter market

    Shares of generally lesser known companies are traded in this market over the telephone.
- Bond market

  Bonds (long-term loans to corporations and governments) are traded over the telephone.
- Mortgage market

  Large institutions buy and sell large blocks of mortgage loans (loans secured by real estate such as houses, apartments, land, office buildings) over the telephone and through face to face dealings.
- Currency market

  Foreign currencies are bought and sold over the telephone.
- Derivatives market

A typical trading room where stocks, bonds, commodities, currencies, options and futures are traded for the firm and its clients.

## Section D—The Products  金融产品

### A. Debt

Debt means money that is borrowed. At some time in the future, debt has to be repaid. Examples are bonds, debentures, operating loans from banks, mortgage loans obtained to buy apartments and houses.

### B. Equity

Equity means the ownership of a company. It is represented by common and preferred shares. Equities are generally not repaid. The investor gets his or her money back by selling them in the secondary market, for example, through the facilities of a stock exchange.

Examples of Chinese bonds

## Section E—The Term  金融产品的期限

Financial instruments are divided into two categories according to how fast the money received from lenders and investors has to be paid back to them.

Short-term—the money is returned within one year.

Long-term—the money is not expected to be returned within the first year.

There are separate and distinct markets for trading these two types of securities.

1. **The money market**—one year or less

Money obtained by issuing these securities has to be returned to the lender or investor in one year or less.

A Chinese share certificate

a. Treasury bills

b. Banker's acceptances

c. Commercial paper

d. Operating bank loans

2. **The capital market**—over one year

Money obtained by issuing this type of instrument is repayable after one year and in the case of most equity securities, it is not expected to be repaid.

a. Bonds and debentures

b. Term bank loans

c. Common and preferred shares

The money market instruments along with bonds, debentures and term bank loans are called debt. Common and preferred shares are called equity.

## Section F—Marketability and Liquidity  适销性及流通性

The marketability is determined by how quickly and easily a particular financial instrument can be bought or sold. In general, for a security enjoying high marketability, there must be a large trading volume and a large number of buyers and sellers interested in it. If a security has high marketability, you can buy or sell a relatively large amount without affecting the price very much.

Liquidity means the ease with which a security can be converted into cash, especially without the seller's having to lower the price. Generally speaking, short-term securities are more liquid than long-term securities.

## Section G—Words and Expressions  术语及解释

**Banker's acceptances**  银行承兑汇票

A draft accepted by a bank and used as a form of borrowing in the money market.

**Bond**  债券

A long-term promissory note issued by a government or corporation; bonds issued by governments are generally unsecured; bonds issued by corporations are secured by a pledge of specific assets.

**Broker** 经纪人

An individual or a firm that acts as an intermediary, putting together willing sellers and willing buyers for a fee (brokerage).

**Capital market** 资本市场

Markets for financial assets and liabilities with maturity greater than one year, including long-term government and corporate bonds, preferred stock, and common stock. Money obtained by issuing this type of instrument is repayable after one year and in the case of most equity securities, it is not expected to be repaid.

**Capital structure** 资本结构

The proportion of debt and equity and the particular forms of debt and equity chosen to finance the assets of the firm.

**Common shares** 普通股

Security representing equity ownership in a corporation; holders of common shares have the right to elect the directors and receive dividends; common shareholders rank after creditors, bondholders and preferred shareholders.

**Commercial bank** 商业银行

An institution that accepts deposits from the public, makes personal, commercial and industrial loans and provides other banking services.

**Commercial Paper** 商业票据

An unsecured IOU issued by large companies and banks.

**Corporation** 股份公司

Form of business organization that is created as a distinct "legal person" composed of one or more actual individuals or legal entities. Primary advantages of a corporation include limited liability, ease of ownership, transfer and perpetual succession.

**Credit union** 信用合作社

A not-for-profit financial co-operative that makes personal loans and provides other consumer banking services to persons sharing a common bond.

**Debenture** 公司债券

A long-term promissory note issued by a corporation and not secured by any pledged assets; it is secured only by the good faith of the issuer. If the issuer were to default, the debenture holders' claims on the assets of the issuer would be secondary to those of investors holding bonds that are secured by assets. Because of this added risk, debentures usually have a higher interest rate than the secured bonds of the same issuer.

**Default**  违约

Failure to perform on a foreign exchange transaction or failure to pay an interest obligation on a debt.

**Default risk**  违约风险

The uncertainty that some or all of an investment may not be returned.

**Derivatives**  金融衍生品

A financial contract, the value of which is tied to something else such as a currency, commodity, stock, etc..

**Equity**  股本

The risk-sharing part of a company's capital, usually made up of "ordinary shares".

**Exchange traded**  交易所交易

A transaction where a specific instrument is bought or sold on a regulated exchange, e.g. futures.

**Face value**  面值

The value of a bond that appears on its face; also referred to as par value or principal.

**Intermediated market**  中介市场

A financial market in which a financial institution (usually a commercial bank) stands between borrowers and savers.

**Investment bank**  投资银行

A firm engaged in raising money for corporations and governments.

**Liquid market**  高流通性市场

An active market in which traders can buy or sell large quantities of an asset when they want without much effect on price.

**Liquidity**  流动性,变现能力

Liquidity is the ease with which financial assets can be converted to cash without creating a substantial change in price or value. Liquidity is influenced by the amount of float in the security, investor interest and size of the investment being converted to cash.

**Liquidity risk**  流动性风险

The risk that a financial market entity will not be able to find a price (or a price within a reasonable tolerance in terms of the deviation from prevailing or expected prices) for one or more of its financial contracts in the secondary market. Consider the case of a counterparty who buys a complex option on European interest rates. He is exposed to liquidity risk because of the possibility that he cannot find anyone to make him a price in the secondary market and because of the possibility that the price he obtains is very much against him and the theoretical price for the product.

**Market maker**　庄家

A participant in the financial markets who guarantees to make simultaneously a bid and an offer for a financial contract with a pre-set bid/offer spread (or a schedule of spreads corresponding to different market conditions) up to a pre-determined maximum contract amount.

**Market risk**　市场风险

The exposure to potential loss from fluctuations in market prices (as opposed to changes in credit status).

**Maturity date**　到期日

The date on which the last payment on a bond is due.

**Marketability**　适销性

The ease with which an asset can be bought and sold.

**Money market**　货币市场

Financial markets for debt securities that are repayable within one year.

**Mortgage**　抵押贷款

A long-term loan secured by real estate.

**Mutual fund**　共同基金

An investment company that pools money from its shareholders in stocks, bonds, government securities and short-term money market instruments.

**Nasdaq**　纳斯达克("美国全国证券交易商协会自动报价"的缩写)

Created in 1971, the Nasdaq (an acronym for National Association of Securities Dealers Automated Quotation) was the world's first electronic stock market. It is a computerized system that facilitates trading and provides price quotations on approximately 5,000 stocks.

**Offer**　出售报价

The wish to sell.

**Offer (ask) rates**　买入(卖出)报价

The rate at which a market maker is willing to sell the quoted asset.

**Orders**　订单

Firm order given to a broker to execute a transaction under certain specified conditions.

**Operating bank loans**　营业贷款

Short-term loans from banks for working capital purposes.

**Over the counter market**　场外交易市场

Market for trading securities that are not listed on organized stock exchanges.

**Par** 面值

Where the market price is the same as the redemption price or the amount to be paid at maturity.

**Portfolio** 投资组合

A collection of securities owned by an investor.

**Price Transparency** 价格透明度

Where a transaction is executed on the floor of an exchange and every participant has equal price.

**Primary market** 初级市场

The function of a stock exchange in bringing securities to the market for the first time.

**Private placement** 私募配售

A securities issue privately placed with a small group of investors rather than through a public offering.

**Promissory note** 本票

Financial document in which the buyer agrees to make payment to the seller at a specified time.

**Pension fund** 养老金

A fund set up to collect regular contributions from a government or corporation and its employees to provide post-retirement income.

**Preferred shares** 优先股

Shares that pay a fixed dividend and have a claim on the assets of a corporation ahead of the common shareholders.

**Risk** 风险

Risk is the financial uncertainty that the actual return on an investment will be different from the expected return. Factors of risk that can affect an investment include inflation or deflation, currency exchange rates, liquidity, default by borrower and interest rate fluctuation.

**Risk averse** 规避风险

Seeking stability rather than risk.

**Risk premium** 风险溢价

The excess return on the risky asset that is the difference between expected return on risky assets and the return of risk-free assets. Risk premium refers to the additional compensation demanded by investors, above the risk-free rate of return, for assuming additional risk. The higher is the additional risk, the larger will be the risk premium.

**Risk profile  风险分析图**

A graph with the value of an underlying asset on the x-axis and the value of a position exposed to risk in the underlying asset on the y-axis. Also used with changes in value. (Contrast with payoff profile.)

**Savings and loan association  储蓄与贷款协会**

Deposit-taking financial institution holding most of its assets in residential mortgages.

**Security  证券**

Certificate representing ownership of equity (stock), debt (bonds) and the rights to ownership (derivatives).

**Stockbroker  股票经纪人**

A financial firm which provides advice and dealing services to the public and which can deal on its own account.

**Stock exchange  证券交易所**

An organized institution where members buy and sell securities.

**Term bank loans  定期银行贷款**

A bank loan for a fixed period of time, usually used to finance fixed assets.

**Treasury bills  短期国库券**

Short-term promissory notes of governments (maturities 91 to 365 days)

**Trust company  信托公司**

A corporation organized for the purpose of accepting and executing trusts and acting as trustee under wills, as executor or guardian; in some jurisdictions trust companies can offer banking services such as taking deposits and making loans.

**Venture capital company  风险投资公司**

Firm providing startup money for high risk companies, especially those specializing in new technologies.

**Volatility  波幅**

The degree to which the price of a financial instrument fluctuates within a short period of time.

# Part III

## Debt Securities 债务型证券

*Wise use of debt in your company's financial plan can reduce the overall cost of financing the assets. Too much debt can lead to bankruptcy.*

## Section A—Introduction 导语

Debt securities are financial instruments that corporations and governments sell to the public to raise money for expanding their businesses, building new factories, developing mines, constructing airports, highways, railways, buying machinery and equipment. They are loans. The issuer borrows money from investors for a period of time—the term. The money is repaid periodically (monthly, quarterly, semi-annually, annually) or in one lump sum at maturity (the last day of the term).

An investor in debt securities earns a return in two ways:

1. By receiving regular interest payments (monthly, quarterly, semi-annually, etc.) and/or;

2. By getting (either by selling in the market or redeeming at maturity) more money for the debt instrument than was paid for it.

Many debt instruments pay interest. The interest rate can be either fixed—does not change during the term of loan or floating—goes up and down as general interest rate levels go up and down.

Other debt instruments do not pay interest but are sold at a discount when they are issued—a price less than the face amount.

The main disadvantage of debt is that making the required interest payments and repaying the money borrowed at the agreed time in the future are legal obligations. If they are not paid, lenders generally have the right to take strong action including putting the company into bankruptcy.

## Section B—General Characteristics of Debt Securities 债务型证券的共性

**Face Value or Principal**

The face value or principal is the amount of money an investor will receive back once a debt security matures. The face value is usually in integral multiples of 100.

It is important to remember that the par value is not the price of the debt instrument. Its price fluctuates throughout its life in response to a number of variables such as general economic conditions and the financial health of the issuer. If a debt security is trading *at par*, the market price is equal to the face value.

**Maturity**

The maturity date is the future day on which the investor's principal will be repaid. Maturities can range from as little as one day to as long as 30 years. Maturities of 5 to 20 years are most common though 100-year bonds and bonds with no maturity date—perpetuals—have been issued.

**Interest**

Interest is the payment investors receive for the use of their money. It is generally expressed as an annual percentage rate. The rate may be constant over the life of the security (fixed-rate) or may change from time to time by reference to an index (floating-rate).

**Coupon Rate**

The coupon is the amount the investor will receive as interest payments. It's called a "coupon" because sometimes there are physical coupons on the bond that you tear off and redeem for interest. This was more common in the past. Nowadays records are more likely to be kept electronically.

The coupon is expressed as a percentage of the par value. If a bond has a coupon rate of 10% and its par value is ￥1,000, then the investor will receive ￥100 of interest a year.

> **A Typical Bond Coupon**
>
> On the due date, in this case February 1870, the bondholder clips (with scissors) the coupon from the bond and takes it to a bank. The bank will pay to the bearer (person presenting the coupon) the amount stated on the coupon, in this case $ 35.00. In this way bondholders received the interest due to them.

**Market Price**

The price a buyer is willing to pay in the secondary market for a particular debt security bond. The price is expressed in the same currency as the security itself and is based on a unit of 100. For example, the price of a US dollar—denominated bond (a bond the interest and principal of which is payable in US dollars) on the secondary market could be US $ 98.05 (trading at a discount). This means that buyers are willing to pay $ 98.05 for each US $ 100 of face value of the bond.

**Discount**

The amount by which the market price of a debt security is less than its face value. When the market price of a bond (or other debt security) is lower than its face value, we say that the bond is trading at a discount.

**Premium**

The amount by the market price of a debt security is more than its face value. When the market price of a bond (or other debt security) is lower than its face value, we say that the bond is trading at a discount.

When the trading price is above the face value, the instrument is said to be selling at a premium and it is below face value, it is said to be selling at a discount.

**Current yield**

The current yield is the annual return on the actual amount paid for a debt security regardless of its maturity. If the security is bought at par, the current yield equals its stated interest rate (coupon rate). Thus, the current yield on a 6% bond is 6%. However, if the market price of the bond is more or less than par, the current yield will be different.

Current yield is calculated by dividing the annual interest received by the market price of the debt instrument and multiplying by 100%.

**Yield to maturity**

A more meaningful figure is the yield to maturity, because it tells you the total return you will receive if you hold a bond until maturity. It also enables you to compare bonds with different maturities and coupons. Yield to maturity includes all your interest plus any capital gain you will realize (if you purchase the bond below par) or minus any capital loss you will suffer (if you purchase the bond above par).

**Issuer**

The issuer is the government, government agency, corporation or organization that sells the securities to investors.

The issuer is an extremely important factor as its stability is the investor's main assurance of getting repaid. Generally speaking, debt instruments issued by governments are less risky than debt securities issued by corporations domiciled within their borders. This is based on the principle that governments have the power of taxation. In theory, if they need more money to pay their debts, they can simply raise taxes. Corporations on the other hand must continue to earn profits in order to stay in business and to honour their obligations.

Many years ago, agencies were formed which created a grading system to reflect the relative credit quality of bond issuers. The bond rating system helps investors assess the credit risk. A bond rating is a report card for the issuer. Blue chip firms, which are safer investments, have a high rating while risky companies have a low rating.

The rating agencies provide an opinion on the ability of an issuer to meet financial commitments such as interest, preferred dividends or repayment of principal on a timely basis.

> An "AAA" (Triple A) rating is the highest rating assigned to a debt obligation by S & P. It indicates an extremely strong capacity to pay principal and interest. Bonds rated "AA" are just a notch below, then single "A", then "BBB" and so on. Some ratings show a + or – to further differentiate creditworthiness. Bonds rated "BBB" and above are considered investment grade, a category to which certain investors, including many pension funds, confine their bond holdings. Bonds rated "BB", "B", "CCC", "CC" and "C" are regarded as speculative. A bond rating of "D" indicates payment default or the filing of a bankruptcy petition.

| BOND RATING CODES | Standard & Poor's | Moody's | Fitch |
|---|---|---|---|
| **Investment grade** | | | |
| Highest quality | AAA | Aaa | AAA |
| Very high quality | | | AA |
| High quality | AA | Aa | A |
| Upper medium quality | A | A | BBB |
| Medium grade | BBB | Baa | |
| **Speculative grade** | | | |
| Somewhat speculative | BB | Ba | BB |
| Highly speculative | B | B | B |
| Low grade, default possible | CCC | B | CCC |
| Low grade, default probable | CC | | CC |
| Default imminent | | Caa | C |
| In default, recovery potential 90% to 100% | | Ca | DDD |
| In default, recovery potential 50% to 90% | SD | | DD |
| In default, recovery potential < 50% | D | C | D |

**Collateral or security**

Collateral means the assets that are pledged by an issuer to secure repayment of a debt security. In the event of non-payment of principal and/or interest, the investors can seize and sell the assets and use the proceeds to apply against the interest and principal they are owed.

**Default**

When an issuer fails to make payments of interest and principal in due or breaches a term or condition of the debt instruments such as failing to maintain a minimum level of working capital or shareholders' equity, the issuer is said to be in default.

## Section C—Short-Term Debt   短期债务

**Treasury Bills**

Treasury bills are promissory notes issued by governments. The bills are not paid periodic interest. Instead, they are sold at a discount from their face value. At maturity, the investor receives the face value. The difference between the face value and the price at which it was sold is treated as interest. T-bills, as they are known for short, are issued for maturities of 90, 180 or 360 days.

### Banker's Acceptances

B/As, as they are called, are an excellent way for companies that are not well known to investors to borrow money in the money market.

The company draws a draft for the amount of money it wants to borrow with a tenor equal to the time period for which it wants the money (e.g. 30 days, 60 days). The company takes the completed draft to its bank with which it has an operating line of credit. If there is room under the line, the bank will stamp the acceptance which means the bank will unconditionally pay the draft on its maturity date. The company then takes the accepted draft to a securities dealer which sells it at a discount in the money market.

```
                TEDDY BEAR MANUFACTURING COMPANY
  ¥1,000,000        SHENZHEN, CHINA            March 1, 2004
                                                    Date
  Thirty days after date
  PAY TO THE ORDER OF         New China Securities
  THE SUM OF         One million renminbi

  To: Bank of China                Teddy Bear Manufacturing Company
      Shenzhen                 Per _____Li Wei_____
                                         Authorized signature

                    ACCEPTED
                 Bank of China 03/01/2004
                 Authorized officer  Gao Yulin
```

> When a bank accepts a company's draft (indicated by the stamp "accepted" across its face and the signature of an authorized bank officer), the bank becomes fully liable to pay the amount of the draft on its due date. Buyers of the draft (investors) do not need to worry about the credit-worthiness of the drawer. They are relying on the strength and reputation of the bank for payment.

### Commercial Paper

Commercial paper is a short term promissory note issued by a corporation. Usual maturities are 30, 60 and 90 days. Most commercial paper bears interest.

# Section D—Long-Term Debt: Bonds and Debentures 长期债务：政府债券及公司债券

Bonds and debentures are long-term promissory notes issued by governments, government agencies, corporations and other organizations and institutions. Government bonds are generally unsecured. Corporate bonds generally have specific assets pledged as security for the payment of principal and interest. Debentures are unsecured debt obligations of corporations.

### Corporate Bonds

Corporate bonds and debentures are issued by companies of all sizes. Bondholders are not owners of the corporation. If the company gets in financial trouble and must be dissolved, bondholders must be paid off in full before stockholders get anything. If the corporation defaults on any bond principal or payment, any bondholder can go into bankruptcy court and request the corporation be placed in bankruptcy.

### Municipal Bonds

Municipal bonds are issued by cities, states and other local agencies and may or may not be as safe as corporate bonds. Some municipal bonds are backed by the taxing authority of the state or town, while others rely on revenue-producing projects to earn income to pay the bond interest and principal.

### Bond Prices

The price of a bond is a function of prevailing interest rates. As rates go up, the price of the bond goes down, because that particular bond becomes less attractive (i.e., pays less interest) when compared to current offerings. As rates go down, the price of the bond goes up, because that particular bond becomes more attractive (i.e., pays more interest) when

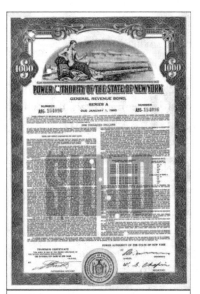

**A Typical Corporate Bond**

Bonds issued by corporations are secured by specific assets which helps protect investors from loss if the company encounters financial difficulties.

compared to current offerings.

The price also fluctuates in response to the risk perceived for the debt of the particular organization. For example, if a company is in bankruptcy, the price of that company's bonds will be low because there may be considerable doubt that the company will ever be able to redeem the bonds.

**Repayment**

At maturity, bonds are usually redeemed at "par", meaning the issuer pays back exactly the face value of the bond. Most bonds also allow the bond issuer to redeem the bonds at any time before the redemption date, usually at par but sometimes at a higher price. This is known as "calling" the bonds and frequently happens when interest rates fall, because the company can sell new bonds at a lower interest rate and pay off the older, more expensive bonds with the proceeds of the new sale. By doing so the company may be able to lower their cost of funds considerably.

**Convertible Bonds**

Another type of bond is a convertible bond. This security can be converted into shares of the company that issues the bond if the bondholder so chooses. The conversion price is usually set considerably higher than the price at which the shares are trading when the bond is issued. Conversion premiums of 15% to 30% are common.

**Coupon Bonds**

Not too many years ago every bond had coupons attached to it. Every so often, usually every 6 months, bond owners would take a pair of scissors to the bond, clip the coupon and present the coupon to the bond issuer or bank for payment. Those bonds could either be "bearer bonds" meaning the person who had physical possession of the bonds owned them or they could be registered in the name of the holder.

Most registered bonds today do not have coupons attached. Instead the issuer sends an interest cheque to the registered holder on every interest payment date. It is as if the issuer clipped the coupons for you and then sent you the money. Even if bonds do not actually have coupons attached, if interest is paid periodically, they are still called coupon bonds.

If, for example, you buy a 20-year bond at issue and hold it until maturity you will collect the face value at that time and will have received interest payments every 6 months for 20 years.

Part Ⅲ—Debt Securities  债务型证券

### Dialogue—The Appointment

**Alan:** Good morning, Fred. I hope I didn't catch you at a bad time. The 12-hour time difference makes it so difficult to co-ordinate communication.

**Fred:** Nice to hear from you, Alan. I know what you mean about dealing across so many time zones! Now is fine. What did you have in mind?

**Alan:** I'm going to be in New York next week. Our company is planning on building a methanol plant near Shanghai. We are going to tap the international financial markets probably for a combination of debt and equity.

**Fred:** Sounds like an interesting project.

**Alan:** It is. There is a rapidly growing demand for industrial chemicals in China. We are operating a near capacity now. The new plant will help us keep pace.

**Fred:** A wise strategy, for sure. Is there a role for us?

**Alan:** That's actually why I'm calling. We're looking for a good investment bank to advise us on the best financing structure and ultimately raise the money we need.

**Fred:** You know the placing power of our firm is among the best. We have been particularly successful in raising money for China-based enterprises. My team just closed a US $ 1.5 billion project financing for a resource development in the western part of China.

Alan: Yes, we think very highly of your firm. However, our board of directors has insisted that we get several competitive bids so you will need to sharpen your pencils.

Fred: Yes, of course. We'll get working on it right away so that we are well prepared when you come. I will also make sure that our industry specialists and other top people are available to meet with you when you come.

Alan: Thank you, Fred. I knew I could count on you to handle this assignment in your usual professional manner. I will be looking forward to seeing you soon. I will send you a copy of my itinerary as soon as I have it firmed up.

**Zero coupon bonds**

A zero-coupon bond has no coupons and there is no interest paid. It is issued at steep discount and redeemed at par maturity. The price in the secondary market depends on: the number of years to maturity, general interest rates, and the financial strength of the issuer (riskiness).

**High-yield or Junk Bonds**

High-yield or junk bonds are issued by start-up companies, companies that have had financial problems, companies employing particularly aggressive financial and business policies. They pay higher interest rates than investment-grade bonds to compensate for the extra risk.

## Section E—Words and Expressions 术语及解释

**Ask (offer) rates** 卖出（买入）报价

The rate at which a market maker is willing to sell the quoted asset.

**Basis point** 基点

One hundredth of one percent (0.01%).

**Bear market** 熊市

A declining market.

**Bid** 买入

The wish to buy.

**Bid rate** 买入报价

The rate at which a market maker is willing to buy the quoted asset.

**Bond rating**　债券评级

A rating given to a bond as the likelihood that the borrower will default on the interest and principal payments.

**Bull market**　牛市

A rising market.

**Capital gain**　资本利得

The amount of profit realized when an asset sold at a price higher than the purchase price.

**Capital loss**　资本亏损

The amount of loss realized when an asset sold at a price less than the purchase price.

**Convertible bonds**　可转换债券

Bonds sold with a conversion feature that allows the holder to convert the bond into common stock on or prior to a conversion date and at a pre-specified conversion price.

**Coupon**　票息

The stated interest on a debt instrument.

**Coupon rate**　票面利率

The fixed rate of interest on a bond.

**Credit rating**　信用评级

Standard & Poor's, Moody's and Fitch Investors Service assign credit ratings to corporate debt, municipal debt and other fixed income securities.

Bond issuers pay credit rating agencies to rate an issue. Once a rating is assigned, it is regularly reviewed by the credit rating agency.

**Credit risk**　信用风险

Credit risk represents the possibility that an issuer of a financial obligation (bond, note, lease, installment debt) will not be able to repay interest and principal on a timely basis. Credit rating agencies analyze the credit quality of an issuer and assign a rating to the issuer's obligations. If the credit risk of an issuer increases, investors will demand a higher yield on that firm's obligations to compensate them for the higher level of risk.

**Discount**　贴现

The margin by which the purchase price is cheaper than the redemption price. If a bond is selling below its face value, it is said to sell at a discount.

**Fixed interest rate**　固定利率

The interest rate is set for the term of the loan.

**Floating interest rate** 浮动利率

The interest rate goes up and down as market conditions change.

**Foreign bonds** 外国债券

Bonds that are issued in a domestic market by a foreign borrower, denominated in domestic currency, marketed to domestic residents and regulated by the domestic authorities.

**International bonds** 国际债券

Bonds that are traded outside the country of the issuer; international bonds are either foreign bonds trading in a foreign national market or Eurobonds trading in the international market.

**Junk bond** 垃圾债券

High risk, low rated speculative bonds.

**Maturity** 到期

The time at which a note, bond, debenture or mortgage becomes due and payable.

**Point/pip** 点

The last decimal place of the quotation.

**Premium** 溢价

The margin by which the purchase price is more expensive than the redemption rate. If a bond is selling above its face value, it is said to sell at a premium.

**Rating agency** 评级公司

A firm that assigns credit ratings to fixed income securities.

**Registered bonds** 记名债券

Bonds for which each issuer maintains a record of the owners of its bonds. Countries requiring that bonds be issued in registered form include the United States and Japan (Contrast with bearer bonds).

**Speculative** 投机性的

High risk securities.

**Stated annual interest rate** 票面年利率

The interest rate expressed as a percentage per annum, by which interest payment is determined.

**Yield** 收益(率)

The return earned on an investment taking into account the annual income and its present capital value. There are a number of different types of yield and in some cases different methods of calculating each type.

**Yield curve** 收益曲线

A curve showing interest rates at a particular point in time for securities with the same risk but different maturity dates; for a particular series of fixed income instruments such as government bonds, the graph of the yields to maturity of the series plotted by maturity.

**Yield to maturity** 到期收益(率)

The discount rate that equates the present value of interest payments and redemption value with the present price of the bond.

**Zero coupon bond** 零息债券

Bonds that are sold at a deep discount and pay no interest.

# Part IV

## Equity Securities 权益型证券

*Bears, bulls and pigs are found in the stock market. Bulls make money. Bears make money. Pigs get slaughtered.*

## Section A—Capital Structure 资本结构

Companies need money to buy the assets like land and equipment and to build factories to produce their products. They get that money from lenders in the form of long-term debt and from the owners who buy shares. The combination of various types of debt and equities that a company uses is called its capital structure.

As we learned in Part III, debt has to be paid back at some point. If the company is unable to do so, it may be forced into bankruptcy. This could happen if the company's sales fall, even temporarily.

On the other hand, owners of a corporation do not have an automatic right to receive dividends or an absolute right to get back the money they paid for their shares. Therefore, the more money the owners have invested a company in relation to the amount of money the company has borrowed, the less likely the company is to go bankrupt if time get tough—the economy slows down, for example.

Shares, stocks, equities are words used to describe ownership of corporations. When we own shares in a corporation, we have the right to "share" along with all the other shareholders in the earnings of the business and in the net assets if it should ever be wound up.

Shares of a company are first issued to investors through a process called an initial public offering, IPO for short. The main reason that a company would issue shares to the public is because

  i. it needs money to grow,
  ii. it cannot produce enough cash from its own operations and,
  iii. it would not be prudent to borrow more money (because of the risk of bankruptcy).

> **Definition**
>
> A capital gain results when an asset is sold at price higher than its cost price. The difference between the selling price and the cost price is called a capital gain. If the difference is negative, in other words, if the selling price is lower than the cost price, we say the investor has incurred a capital loss.

Once a company's shares have been offered to the public in an IPO, they can be bought and sold at any time in the secondary market, on a stock exchange for example.

Investors buy shares for two reasons:

1. receive regular income (cash) in the form of dividends and,
2. earn capital gains—selling shares in the secondary market for more than was paid for them.

There are two main types of shares: preferred shares and common shares. Each type has particular rights and benefits, advantages and disadvantages.

## Section B—Preferred Shares  优先股

Preferred shares are somewhat like bonds. They generally entitle the holder to receive fixed quarterly payments called dividends so investors buy them to produce income. There are two big differences, however, between bonds and preferred shares. Bond interest is paid first and then preferred dividends. Bond interest is a legal obligation of the issuer. If it is not paid, bondholders can force the company into bankruptcy. While preferred shareholders expect to receive dividends, they have no legal right to force the company to pay them. If the company incurs a loss or is short of cash, it may not pay the expected dividends.

The other difference relates to income taxes. Bond interest is paid before corporate income taxes are calculated whereas as dividends are paid out after tax income. Individuals pay income tax on interest they receive on bonds. The tax rate on dividends, however, is often lower to compensate for the double taxation—the same income being taxed twice, once when it is earned by the corporation and again when it is paid to the shareholders.

## Section C—Common Shares  普通股

Common shares are at the very bottom of a company's capital structure. Common shareholders are entitled to whatever is left after all of the company's expenses such as wages, materials, interest and so on, have been paid and after preferred dividends have been provided for.

Common shares are the most risky of the three types of investments we have been discussing—bonds, preferred shares and common shares—because they rank last. However, the potential rate of return is the highest because there is no upper limit on how high the price of the shares can rise. Common shares can be grouped into the following main categories:

### A. Income shares

Many companies pay regular quarterly dividends on their common shares. In practice, these dividend payments are rarely missed, so investors can depend on them to supplement their ordinary income. Furthermore, the dividend payments rise as the company's earnings grow, so the investors are protected somewhat from inflation.

### B. Growth shares

Other companies, however, pay no dividends to their common shareholders, preferring to retain the cash flow from their operations and invest in expanding the business. As the company's sales and profits increase, the price of its common shares generally rises as well. An important advantage of growth shares is that the investor is not taxed on the increasing price of the common shares until the shares are actually sold.

### C. Speculative shares

These common shares are very high risk. The issuers tend to be small or newly-formed companies often in mining or oil and gas development or in high tech industries. There is the potential of earning big capital gains, but losing all or at least part of one's investment is much more likely. These companies do not pay dividends.

In this category are what we call "penny stocks". These are high-risk shares of companies often in mining or oil and gas exploration and development.

### D. Blue-chip stocks

Called red chips in China, these are shares of the largest, most stable companies in the country. They appeal to conservative investors because they provide a more consistent stream of income than most stocks.

### E. Penny stocks

Penny stocks are very volatile and usually trade for under a dollar per share. They're offered by speculative ventures and can go boom or bust overnight. They are very risky and should only be bought with money you can afford to lose.

### F. American depositary shares (ADS)

Depositary receipts were created in 1927 to aid US investors who wanted to purchase shares of non-US corporations. Since that time, depositary receipts have grown into a popular and flexible structure which enables issuers worldwide to access investors outside their home markets.

Global depositary receipts (GDRs) are depositary receipts that are available in two or more markets outside the issuer's home country. Singapore depositary receipts are listed on the Singapore Stock Exchange and allow non-Singapore companies to access Asian investors.

A depositary receipt is a negotiable certificate evidencing ownership of shares in a corporation domiciled in a country outside the market in which it is traded. An American Depositary Receipt (ADR) is the actual physical certificate whereas an American Depositary Share (ADS) is the actual share.

Each depositary receipt represents a specific number of the underlying shares remaining on deposit in the issuer's home market. Each depositary receipt can represent one, more than one or a fraction of underlying shares. The relationship between the depositary receipt and the ordinary share is referred to as the ratio. While many depositary receipt programs are established with a 1∶1 ratio (one underlying share equals one depositary share), current programs have ratios ranging from 100,000∶1 to 1∶100.

Depositary receipts are quoted and traded in the currency of the country in which they trade and are governed by the trading and settlement procedures of that market. The ease of trading and settling depositary receipts makes them an attractive investment option for investor wishing to purchase shares in foreign companies.

### Example

Shanghai Sinopec Petroleum Co., Ltd. is a good example of an American depositary receipt. The company is domiciled in the People's Republic of China. A Chinese bank holds a certain quantity of Sinopec shares in trust for an American bank. On the strength of the undertaking of the Chinese bank to always hold that quantity of shares in trust, the American bank issues what are called American Depositary Receipts. These take the place of the share certificates—the pieces of paper we normally associate with of ownership companies. A Sinopec ADR for 1,000 shares tells us that there are 1,000 actual Sinopec shares held on deposit for the benefit of the holder of the ADR. Shares traded under an ADR agreement are called American Depositary Shares to distinguish them from "normal" shares. Holders of ADS are entitled to all of the rights and benefits that holders of ordinary shares enjoy.

## Investment Banking 投资银行

## Dialogue—The New Client

**Mark:** I think that meeting went well, don't you?

**Jenny:** Yes, I totally agree. The VP Finance seemed particularly interested in our proposal.

**Steven:** That company is about to take off! They have very ambitious growth plans. I know we can help them get the money they need to meet their goals.

**Jenny:** No doubt about that. And we can contribute in many other ways also. They do a lot of business in foreign currencies so our FX traders should be able to get them the best rates.

**Mark:** We should talk to our derivatives people also. They can probably come up with some ways to help the company manage its interest rate and foreign currency risk.

**Steven:** Good thinking. I'll call Norman this afternoon and see what ideas he has.

**Jenny:** I also think that the company is a prime candidate to take public. It will give the company much greater access to capital and provide the owners with liquidity for their stock.

**Mark:** I totally agree. I think we should work up an analysis of the company, crunch some numbers and see what kind of size we could be talking and what kind of multiple we might be able to get.

**Steven:** Good idea. I suggest that when we are ready, we call the VP Finance and try to meet with him informally, say over lunch in a private room at our club rather than making a formal presentation. Going public requires a big change in corporate thinking. It seems to me that if we try to introduce the idea gradually in relaxed surroundings, we can gain his confidence and significantly improve our chances of success.

**Jenny:** That makes a lot of sense. It seems to me that the reason a lot of IPOs ultimately fail is that management rushes into them without adequate preparation and no plans for follow-up.

**Mark:** You are quite right. There are a lot of advantages to being a public company, but the demands of the market, the scrutiny of the regulators and keeping the investors, fund managers and analysts happy are big challenges for people who are not used to it.

**Steven**: Our experience certainly has been that working carefully and steadily with clients in order to build a solid base takes a bit longer, but it sure pays off in the long run.

**Mark**: Very true. Say, it's coming up to 12. Do you guys have any plans for lunch?

**Jenny**: No.

**Steven**: Me neither. What did you have in mind?

**Mark**: I was thinking of the Harbourside at the Regent Hotel. The view is terrific and they have a great buffet. I think we've earned a bit of a treat after all our hard work and successful meeting, right?

**Steven**: Sounds great. I've worked up a real appetite.

**Jenny**: Me too. I love the seafood there.

**Mark**: Well, let's go then. We should be able to get a taxi from here. Should only take 15 or 20 minutes. You two attend to the taxi and I'll take care of the reservation.

**Steven**: Right you are!

## Section D—Words and Expressions  术语及解释

**American depositary receipt（ADR）  美国存托凭证**

Certificates which represent ownership of a given number of a company's shares, which can be listed and traded separately from the underlying shares. American Depositary Receipts are receipts held by a US bank that represent stock in a foreign firm. ADRs trade in US dollars, making it simpler for US investors to invest on overseas markets.

**American depositary share（ADS）  美国存托股票**

The share certificate (piece of paper) evidencing ownership of an American depositary receipt.

**Blue chip  蓝筹股**

Large established company-in China known as "Red Chips".

**Depository receipt  存单**

A derivative security issued by a foreign borrower through a domestic trustee representing ownership in the deposit of foreign shares held by the trustee.

**Global depositary receipt   全球存托凭证**

These negotiable certificates are held by one country's bank and represent a certain number of shares of a foreign stock which is traded on another exchange; similar to American depositary receipts.

A bank issued certificate in more than one country for shares in a foreign company. The shares are held by a foreign branch of an international branch. The shares trade as domestic shares but are offered for sale globally through the various bank branches.

**Growth stocks   增长型股票**

Stocks with high price/book or price/earnings ratios. Historically, growth stocks have had lower average returns than value stocks (stocks with low price/book or PE ratios) in a variety of countries.

**Initial public offering (IPO)   首次公开发行**

When a private company "goes public", it offers shares on the market for the first time in an initial public offering.

**Preferred shares   优先股**

Normally fixed income shares, where holders have the right to receive dividends before ordinary shareholders. In the event of liquidation preference shareholders rank above ordinary shareholders.

**Share   股份**

A document signifying part ownership in a company; the terms "share" and "stock" are often used interchangeably.

**Stocks   股票**

A share of ownership or equity in a corporation; for example, if you buy 10,000 shares in a company with 1 million shares outstanding, you own 1 per cent of the company. Ownership of a corporation which is represented by shares which are proportionate a piece of the corporation's assets and earnings; stocks are also known as equities.

**Value stocks   价值型股票**

Stocks with low price/book ratios or price/earnings ratios. Historically, value stocks have enjoyed higher average returns than growth stocks (stocks with high price/book or PE ratios) in a variety of countries.

Investment Banking 投资银行

# Part V

## Research 研究金融市场

*Picking the right stocks is easy if you study the market and your financial needs. Carefully think about your financial goals and your time frame for meeting them.*

### Section A—The Research Department 研究部门

In order to determine which stocks are likely to be good investments, investment dealers employ large numbers of highly trained, experienced financial analysts. These individuals are grouped together in the firm's research department.

Research departments are generally divided into teams. Each team specializes in a specific industry, such as telecommunications, autos, high tech, healthcare and so on. This allows them to develop in-depth knowledge, to keep current with changing conditions and to anticipate future trends and predict the impact they will have on individual companies.

Research analysts meet with top company managers, attend industry conferences, study financial statements, talk to customers, bankers, suppliers, analyze economic indicators all in an effort to fully understand each company, its past performance—what made it successful or caused it problems—and what it can be expected to do in the future.

Equity research helps investors and fund managers decide which stocks to buy and when to sell the stocks they hold.

#### A. Supply and demand

Shares are just like any other product we buy and sell. The price of a particular company's shares is subject to the same laws of supply and demand that affect most goods and services. The more people there are who want to buy a particular share, the higher the price will be—and it will keep rising until the number of shares people are willing to sell is exactly equal to the number of shares other people are willing to buy. Conversely, if there are more sellers than buyers, the price will fall until a balance is restored.

### B. Over valued and under valued

The objective of research is to evaluate companies, study how they have performed in the past and predict how they will do in the future. Research analysts determine the price for each company's shares that they think represents the true value of the company today. Then they compare the market price of the shares with the price they have calculated. When the market price is less than the calculated price, we say that the shares are under valued (by the market) and they would make an attractive investment. The principle is that just as water reaches its own level, share prices will move towards their real value based on the company's expected future performance.

---

**Definition**

**Fundamental analysis** is the study of interest rate trends, unemployment, gross domestic product and other factors to predict growth patterns for the economy and the analysis of companies using balance sheet and income statement ratios, trends, evaluation of management, comparison with other companies.

---

If the market price is higher than the calculated price, the shares are considered to be over valued. In other words, the research analyst feels that the market is placing too high a value on the company and there is a high probability that the market price will fall. As more and more investors realize that the company's future prospects are not nearly as good as they thought when they first bought the shares, they will sell them. When there are more sellers than buyers, the price will go down.

## Section B—What Buying a Share of Stock Gives Us? 购买股票的意义

Ownership of shares gives us the right to participate in the company's earnings. Therefore, the true worth of a share of stock should be the present value—the value today—

of all the future earnings attributable to that share. This is the principle of "intrinsic value". All of our research recommendations are based on it because we believe that the market price of a stock will, over time, move towards its intrinsic value. If the market price is above the intrinsic value, we would recommend selling the stock. If it is below the intrinsic value, we would recommend buying. If the difference between the intrinsic value and the market price is large, we would rate the stock a strong sell or a strong buy respectively.

A share of stock gives us a share of the pie, the pie in this case being the company's earnings and assets.

## Section C—The Company Under a Microscope　显微镜下的公司

### A. The broad view—the economy and the industry

Before valuing an individual company's shares, we first consider the present and expected strength of the economy. Next we look carefully at the industry in which the company operates. Is it growing? What problems, opportunities does it face? Is the industry countercyclical—does it grow when the general economy is shrinking? Is the industry recession—proof—that is, will consumers buy its products even during a recession?

### B. What is unique about the company?

Finally we come to the evaluation of the particular company. What are the factors that give it a competitive edge? Is it a "low-cost" producer? Does it have unique technology? How strong is its management? What competitive threats does the company face? Answers to these questions will give us the ability to predict the company's future performance with a high degree of certainty.

A company's balance sheet is like a lake. Water comes into one end of a lake and leaves from the other end. Water is constantly being added and removed. At any point in time, however, there is a large quantity of water sitting there not moving. It is a stock or pool of water rather than a flow of water.

Likewise, the balance sheet records the company's stock of assets—the things that it owns and which it uses in its business to earn money measured at a point in time. Accountants call this a "stock", that is a pool of assets. As time passes, money is added to the stock from sales of the company's product or service just like the water coming into the lake. And money is steadily taken away from the assets as the company pays its bills, suppliers, workers, utilities, taxes, etc.. This is the same as the water leaving the lake.

Investment Banking 投资银行

### C. The financial statements

Let us go through some of the basic measures that we commonly use to value common and preferred shares. Here is a simplified version of Sinopec's financial report to shareholders.

The income statement is like a river flowing from one town to another. It records the money the company earns from all sources and the expenses it incurs during a specific period of time, for example, three months—quarterly report; a year—annual report.

The balance sheet, on the other hand, shows the company's financial position at a particular point in time. On the left side are the assets—what the company owns. The right side is divided into two main parts: first the liabilities. This is what the company owes to its creditors. Second is the shareholders' equity. This is the money the shareholders have invested in the company.

## Section D—How Much Money Is Company Earning? 公司收益情况

Let us work through the income statement. First we have sales—the total revenue the company earns from selling its product or service. From that we deduct "cost of goods sold". This figure includes all the money the company spends on production and delivery—such items as wages, materials and supplies, energy, transportation. The difference between sales and cost of goods sold is called the gross margin. Next we deduct "general and administrative costs"—salaries of managers, executives and office personnel, accounting, legal and insurance costs, communications expenses, business and property taxes.

Deducting G & A, as these costs are referred to, from the gross margin gives us

The income statement is like a river. Money is flowing through the company all the time. Cash is received from sales and collection of receivables and is used to pay operating expenses. Accountants call income and expense items "flows".

"earnings before interest and taxes"—EBIT for short. Now we deduct interest expense. This includes all expenses relating to borrowed money. The difference is called "earnings before tax"—EBT. Taxes here means income taxes—taxes which vary directly with income earned unlike property taxes which a company has to pay whether it earns any money or not. After deducting income taxes we are left with net income—sometimes referred to as net income after tax. These are the earnings that belong to the shareholders and they are divided among the shareholders according to the rights and privileges set out in the share conditions. For example, if the company has preferred shares outstanding and has paid dividends during the period covered by the income statement, the total amount of dividends paid will be deducted from the net income.

## Section E—Earnings Available for the Common Shareholders 可分给普通股股东的收益

The earnings remaining after deducting preferred dividends accrue to the benefit of the common shareholders. We call this number "earnings available for common shareholders". This brings us to one of the most important measures used in the valuation of common shares—earnings per share—EPS for short. It is calculated by dividing "earnings available for common shares" by "the number of common shares outstanding". If you hold common shares of that company, that is your share of the company's earnings for each share you own.

---

Research Tip

When evaluating a stock, examine the company for the following characteristics:
- Respected brand name
- Dominant market share
- A clear mission
- Strong leadership
- A solid financial foundation

Investment Banking  投资银行

## Section F—What Are the Earnings Worth  收益的价值

EPS by itself may be interesting but is not very useful. We need to relate it to the company's share price. We do this by dividing the market price of the company's common shares by the EPS to get the "price-earnings ratio", P/E ratio for short. This tells us how much the market, that is all investors taken together, is willing to pay for one renminbi of earnings. The amount the market is willing to pay is largely dependent on general interest rate levels and on investors' expectations concerning the economy in general and the company in particular. For example, if investors think that a company's earnings will rise steadily, they will likely pay more for each renminbi of earnings than they would if the company's earnings are likely to remain flat, or worse, fall.

**China Petroleum & Chemical Corporation**

|  | 2004 | 2003 |
|---|---|---|
| Net revenues | ¥575,531 | ¥404,676 |
| Deduct cost of goods sold | ¥465,603 | ¥329,237 |
| Gross profit from operations | ¥109,928 | ¥75,439 |
| Deduct selling, general and administrative expenses (S, G & A) | ¥52,062 | ¥41,295 |
| EBIT | ¥57,866 | ¥34,144 |
| Deduct financial expenses | ¥4,331 | ¥4,129 |
| EBT | ¥53,535 | ¥30,015 |
| Deduct income tax | ¥21,260 | ¥11,004 |
| Net profit | ¥32,275 | ¥19,011 |
| Deduct preferred dividends | – nil – | – nil – |
| Income available for common shareholders | ¥32,275 | ¥19,011 |
| Earnings per share (EPS) | ¥0.372 | ¥0.219 |
| Share price — Shanghai Stock Exchange April 21/05 | ¥4.22 | |
| Price — earnings (P/E) ratio | 11.3 x | |

In the above example, a simplified version of Sinopec's income statement for the year ended December 31, 2004, the company earned net profit after tax of RMB ¥32,275 million—almost US $4,000,000,000.

If the company had preferred shares outstanding on which it paid a dividend, the amount of those dividends would be deducted from the net profit after tax. Since Sinopec has no preferred shares, there is no deduction. Therefore, the amount of earnings available for the common shareholders is equal to the net profit after tax—RMB 32,275 million. This is the amount in which the common shareholders participate based on the number of shares they hold. The more shares you own, the bigger your share of the pie is. Some of the pie is paid out to shareholders in the form of dividends. The rest is kept by the company to reinvest in the business providing money to help it grow.

The EPS is calculated by dividing the earnings available for the common shareholders by the number of common shares outstanding—86,702,439. Dividing the market price of the shares (RMB 4.22) by the EPS gives us the P/E ratio of 11.3 times. This means that investors in the market are willing to pay RMB 11.3 for each one RMB that Sinopec earns.

## Section G—Consider the Dividend  股息

Some companies pay out a portion of these earnings in cash to their common shareholders in the form of dividends. The total amount of dividends paid to common shareholders is deducted from the "earnings available for common shareholders" and the difference is retained by the company to help finance growth. These amounts are cumulated from the time the company was formed. They appear on the company's balance sheet as retained earnings.

Two other common measures of valuation of common shares relate to dividends. The first is, the dividend payout ratio calculated by dividing the dividends paid to per common share by EPS and multiplying the result by 100%. It tells us what percent of a company's earnings are paid out in cash to common shareholders. For those companies which pay dividends, a payout ratio around 50% is common.

As EPS rise, companies generally raise the dividends they pay per share. However, directors do not like to ever reduce the dividend. It is a sure sign that the company is encountering financial difficulties. This will likely cause the share price to fall and may make it more difficult and expensive for the company to borrow the money it needs to operate. Therefore, the directors will want to be as sure as possible that the company can continue to produce profits at the higher rate before increasing the per share dividend.

The other measure we regularly use is dividend yield. We find this by dividing the dividend per share by the market price per share and multiplying by 100%. This tells the current cash rate of return on an investment in the shares. It includes only dividends, not capital gains or losses. Moreover, it does take into account how long we hold the investment. Therefore, it does not measure our actual total return on investment. It is, however, particularly useful if our primary investment goal is earning income. It is important to note that we use this measure for both common and preferred shares.

### The Week Ahead

(Most large investment dealers hold regular early morning meetings at which information about the previous day's market activity, developments expected to occur during the week ahead and securities which the firm is promoting to customers is passed along to senior managers, account executives and traders in offices all over the country by conference call. The following report is typical.)

Good morning, everyone. The news today is mixed. We saw the market fall to its lowest level in over five months yesterday largely as a result of disappointing earnings from IBM. This increased everyone's concerns about an economic slowdown. The market is nervous about a lot of earnings reports due next week. Profit reports are expected from General Motors, Intel, Johnson, Ford and Merck. Our analysts believe that if these reports are good, the market's recent slump can be reversed.

Two government reports showed a sharp drop in manufacturing output and import prices being driven up by higher oil costs. Crude oil futures rose for a fifth straight day Monday. A barrel of light crude closed at \$53.32, up 79 cents. These reports have increased our concern about inflation.

General Electric reported a 25 percent jump in first-quarter profits. Its shares rose 25 cents to \$35.75. The company's forecasts for the second quarter and full year are in line with our estimates.

The press reported that Wal-Mart Stores Inc. Vice-Chairman Thomas Coughlin resigned for falsifying expense reports. The Justice Department has begun an investigation. Wal-Mart fell 33 cents to \$48.57.

Microsoft will host two analyst meetings next week to discuss its security business. Hewlett-Packard's Chief Executive, Carly Fiorina resigned yesterday. The company will report first-quarter earnings tomorrow. Our analysts expect earning of 34 cents per share. We think Fiorina's resignation will help the company so we have upgraded HP to buy from neutral. Its shares are trading at a significant discount to those of its competitors.

Traders and account executives listen to the Tuesday morning report from their firm's head office. This keeps everyone up-to-date about what is going on. Markets move quickly so current information is vital to effectively serving clients' needs.

## Section H—Words and Expressions  术语及解释

**Balance sheet**  资产负债表

A statement showing a firm's accounting value on a particular date. It reflects the equation, Assets = Liabilities + Stockholders' equity.

**Cost of equity capital**  股权资本成本

The required return on the company's common stock in capital markets. It is also called the equity holders' required rate of return because it is what equity holders can expect to obtain in the capital market. It is a cost from the firm's perspective.

**Gross domestic product (GDP)**  国内生产总值

A measure of the market value of goods and services produced by a nation.

**Income statement**  损益表

Financial report that summarizes a firm's performance over a specified time period.

**Inflation rate**  通胀率

The general increase in the price level.

**Merger**  合并

A form of corporate acquisition in which one firm absorbs another and the assets and liabilities of the two firms are combined.

**Multinational corporation**  跨国公司

A corporation with operations in more than one country.

**Payout ratio**  派息率

Proportion of net income paid out in cash dividends.

**Price/earnings ratio (P/E ratio)**  市盈率,本益比

A measure of investor confidence, normally the higher is the figure, the higher will the confidence calculated as current share price divided by earnings per share be.

**Private company**  私人持股公司

A company which is not a public company and cannot offer its share to the public.

**Privatization**  私有化

Conversion of a state-run company to public limited liability status.

**Public company**　股票上市公司

A company that does not fulfill the criteria of a private company, whose articles of incorporation (charter) limit the number of shareholders to 50 (with the exception of anyone salaried by the company or a subsidiary), prohibit the distribution of securities to the public and restrict the free transfer of the company's shares.

**Return on equity (ROE)**　资本收益率

Net income after interest and taxes divided by average common stockholder's equity.

**Trillion**　万亿

One thousand billion (12 zeroes).

# Part VI　Trading　股票交易

*Bears, bulls and pigs are found in the stock market. Bulls make money. Bears make money. Pigs get slaughtered.*

## Section A—Putting Our Knowledge into Action　变知识为行动

We have a good understanding of how financial markets work. We know the advantages and disadvantages of different kinds of securities. We have established our risk profile. We have done our research. We have selected a great stockbroker and opened an account with his firm. Now it is time to put all this knowledge to work. We are going to start trading!

## Section B—Opening an Account　开户

Before we can begin trading securities, we must open an account with a securities firm— a stockbroker or an investment bank.

## A. New Client Account Form

Securities firms generally require that all customers fill out and deliver a very detailed personal information report called a New Client Account Form. In order for a securities firm to effectively serve traders and investors alike and to offer advice and guidance that specifically meets each client's particular needs, it must have a thorough understanding of the individual's personal financial situation.

Therefore, in addition to your name, address and telephone number, as a new client you will be asked

---

**Cautionary Note**

The cardinal rule for every investment banker or adviser is that he or she must know his or her client extremely well. In other words, he or she must learn the essential facts relative to every client and must determine the general investment needs and objectives of the client. The banker or adviser should only make recommendations that are consistent with those investment needs and objectives.

---

- to provide information about your employment,
- how much you earn and from what sources,
- what your net worth is,
- how much investment experience you have,
- what your attitude towards risk is,
- if anyone else has an interest in or control over your account,
- if you are you an insider or control person of any public companies and finally
- what your investment objectives are?

## B. Shareholder Communication Form

This document asks you to indicate the amount of information, such as annual reports, financial statements, proxy circulars and notices of shareholder meetings, which you wish to receive from the companies in which you invest. The form will also ask whether or not you are willing to disclose your name and securities holdings to those companies.

### New Client Account Form Tips

The New Client Account Form will generally include your name, address, employment information, credit references, income, net worth, investment experience, attitude toward risk and investment objectives. Most forms also ask whether anyone else has any interest in or authority over your account and whether you are an insider or control person of any public companies. They may also include information relating to the transfer and registration of securities held in your account.

Before you sign the form, make sure that everything in it is correct. Errors in the form may lead to inappropriate advice and may erode the legal protections you are entitled to if something goes wrong. Get a copy of the form and keep it with your account records. Make sure that you contact the firm (preferably in writing) to have the form updated whenever the information in it changes. This is particularly important with key information such as your address, your personal financial circumstances and your investment objectives.

In most cases, you will also be asked to complete a shareholder communication form in which you will indicate the amount of information, such as annual reports, financial statements, proxy circulars and notices of shareholder meetings, that you wish to receive from the companies in which you invest. The form will also ask whether or not you consent to the disclosure of your name and securities holdings to those companies.

## Section C—What the Client Should Expect from the Securities Firm? 证券公司提供的服务

**SHANGHAI INTERNATIONAL SECURITIES COMPANY**

*We promise...*

✓ To be competent and ethical and to act in your best interest at all times.
✓ To deal with you fairly, honestly and in good faith.
✓ To find out your investment needs and objectives.
✓ To make recommendations that are consistent with those needs and objectives.
✓ To disclose the risks associated with our recommendations.
✓ To disclose any conflicts of interest we may have concerning our recommendations.
✓ To provide you with prompt written confirmation of trades made on your behalf.
✓ To show you clearly the details of all transactions including the fees and commissions charged.
✓ To provide monthly statements of account detailing the activity in your account, the fees charged and the securities we hold for you.
✓ To obtain your authorization in advance of every trade made on your behalf unless you have provided a power of attorney to us.

## Dialogue—establishing report

**Bob:** Bob Smith speaking. How may I help you?

**Lucy:** Good morning, Mr. Smith. My name is Lucy Brown. I don't know much about the stock market. However, I saw your firm's advertisement on TV last night. That made me interested in finding out more about investing. I am thinking about buying some shares in Sinopec.

**Bob:** I am so glad that you called. I would be delighted to tell you how it all works. It's quite simple really. But first do you mind if I take down a little information from you?

**Lucy:** Certainly. What would you like to know?

**Bob:** For now let me take down your address and telephone numbers. I will send you a package of information describing our products and services in the mail today. It shows how we can work together to achieve your financial goals. Also included is our new client account form. Please fill it out and return it to me. Then when you are ready to begin investing, all of the paperwork will be complete.

**Lucy:** That sounds fine. My name is Lucy Brown. I live at 345 Main Street apartment #1201 in Shanghai. The postal code is 200050. My telephone number is 54081186.

**Bob:** Thank you, Ms. Brown. May I ask where you work?

**Lucy:** Of course. And please call me Lucy. I am an account executive at Creative Advertising Agency. Our firm does a lot of work in the banking industry here in China. We are helping some of the major banks broaden their client base by directing their promotional activities on satisfying customer needs.

**Bob:** Thank you, Lucy. That sounds like a very challenging and exciting business. Can you give me an estimate of your annual income and your net worth?

**Lucy:** My earnings generally range between ¥20,000 and ¥30,000 each month. I have my own car and I own my apartment. What do you mean by "net worth"?

**Bob:** Your net worth is the difference between the value of all of the things you own—we call these your assets—minus the amount of money you owe to others—these are called your liabilities.

**Lucy:** I would have to sit down and do an accurate calculation. My best guess now is that my net worth is approximately ¥1,500,000.

**Bob:** That is fine for now, Lucy. Do you have any dependents?

**Lucy:** No. I live alone and have no one who depends on me for support.

**Bob:** From your earlier comment I understand that you have not done much direct investing in the stock or bond markets. Is that the case?

**Lucy:** Yes, that is true. I own some mutual fund shares that a neighbor who is a commission salesman persuaded me to buy. And from time to time I have purchased bank certificates of deposit. However, I have never played the stock market directly.

**Bob:** I am glad you have decided to make a move towards investing for yourself. I think your timing is very good. The market seems poised for a strong rally.

**Lucy:** That sounds very encouraging. I am looking forward to learning all about investment markets.

## Section D—Stock Symbols  证券交易代码

Each company that has securities traded on an organized exchange or over-the-counter market is assigned a symbol or numerical code. If a company has more than one class of shares trading, there will be a modifier after the company symbol to indicate the particular class. This shorthand form is a convenient way of referring to a particular share instead of using the company's actual name which, in many cases, is somewhat long and complex.

On the New York Stock Exchange, companies are assigned one, two or three letter codes. On the Nasdaq, the code is four letters. On the Shanghai and Shenzhen Stock Exchanges, six digit codes are used. Here are some examples:

| Company | Code | Exchange |
|---|---|---|
| China Mobile (Hong Kong), Ltd. | | |
| American depositary receipts | CHL | New York Stock Exchange |

| | | |
|---|---|---|
| Common shares | 0941os | Hong Kong Stock Exchange |
| Common shares | 120101 | Shanghai Stock Exchange |
| Coca-Cola Co. | | |
| Common shares | KO | New York Stock Exchange |
| Intel Corp. | | |
| Common shares | INTC | Nasdaq |
| Common shares | 4335 | Hong Kong Stock Exchange |
| Microsoft Corp. | | |
| Common shares | MSFT | Nasdaq |

## Section E—Where Are The Company's Shares Traded? 交易场所

The shares of public companies are traded on stock exchanges, Nasdaq (an electronic marketplace) and in over-the-counter markets around the world. The highest profile for a company and the broadest exposure to investors comes from having its shares trade on a stock exchange or Nasdaq.

---

**Definition**

A **Publicly - traded company** is a company whose shares can be bought and sold by members of the general public. In order for a company's shares to trade publicly, the company will go through a formal registration process with securities regulators. This involves filing detailed information about the company, its owners and managers, its business and its finances.

---

### A. Senior stock exchanges and the Nasdaq

In order for a company's securities to trade on a stock exchange or Nasdaq, the company must qualify for listing. Senior stock exchanges such as Shanghai, Hong Kong, New York, London and Toronto have very stringent tests that must be met. These tests relate to the company's operating history, its financial strength (shareholders' equity, working capital, net profit), the total market value of its equity securities and the breadth of ownership.

> **Definition**
>
> An interlisted security is one which is listed on more than one exchange. Interlisting generally raises the profile of issuers in the global market and trading volumes for their securities increase across all markets.

In order to maintain its listing, a company must continue to meet similar standards. Operating history and financial strength standards are designed to ensure that shares of the highest quality companies are traded in these markets. The requirement that a company's shares be widely held in order to qualify for and maintain a senior stock exchange listing is to ensure adequate liquidity. If there are few shares in the hands of the public, it will likely be difficult to buy or sell them without significantly increasing or decreasing the price.

Companies are required to file on a timely basis detailed quarterly and annual financial information. The objective is to ensure that investors have current financial information on which to make informed investment decisions. Failure to meet the reporting requirements can result in suspension of trading and ultimately delisting.

### B. Junior or venture exchanges

Emerging companies that have not yet attained the financial strength to qualify for listing on one or more of the senior stock exchanges, can apply for listing on a venture exchange such as the Toronto Venture Exchange or the Canadian Venture Exchange. The listing requirements on these exchanges are much less onerous than on the senior exchanges. This provides emerging companies with access to capital, while offering investors a well-regulated market for making venture investments. These exchanges are particularly attractive for companies in the mining, oil and gas and high technology sectors. They enjoy a wide range of benefits including opportunities to efficiently access public equity capital, liquidity for existing investors and the prestige and market exposure associated with being listed on an internationally recognized exchange.

### C. Unlisted markets

The OTCBB, short for Over-the-Counter Bulletin Board is an electronic trading service offered by the National Association of Securities Dealers (NASD) in the United States. There

## Investment Banking  投资银行

is little regulation of this market so buying shares traded in it is quite risky.

Most speculative of all are shares listed on "pink sheets", a daily publication compiled by the National Quotation Bureau containing price quotations for shares of companies which have not registered with securities regulators and which are not required to meet minimum standards. There is nothing much more speculative than trading shares listed on the pink sheets! They are called "pink sheets" because for many years the quotes were printed on pink sheets distributed to stockbrokers.

## Section F—The Quote  报价

Once we have decided what we want to buy or sell and we are ready to deal, the next step is to find out what the market is for the shares we want to buy or sell. We can do this by telephoning a stockbroker or by checking one of the numerous financial sites on the Internet.

Suppose we want to buy 2,500 shares of Sinopec Shanghai Petrochemical Co., Ltd. Its American depositary receipts are traded on the New York Stock Exchange. The symbol is SHI.

We call our broker and he tells us that the stock is 32.65 bid 32.75 asked. That means that the highest price someone is willing to pay for Sinopec shares at the moment is US $32.65 and the lowest price sellers will accept is US $32.75.

> **What's the Market?**
>
> SHI is 32.65 bid 32.75 asked, last trade 32.65 on 15,000 shares, up 30 cents on the day.

The difference between the bid and ask prices is called the spread. We see that 15,000 shares have traded so far today. We refer to that as the volume. The last trade was at 32.65. The highest price paid today was 32.78 and the lowest price was 32.60.

Shares trade in units of 100 shares. These are called board or round lots. Trades of less than 100 shares are called odd lots. The bid and ask quotes are always for at least one board lot-they could be for more in each case, however—integer multiples of 100.

## Section G—Placing an Order  下达买卖指令

We need to tell our broker how many shares we want to buy or sell and what price we are willing to pay (buy) or accept (sell). We have several options with respect to price. We can use any one of the following ways:

---

### Dialogue—Placing the Order

**Bob:** Bob Smith speaking. How may I help you?

**Lucy:** Hello Bob. This is Lucy Brown calling. I would like to place an order.

**Bob:** Good morning, Lucy. So nice to hear from you. What did you have in mind doing today?

**Lucy:** I would like to buy 2,500 shares of Sinopec. What's the market?

**Bob:** Let me check for you. Just a moment, please. Here we are. SHI is presently 32.65 bid, 32.72 asked, last trade at 32.68 up a nickel. Volume is 12,500. The Dow is down 33 points.

**Lucy:** How many shares are offered at 32.72?

**Bob:** 1,000 are offered at 32.72 and another 500 at 32.75.

**Lucy:** Please buy 2,500 Sinopec at 32.70 with 10 cents discretion good for today only.

**Bob:** Thank you, Lucy. I will call you as soon as we have a fill.

**Lucy:** Thank you, Bob. I am looking forward to hearing from you.

---

**At the market**

This means you are willing to buy or sell at whatever price the market forces determine. It is your broker's job to get you the lowest possible price if you are buying and the highest possible price if you are selling.

**At the market limit 32.80**

If you are a buyer, this means you are willing to pay the price as set by the market up to a maximum price of US $ 32.80. This protects you if a stock's price is rising quickly or it is very volatile. You won't suddenly find yourself paying a price higher than you are prepared for.

**At a specific price**

You specify the specific price at which you are willing to buy or sell the shares. If you are buying, the most he can pay for shares to you is the price you have set. He can, of course, buy them at a lower price if the price falls.

If you are selling, this is the minimum price you will accept. Your broker cannot sell them at a lower price but he may sell them at a higher price for you if the market rises.

**At a specific price with some discretion**

You specify the specific price at which you are willing to buy or sell the shares but you give your broker to change the price you have set by a small amount if he considers it necessary and in your interest to do so.

This gives your broker some flexibility, a little room to manoeuvre. For example, you could buy 1,000 SHI at 32.70 with a nickel discretion. Share prices move up or down in increments of one cent—a penny. So what you are saying here is that you want to buy the shares at 32.70 but if your broker thinks it is absolutely necessary, he or she can pay up to 32.75. This might happen if the share price seems to be rising and there is a risk that you will miss buying the shares.

**An open order**

Also called good till cancelled or GTC, this order stays alive until you specifically call to cancel it.

**A day order**

If this kind of order is not filled by the time trading ends that day, it dies. A new order would have to be placed the next day if you still wanted to buy or sell the shares.

**A fill or kill order**

This means that you want to buy the total number of shares in your order, 2,500 for example, or none at all.

> **Dialogue—Confirming the Fill**
>
> **Secretary:** Lucy Brown's office.
> **Bob:** Hello. May I please speak to Ms. Brown?
> **Secretary:** Yes. May I ask who is calling please?
> **Bob:** My name is Bob Smith. I am with Shanghai International Securities. Ms. Brown is expecting my call.
> **Secretary:** Thank you, Mr. Smith. I will put you through now.
> **Lucy:** Lucy Brown.
> **Bob:** Hello Lucy. This is Bob Smith speaking. I am pleased to confirm that we bought for you 2,000 SHI at 32.70 and 500 SHI at 32.73.
> **Lucy:** That is wonderful. Thank you for being so quick and for getting me such a good price.
> **Bob:** You are most welcome. We pride ourselves on being one of the best firms in the business when it comes to execution of orders.
> **Lucy:** What happens now?
> **Bob:** Today is Tuesday. Settlement is three business days from now-that is Friday. That means that payment is due from you on or before that date.
> **Lucy:** I will come in tomorrow. I will bring the New Client Account Form you sent me and my cheque. What time would be convenient for you to see me.
> **Bob:** Would 2:00 p.m. suit you? I will give you your contract for your purchase at that time.
> **Lucy:** Yes, thank you. I will look forward to seeing you at 2:00 p.m. tomorrow.

## Section H—The Reporting  公司报告

### A. The ticker tape

Timely reporting of all information relating to publicly-traded companies is vital to maintaining efficient securities markets. A crucial part of that information is how much people are actually paying for a particular security and how much they are buying at that price. Within seconds (or minutes if trading is particularly heavy), details of all trades are passed electronically to the market's computers and flashed instantly to traders and investors everywhere.

The ticker symbols designate the securities that were traded (issuer, type or class of security). Red indicates that the price is lower than the previous trade, green means it is higher and blue indicates that there was no change.

"Bulls" expect the market to rise; "bears" expect it to fall.

$$ACO.PR.A_{5K@}\ 27.8\ \blacktriangledown\ 0.4\quad SHI_{2@}\ 32.8\ \blacktriangle\ 0.12\quad IBM_{330k@}\ 89.29\quad SNP\ 36.76:36.86$$

- Ticker symbol: ACO.PR.A
- Price of the trade: 27.8
- Change amount: 0.4
- Shares traded: 5K@
- Change direction: ▼
- Bid / Ask: 36.76 / 36.86

K = 1,000 (thousand)
M = 1,000,000 (million)
B = 1,000,000,000 (billion)

From time to time the tape will report bid and ask prices as well as actual trades. These are shown in black.

The small numbers (subscripts) show the quantities traded. If there is no modifier (K, M of B), the subscript is the number of board lots traded. In the above example $SHI_{2@}$ means that two board lots (200 shares) of Shanghai Sinopec Petroleum Co., Ltd. traded at 32.8. Similarly, $IBM_{330K@}$ means that 330,000 shares of IBM traded at 86.29.

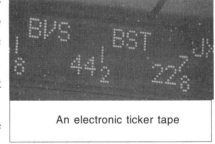

An electronic ticker tape

In summary, the above portion of a ticker tape gives us the following information:

1. 5,000 Atco Ltd. 5.75% series 3 preferred shares traded at 27.80 down 0.40 from the last trade.

2. 200 Shanghai Sinopec Petroleum Co., Ltd. American depositary receipts traded at 32.80 up 0.12 from the last trade.

3. 333,000 International Business Machines Corp. common shares traded at 89.29 unchanged from the previous trade.

4. China Petroleum and Chemical Corp. ADRs are 36.76 bid 36.86 asked.

## Evening Stock Market Report

Hong Kong stocks closed higher Monday with many investors bargain hunting following two straight sessions of losses. Turnover rose to 22.58 billion Hong Kong dollars (US $ 2.89 billion; euro2.19 billion), up from Friday's HK $ 19.66 (US $ 2.52 billion, euro1.90 billion).

Banking stocks suffered on worries about their earnings growth amid weak loan demand. Hang Seng Bank, Ltd. fell 0.4 percent to HK $ 107.50 while HSBC Holdings PLC closed unchanged at HK $ 131.50.

Among real estate stocks, Cheung Kong (Holdings), Ltd. rose HK $ 1.25 to HK $ 74.75 and Sun Hung Kai Properties rose 75 cents to HK $ 77.50. Traders bought Chinese telecommunication companies. China Unicom, Ltd. jumped 4.2 percent to HK $ 6.15, while China Mobile (Hong Kong), Ltd. added 0.6 percent, closing at HK $ 26.60. China's biggest airline, Air China, Ltd., rose 8.2 percent in its debut on the Hong Kong bourse last week, lifted by robust growth in China's air traffic. The carrier's stock closed at HK $ 3.23.

## B. The newspaper

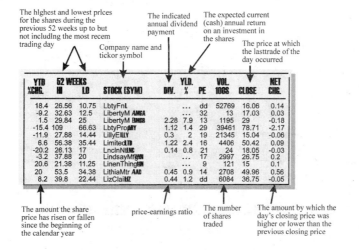

## Investment Banking  投资银行

The chart above is typical of how the financial press reports trading activity in stocks, bonds and other securities. The first column shows the percentage change in the stock price since the beginning of the year. The second and third columns show the highest and lowest prices at which the stock has traded during the previous 52 weeks. The fourth column is the name of the company and the type of security-preferred shares for example. The fifth column shows the amount of dividends the company expects to pay on each share during the current year. The sixth column tells us what the dividend yield is. It is calculated by dividing the expected annual dividend by the closing price and multiplying by 100%. The seventh column is the price-earnings ratio. If the company lost money last year, there is no price-earnings ratio shown. The eighth column shows the volume—the number of shares traded during the day. In our example, the volume is shown in units of 100 shares—board lots. The ninth column shows the price at which the last trade of the day in the particular stock took place. The final column shows whether today's closing price was higher or lower than the closing price the previous trading day and by how much.

## Section I—Measuring Movements in the Overall Market  交易指数

Stock indices such as the Dow Jones Industrial Average (New York), the Hang Seng Index (Hong Kong) and the Toronto Stock Exchange 300 composite (Canada) are measures of whether the market is generally rising or falling. They are based on a representative sampling of important publicly-traded companies.

### A Final Note

You can make money in the stock market if prices are rising—a bull market.

You can make money in a bear market—prices are generally falling.

You cannot make money if you are greedy—being a "pig". These market players almost always end up losing lots of money.

## Section J—Words and Expressions  术语及解释

**Depository receipt  存单**

A derivative security issued by a foreign borrower through a domestic trustee representing ownership in the deposit of foreign shares held by the trustee.

**Index  指数**

A relative expression of the weighted value of a group of securities used as a performance indicator.

**Inflation rate  通胀率**

The general increase in the price level herein measured by the growth rate in the GNP Implicit Price Index or the general price deflator.

**Insider  内线**

An insider is a person who owns more than 10% of the voting shares of an issuer. All issuers and directors and senior officers of a corporation are deemed to be insiders.

**Intermediated market**　中间市场

A financial market in which a financial institution (usually a commercial bank) stands between borrowers and savers.

**Lead manager**　主承销

The lead investment bank in a syndicate selling a public securities offering.

**Limit order**　限价单

An order given at a certain price.

**Liquidation**　清仓

The closing of an existing position.

**Long**　多头

More purchases than sales.

**New Issue**　新股发行

An issuer coming to the market for the first time.

**Offering memorandum**　股票发行备忘录

An information document drafted by an issuer, for the same purposes as a prospectus (see definition below), but which contains fewer sections because the issuer obtained certain exemptions from the securities regulator.

**Payout ratio**　派息率

Proportion of net income paid out in cash dividends.

**Price/earnings ratio (P/E ratio)**　市盈率，本益比

A measure of investor confidence, normally the higher the figure the higher the confidence. Current share price divided by earnings per share.

**Price Transparency**　价格透明度

Where a transaction is executed on the floor of an exchange and every participant has equal price.

**Price uncertainty**　价格不确定性

Uncertainty regarding the future price of an asset.

**Primary market**　初级市场

The function of a stock exchange in bringing securities to the market for the first time.

**Private placement**　私募配售

A securities issue privately placed with a small group of investors rather than through a public offering.

**Private company**　私人持股公司

A company which is not a public company and cannot offer its share to the public.

**Privatization**　私有化

Conversion of a state-run company to public limited liability status.

**Project financing**　项目融资

A way to raise non-recourse financing for a specific project characterized by the following：(1) the project is a separate legal entity and relies heavily on debt financing and (2) the debt is contractually linked to the cash flow generated by the project.

**Promissory note**　本票

Financial document in which the buyer agrees to make payment to the seller at a specified time.

**Prospectus**　招股说明书

A prospectus is a disclosure document prepared by an issuer—a company that wants to distribute securities to the public—which is distributed to potential investors. The prospectus must contain very specific information about the company issuing the securities. It describes the company and its business sector and contains the company's articles of incorporation, its history, a list of its directors, its financial statements, a description of the issue and the risk factors associated with the investment. Before it can be distributed to investors, the prospectus must be issued a receipt by the Commission des valeurs mobilières du Québec indicating that it complies with the requirements of the Securities Act.

**Public company**　股票上市公司

A company that does not fulfill the criteria of a private company, whose articles of incorporation (charter) limit the number of shareholders to 50 (with the exception of anyone salaried by the company or a subsidiary), prohibit the distribution of securities to the public and restrict the free transfer of the company's shares.

**Public securities offering**　公开发行证券

A securities issue placed with the public through an investment or commercial bank.

**Return on equity (ROE)**　资本收益率

Net income after interest and taxes divided by average common stockholder's equity.

**Rule of 72**　72法则

The rule of 72 is a simple estimate of how long it will take an investment to double for a given interest rate. By dividing 72 by a given interest rate, the result will be an approximate time period for the investment to double in value. For example, if you had an investment that you know would produce a 10% return each year, you could divide 72 by 10 ( = 7.2) and figure out it would take just over 7 years for your investment to double.

**Stop loss order** 停止损失指令

A order at best after a certain rate has been reached or passed or dealt, depending upon the specified conditions previously agreed between the parties.

**Subsidized financing** 融资津贴

Financing that is provided by a host government and that is issued at a below—market interest rate.

**Syndicate** 银团

The selling group of investment banks in a public securities offering.

**Trillion** 万亿

One thousand billion (12 zeroes).

**Underwriting** 承销

An arrangement by which a company is guaranteed that an issue will raise a given amount of cash. Underwriters undertake to subscribe for any of the issue not taken up. They charge commission for this service.

# Exercises

练习

## Listening Comprehension Exercises 听力综合练习

### A. Dialogue—The investment bankers

With your book closed, have two people read aloud the dialogue in which the three investment bankers are discussing their strategy.

1. What is the purpose of their trip?
2. Where are they?
3. What is Gerald's position and what is he concerned about?
4. Why does he think the stock price of Sterling Chemical will rise if people find out that they are in that city.
5. Do you think there is anything else they could do to keep their plans from being discovered?

### B. Dialogue—The new client

With your book closed, have three people read aloud the dialogue following the meeting with a new investment banking client and answer the following questions:

1. Who did the three investment bankers meet with?
2. What is the feeling the three investment bankers had when they left the meeting?
3. What else do they plan to do to help the client?
4. Why do they want to avoid a formal presentation in trying to persuade the VP Finance to consider an IPO?
5. Why did they decide to go to the Harbourside Restaurant for lunch?

### C. Evening stock market report

With your book closed, have someone read aloud the evening stock market report and answer the following questions:

1. Why did the prices of bank stocks fall?
2. What happened to the price of shares of Air China and why?
3. What investment strategy were many traders following?

## Speaking Exercises  对话练习

### A. Dialogue—The appointment

Choose a partner. One takes the role of Alan, the other the role of Fred. Read the dialogue out loud. Work hard at developing a smooth style.

Create a dialogue of your own for making an appointment with a prospective investment banking client. Choose a partner and practice reading each other's dialogue. Exchange your dialogues with other class members and practice reading them. Try to communicate the information or ask the questions without actually reading the text.

### B. Building a portfolio

Choose a partner. One of you is an account executive at an investment bank. The other is a new client. The person who is the account executive is helping the new client establish financial goals by asking questions. Based on the answers given to the questions by the "client", develop a portfolio that best meets the objectives of the client. It is not necessary to choose specific stocks, only the types of securities and the proportion of each in the portfolio. Suggested questions are given below.

　　a. How much money do you have to invest now?
　　b. Will your employment income allow you to invest additional money in the future? How much? Are you confident that will continue?
　　c. What are your monthly financial obligations and how much do those obligations change from month to month or year to year?
　　d. Do you have other valuable assets that will play a role in your financial future?
　　e. Do you have outstanding debts that you would like to pay off?
　　f. Do you plan to make any major purchases in the future?
　　g. Do you need money from your investments each month to supplement your regular income? If so, how much?
　　h. Do you have dependents to care for and will their needs be changing over time?
　　i. Have you considered your life and property insurance requirements?

j. Are there income tax considerations that are particularly important to you?

k. Are you a participant in a retirement savings plan or registered pension plan?

l. Do you expect to inherit money at any point in the future?

m. How much money would you like to have readily accessible in case of emergency?

**C. Choosing an investment advisor**

Choose a partner. One of you will play the role of an investor who has decided to choose a securities firm to help you manage your money. The other team member will play the role of an account executive at a major investment bank. The "prospective client" is trying to determine if this is the right firm. Suggested questions for the "prospective client" to ask are given below. The "account executive" is anxious to be chosen.

1. Is the firm in the market for new clients such as you, with your expected account size and your general investment objectives?

2. Do the firm and its staff specialize in a particular type of investment product or a particular clientele? (For example, does it focus on speculative securities, mutual funds, blue chip stocks? Does it cater to conservative retail investors, high net worth clients, institutions or speculators?)

3. Do the firm and its staff have any special expertise in the types of investments that might be of interest to you?

4. What products is the firm and individual registered to sell or advise on? How long has the firm been registered? Does it operate in other provinces as well? How many employees does it have? How many clients?

5. What services does it provide to clients like you? For example, does the dealer provide trade execution only or does it provide advice, research and trading?

6. Does the firm have an internal research department that provides research reports to clients? Does it offer any educational seminars for its clients?

7. How does the firm charge for its services? What commission rates or brokerage fees would a client like you expect to pay?

8. If you opened an account, what representative(s) might be available to you? What are their experience and qualifications?

9. Has the firm been subject to any disciplinary proceedings in the past few years? What about the individuals you might be dealing with?

10. Is the firm a member of a contingency fund designed to protect clients in the event of its insolvency? If so, what coverage does the fund provide?

## Skill-building Exercises—Research   阅读与研究练习

Read the stock market section of the business page of a newspaper for three days. Identify five terms or ideas you do not understand which seem important to understanding how the stock market works. Share these unknowns with your classmates and teachers so everyone can help one another understand key ideas while learning about the stock market.

## Skill-building Exercises—Writing and Speaking   说写练习

Look at the picture below.

1. What do you think the man and woman are looking at?
2. They seem happy. Why do you think this might be?

Write a dialogue for the two people in which they discuss what they are reading and what they will do in the future as a result of what they have learned from reading the newspaper.

## Skill-building Exercises—Writing   写作练习

Imagine that you are an account executive with a major investment bank. One of your new clients, Mrs. Smith, is on the phone. Recently widowed, she inherited a large sum of money and has become interested in learning about the stock market. She is not happy because the price of stock that you recommended her to buy has fallen sharply. This is what she has just said to you:

"Stock prices are fixed. Every day they change, up or down. It is just a way to cheat the public and take their money. I don't understand why the government keeps changing those prices."

Based on what you have learned in this chapter

a. write down what you would say to Mrs. Smith on the phone; remember that she could become a very valuable client and you want to retain her goodwill;

b. follow up by writing a letter to her commenting on her misunderstandings. (Hint: Stock prices do change, but the government does not change them. Buyers and sellers of stocks cause the prices to change each day as they decide how valuable those stocks are to them. Changing stock prices show how people's buying and selling decisions will change when they hear news that indicates how well this company is performing in the economy.)

## Building Vocabulary Exercises  词汇练习

**A. Match the definitions below with the words in the list that follows:**

1. A portion of a company's profit paid out to common and preferred shareholders, the amount having been decided on by the company's board of directors. _____

2. A company whose securities are traded on a stock exchange. _____

3. A method of evaluating the future prospects of a company by analyzing its financial statements. _____

4. 1/100 of one percent (0.01%). _____

5. Stocks of stable companies that have a low to moderate risk and pay regular dividends. _____

6. The annual rate of return on a bond taking into account both the interest income and the difference between the current market price and the par value. _____

7. For stocks, indicators of broad market performance. _____

8. The process by which a private company offers shares to the public for the first time and thereby becomes a public company. _____

## Investment Banking 投资银行

9. A combination of letters that identifies a stock-exchange security. _____

10. The rate that the most creditworthy international banks charge each other for large loans in Eurodollars; the rate that a bank demands in order to place a Eurodollar deposit at (or make a loan to) a top credit-rated bank in London, England. _____

11. A participant in the financial markets that maintains a firm bid and offer price in a given security by standing ready to buy or sell at publicly quoted prices. _____

12. Stocks with good investment qualities; shares of well-established companies with good earnings records and regular dividend payments and whose products and/or services are widely accepted and universally known for their quality. _____

13. The market for securities not listed on an exchange. _____

14. A high risk, high yield bond generally with a credit rating of BB or lower; often used as a means of financing takeovers. _____

15. Loss that is incurred from the sale of assets at a price below the purchase price. _____

16. The amount returned to bondholders at maturity. _____

17. A member of some stock exchanges who is responsible for maintaining a fair and orderly market in the stocks they are allocated. _____

18. A class of stock that represents ownership in a company. _____

19. All directors and senior officers of a corporation and those who may also be presumed to have access to confidential information concerning the company; also anyone owning more than 10 per cent of the voting shares in a corporation. _____

20. Shares of companies whose earnings are expected to increase at an above-average rate; these stocks typically have low yields and relatively high price/earnings rations. _____

21. The price at which a seller offers securities or property for sale. _____

22. The ease with which financial assets can be traded in a market without creating a substantial change in price or value. _____

23. A class of stock with a claim on the company's earnings before payment may be made on common stock and usually entitled to priority over common stockholders if the company fails or liquidates. _____

24. A financial institution whose primary function is to obtain capital for companies and individuals to expand their wealth through investment. _____

25. The process of converting paper profits into cash. _____

26. A registered offering of a large block of a security that has been previously issued to the public. The blocks being offered may have been held by large investors or institutions and proceeds of the sale go to those holders, not the issuing company. _____

1. Ask (offer)
2. Average or Index
3. Basis point
4. Blue-chip stocks
5. Capital loss
6. Common share
7. Dividend
8. Fundamental Analysis
9. Growth stock
10. Income stocks
11. Initial public offering (IPO)
12. Insider
13. Investment bank
14. Junk bond
15. Liquidity (or marketability)
16. Listed company
17. London Interbank Offer Rate (LIBOR)
18. Market maker
19. Over the counter (OTC)
20. Par (or face) value
21. Preferred stock (or shares)
22. Profit taking
23. Secondary offering (secondary distribution)
24. Specialist
25. Ticker symbol
26. Yield to maturity

**B. Match the definitions below with the words in the list that follows:**

1. An order to buy or sell securities immediately at the best possible price. _____

2. The total proceeds (defined broadly to include both cash distributions and capital gains) derived from the investment calculated as a percentage of the amount initially invested. _____

3. Failure to perform on a foreign exchange transaction or, failure to pay an interest obligation on a debt. _____

4. Bonds for which the issuer maintains a record of the owners. _____

5. Negotiable certificates held by US banks representing a certain number of shares of a foreign stock. _____

6. The market in which existing securities are traded among investors. _____

7. A basket of stocks used to track the market. _____

8. An order to buy or sell a security if it reaches a specified price. _____

9. A method of evaluating future security prices and market directions based on statistical analysis of variables such as trading volume, price changes, etc., to identify patterns; a graphical analysis of historical price trends, used to predict likely future trends in the market. _____

10. The payments that a borrower must make to a lender for the use of a fixed sum of money. _____

11. A market in which traders can buy or sell large quantities of an asset whenever they want with minimal effect on price. _____

12. The market price of a common stock divided by annual earnings per share. _____

13. The actual issued share that is traded under an American Depositary Receipt (ADR) agreement. _____

14. Short-term government debt; paying no interest, these instruments are sold at a discount; the difference between the discount price and par value is the return to be received by the investor. _____

15. A stock market whose index of representative stocks (for example, the Hang Seng Index) is declining. _____

16. The rate of interest charged by chartered banks to their most credit-worthy borrowers. _____

17. An order to buy/sell at the current trading level. _____

18. An investment dealer that purchases securities directly from the issuer for resale to other investment dealers or the public or for resale to the public in the issuer's name. _____

19. The stated interest on a debt instrument. _____

20. A stock of a company with a record of stable earnings and continuous dividends, which has demonstrated relative stability in poor economic conditions. _____

21. The profit you would earn if you sold an asset which has increased in value. _____

22. The date on which the last payment on a bond is due. _____

23. Short-term bank paper traded in the money market with the repayment of principal and payment of interest guaranteed by the issuer's bank. _____

24. A standard number of shares for trading transactions. _____

25. Stocks with low price/earnings ratios. _____

26. An order given at a certain price. _____

| | |
|---|---|
| 1. American depositary receipt (ADR) | 15. Maturity date |
| 2. American depositary share (ADS) | 16. Price-earnings ratio (P/E ratio or P/E multiple) |
| 3. At-market | |
| 4. Bankers' acceptance | 17. Prime (interest) rate |
| 5. Bear market | 18. Rate of return |
| 6. Board lot | 19. Registered bonds |
| 7. Coupon | 20. Secondary market |
| 8. Default | 21. Stop price |
| 9. Defensive stock | 22. Technical analysis |
| 10. Index | 23. Treasury bill (T-bill) |
| 11. Interest | 24. Unrealized gain (paper profit) |
| 12. Limit order | 25. Underwriter |
| 13. Liquid market | 26. Value stocks |
| 14. Market order | |

**C. Match the definitions below with the words in the list that follows:**

1. Quotations which are not firm. _____

2. A curve showing interest rates for securities with the same risk but different maturity dates. _____

3. Stocks of companies with a total market value (or market capitalization) of $1 billion or more. _____

4. A bond that pays no interest and is initially sold at a discount. _____

5. Someone who represents another. _____

6. A low priced, speculative security. _____

7. Negotiable certificates held by a bank in one country and representing a certain number of shares of a stock of a company based in another country. _____

8. The practice of buying and selling foreign exchange, stocks, bonds, commodities in different markets in order to profit from minute differences in price between the two markets. _____

9. The amount by which a bond sells in the secondary market at less than its par value or

face value. _____

10. The price a buyer offers to pay for a security or property. _____

11. The amount of interest or dividend paid on an investment expressed as a percentage of the market price. _____

12. A long-term debt instrument with the promise to pay a specified amount of interest and to return the principal amount on a specified maturity date. _____

13. London Interbank Eurodollar Offer Rate. _____

14. A condition of a financial market characterized by generally rising prices. _____

15. Certificates representing ownership in a corporation. _____

16. A profit made on the sale of an asset when the selling price is above the purchase price. _____

17. An arrangement by which a company is guaranteed that an issue will raise a given amount of cash. _____

18. The number of shares being offered for sale at the ask price. _____

19. The possibility of loss; the uncertainty of future returns. _____

20. A company whose common shares can be freely bought and sold by anyone. _____

21. A market in which there are comparatively few bids to buy or offers to sell or both. _____

22. The value of a company; the amount of money someone would have to pay to buy the company. _____

1. Agent
2. Arbitrage
3. Ask size
4. Bid
5. Bond
6. Bull market
7. Capital gain
8. Discount
9. Derivative
10. Global depositary receipt (GDR)

11. Indication only
12. Large-cap stock
13. LIBOR
14. Market capitalization
15. Penny stock
16. Public company
17. Interest rate
18. Risk
19. Shares
20. Thin market

21. Underwriting
22. Yield
23. Yield curve
24. Zero coupon bond

## Test Your Knowledge  知识测试

**General questions:**

1. In what way can investment banking be compared to the oil used in your car's engine?
2. What are the main investment banking activities?
3. What are some investment goals?
4. Why is it important to set financial goals?
5. What will a good investment banker do for his or her client?
6. A place where people with money meet people who have money is called a _____.
7. What are the different types of bonds?
8. Why might an investor want bonds in his or her portfolio?

**Multiple choice questions:**

1. Which of the following decisions will guarantee that a person will make money in the stock market? _____
   a. Buy the stock of a big company like IBM.
   b. Buy the stock of a small company like Starbucks Coffee.
   c. Purchase stocks after the stock market has dropped for two days in a row.
   d. None of these decisions will guarantee that an individual will make money in the stock market.

2. If a company starts purchasing its own stock, what will the company leaders attempt to do? _____
   a. To raise company profits.
   b. To increase company expenses.
   c. To show that the company believes the price is too low.
   d. To confuse the regulatory authorities.

3. What does "spread" mean? _____
   a. The difference between the rates at which money is deposited in a financial

institution and the higher rates at which the money is lent out.

b. The difference between the bid and ask price for a security.

c. The difference between buying and selling rates for foreign exchange.

d. The difference between the rate of return on an investment (or asset) and the cost of the funds used to buy it.

e. All of the above.

**Answers**: 1 (d) 2 (c) 3 (e)

**True or false questions**:

Answer the following questions and provide an explanation in the space below:

1. Stocks are items found in the storeroom of a grocery store. _____

2. Only rich people invest in the stock market. _____

3. Governments sell most stocks on the stock market. _____

4. If the stock market goes up 30 percent one year, it will fall by 30 percent in the next year. _____

5. Any stock that goes up in price must eventually come back down. _____

6. Bears, bulls and pigs are found in the stock market. _____

7. Stock prices are set by the regulatory agencies of governments. _____

8. Stock markets are open on business days around the clock around the world. _____

9. Sometimes companies buy their own stocks on the stock market. _____

10. It is hard to buy a good stock today because all the good ones have already been purchased. _____

11. Buying stocks is a sure way to make money. _____

12. Corporations sell new issues of stock on stock exchanges such as the Shanghai Stock Exchange and the New York Stock Exchange. _____

13. "Insider" stock trading means that trading stocks takes place inside a building. _____

14. People can buy stocks on the Internet. _____

15. When the stock market goes up, it causes the economy to grow. _____

**Answers:**

1. **False.** Stocks are shares of ownership of companies. These shares are sold to the public in markets around the world.

2. **False.** Millions of people invest in the stock market through mutual funds, individual purchases of stock and pension investments. Very wealthy people make up only a small portion of stock market investor population.

3. **False.** Governments do not sell stocks of private companies.

4. **False.** The prices of stocks on the stock market change as the supply and demand for stocks change. They can change at any rate or prices or can stay the same for a long time. How much they move up does not forecast how far they may fall. Over the long term, stocks have appreciated by 9 percent.

5. **False.** Stock prices will usually not fall if the company remains successful and other investments do not become more attractive. Stock prices reflect the interests of investors. The law of gravity does not apply to stock prices.

6. **True.** These names refer to people and their attitudes toward stock market

performance. Bulls are people who think the market will continue to rise. Bears think stock prices are very likely to fall. Pigs are people who try to make a big killing on the market in a short time and tend to get "slaughtered". In other words, they lose all their money on high-risk investments.

7. **False.** Stock prices are set by the supply and demand for stocks. Government agencies regulate the stock markets to insure honest practices are followed and accurate information is provided to buyers and sellers of stocks.

8. **True.** Stock markets exist in many different countries located in different time zones, so markets in Europe and Asia are open and in operation while US markets are closed.

9. **True.** A company for a variety of reasons may wish to have its stock price increased in value. One way a company might be able to increase the price of its stock is by buying its own stock.

10. **False.** All "good" stocks are available for sale in large quantities. Just because someone currently owns them does not prevent investors from buying the stocks. The new investor must offer a price attractive enough so current owners have an incentive to sell their stocks.

11. **False.** The prices of stocks rise and fall depending upon economic conditions and business success. Many people have lost money by buying stocks when the prices were high and selling them after prices fell. There is risk in the stock market. It is not a sure way of making money.

12. **False.** New issues of stock are purchased by investment bankers (primary market) who will offer stocks to be resold to the public (secondary market).

13. **False.** "Insider" stock trading refers to the illegal practice of people related to a company who find out important information about a company that will affect the stock price and buy or sell the stock before the information is made available to the general public. An "insider" may be an accountant who knows that a company's profits are greater than anticipated by the public because that accountant just finished preparing the accounting report for the company. If that accountant buys stocks before the report is made, she or he could buy the stock at a lower price than what other buyers will have to pay after the report is made public. In such a case, she or he would illegally benefit from this "Insider" information.

14. **True.** Many electronic methods exist that allow people to buy stocks without talking directly with a person. One method brokerage firms use is to allow people to buy stock with

computers using the Internet (the electronic information superhighway). It allows people to make trade quickly and inexpensively.

15. **False.** The stock market is a very small part of the economy. It cannot cause the economy to grow or decline. It is one leading indicator of the economy, so when the stock market goes up it does signal that many people think the economy will grow in the near future. Sometimes they are right and sometimes they are wrong. The stock market cannot make people and companies in the economy improve their production of real goods and services.

## Case Study  案例分析

**Uncle John's Money**

Jody loved Uncle John. When John died, she missed him. It was only five years ago that Uncle John had bought a home two blocks away from her home. She visited him every day just to enjoy his company and to help him remember where things were. He was forgetful about everything except Jody. He forgot where he left his car keys, his eyeglasses or the TV remote, but forgetting about money was the really big problem. He always left cash around the house. Jody would find dollar bills scattered around the house and give them back to Uncle John. "You should put this money in a safe place, Uncle John," she would say. Uncle John would reply, "Jody, there is no safe place for money."

Uncle John could not travel much. His lungs were bad. Jody asked her father why Uncle John had such health problems and why he was so forgetful.

"It's probably a result of the blow to the head he received in the Honduras demonstrations," Jody's father explained. "Your Uncle John has lived an interesting life. He was a brilliant student who dropped out of college to write educational software for schools. His specialty was economic fables and myths, which became classics both in the computer software field and in children's literature. He retired early—a wealthy man determined to help people in poor countries. For 20 years he worked in Latin America, helping farmers in Honduras and Colombia switch to profitable crops other than bananas and cocaine. Later he helped Brazilian Indian tribes sell Rain Forest products, before moving on to encourage Chinese government workers to set up their own businesses. In each country he got into trouble with authorities who didn't like the changes. This trouble resulted in an occasional beating or prison stay, but he avoided even more trouble because he always carried cash, US dollars. He used the money to pay people not to harm the poor people he worked with. He always carried US dollars and he never used banks."

After Uncle John's death, Jody helped her father clean up Uncle John's home and prepare it for sale. It was at that time she found out about Uncle John's will. According to Dad, Uncle John left all his belongings to his brother, Jody's father, except for the money in the house. Any money found in the house was Jody's to use as she wished. In his will, Uncle John asked her to find a safe place for the money.

It took Jody and her father two days to clean John's house completely. As they cleaned, they kept finding money in different places— $100 in the cupboard, $10 in the cookie jar, a bag of coins in the toilet tank. But the real discovery came when they took the mattress off the bed. Money fell out of a slit in the bottom of the mattress. When they gathered it all up and added it together with the other money found earlier, the total came to $100,000.

"Well, Jody," her father asked, "what is the safe place where you are going to put the money?"

**Questions for Discussion**

As a group, decide what do you think Jody should do with the money. You can choose among the following alternatives. Discuss the potential costs and benefits of each. Prepare a chart that summarizes your thinking about the costs and benefits of each alternative. Make a short presentation to the class, explaining how you weighed the costs and benefits as shown on your chart. Conclude by stating your group's decision. Be prepared to answer questions.

# Sample Examination Questions 模拟试题

## Vocabulary

1. Use the following words or phrases in a sentence.

    a. market

    b. shareholder communication form

    c. client

    d. spread

    e. junk bond

    f. rate of return

    g. default

2. Define the following words and phrases and provide a Chinese translation.

    a. bid

    b. dividend

    c. quote

    d. interest

    e. current yield

## Understanding

1. What is the role of an investment banker?
2. Why is it important to set goals? Give some examples of financial goals.
3. Why might a government department use an investment bank?
4. What is a market? What is a financial market?
5. What is the difference between primary and secondary markets?
6. What are the differences between common and preferred shares?
7. Why do investors buy bonds?
8. What is the relationship between term and rate of return?

9. What is liquidity and why is it an important consideration when deciding whether or not to make an investment?

10. What are the advantages and disadvantages to a corporation of issuing bonds?

11. What are some categories of common shares?

12. To what type of investor would you recommend the purchase of penny stocks?

13. Explain how depository receipts work and what the advantages to the issuing corporation are.

# Derivatives

# 金融衍生品

## Part I  Introduction  导语

Derivatives are like aspirin. If you have a headache and you take one or two, they will help alleviate the pain. If you take the whole bottle at once, you may kill yourself.

## Derivatives 金融衍生品

## Part I — Introduction 导语

### Dialogue-What's new?

**Ken:** Hello, Brian. What a pleasant surprise meeting you on the street like this. I have been meaning to call you. How are you? How is the family? Is everything going smoothly at work?

**Brian:** Good morning, Ken. It's great to see you also. Everything is fine with me, but how about you? What did you want to talk to me about?

**Ken:** I wanted to see if you have any idea how I can reduce some of the risks that I face every day in my business. It's driving me crazy. Sometimes I think I would be better off by selling everything and taking the money to the casinos in Macau. If I am going to lose money, I might as well have fun doing it!

**Brian:** That does sound serious. We all face risks in our businesses. We just have to find ways of reducing them. I have an idea. For some time now, I have had a lady from a local securities firm helping me. She is a very experienced investment banker. She and her associates are experts in developing and implementing strategies to manage all kinds of risk. I could see if she is available for lunch. The three of us could meet and discuss these weighty matters in relaxing surroundings over a nice glass of wine. I still have a lot to learn so I would enjoy the opportunity hear about your particular problems and how she suggests handling them.

**Ken:** That is very considerate of you, Brian. I really would appreciate it. I knew you would have some good ideas.

**Brian:** Let me call her now and see when she is free. Is today convenient for you?

**Ken:** Yes, today would be great. The sooner the better. I know I can't continue the way I am for much longer. Is today ok for you?

**Brian:** I was going to be meeting a client for lunch today, but he had to go to Shanghai on business for a couple of days so my calendar is clear.

**Sandra:** Sandra Porter speaking. How may I help you?

**Brian:** Good morning, Sandra. This is Brian Kendall speaking.

**Sandra:** Hello, Brian. It is nice to hear from you. I was thinking of you just yesterday when the US Federal Reserve Chairman announced another increase in the fed funds rate. You must be feeling pretty happy about that interest rate swap we put in place for your company.

**Brian:** Yes, I am very happy and what is more important, so is my boss! If we had not done that swap, the higher interest costs we would be now paying would be really squeezing our profits.

**Sandra:** I am glad we were able to help.

**Brian:** That is the reason I am calling. One of my closest friends runs a large exporting business. He is having some problems managing risk. You have done such a great job for me that I thought you might be able to help him also.

**Sandra:** Thank you for thinking of me. I would be delighted to meet with him. Did you have a time in mind?

**Brian:** I am with him now. We were hoping that we could buy you lunch today.

**Sandra:** That would be fine. What time and where would you like to meet?

**Brian:** There is a new restaurant just opened near the Mandarin Hotel. How about meeting there at 12:15?

**Sandra:** Yes, I have heard about it. People say it is very good. 12:15 is fine. I will look forward to seeing you then. Bye.

## Section A—A Common Business Problem 一个普遍的商业难题

Do you often feel like running your business is like playing roulette? There are so many risks that you face:

Commodity prices, interest rates, fx rates can go up and down without warning. These price movements can bring us to considerable risk so that at times it seems like we are gambling at a casino instead of running a business.

- Interest rate risk—your profits may fall when interest rates rise.
- Commodity price risk—when raw material prices rise, your business loses.
- Foreign exchange risk—if the value of your country's currency falls, you have to pay more for the products you have to import.
- Credit risk—If an important customer doesn't pay on time, your company may have cash flow problems.
- Sovereign risk—Changes in foreign countries' laws, rules and regulations can cost your business more money.

Derivatives are effective tool for managing many kinds of financial risks, helping you concentrate on running your business, making a normal profit from the product or service that you supply. You can largely insulate your business from powerful forces over which you have no control.

A cotton blouse
A typical end product made from raw cotton.

## Derivatives 金融衍生品

### Dialogue—Defining the Problem

**Brian:** Hello, Sandra. I would like you to meet my friend, Ken Smithson. Ken, this is Sandra Porter, one of the most capable investment bankers in the city.

**Sandra:** How do you do, Ken? It is a pleasure to meet you.

**Ken:** How do you do, Sandra? The pleasure is all mine I assure you. It is very good of you to take time out of your busy schedule to meet with us on such short notice.

**Sandra:** I am very glad to have the opportunity to help. Let's get seated and then you can tell what difficulties you are facing.

**Brian:** (To the Maître d') Reservation for Kendall, please.

**Maître d':** Yes, Mr. Kendall. Please come this way.

**Ken:** Let me give you some background about my company. We manufacture sportswear—T-shirts, shorts, casual slacks. Most of our products are made from cotton which we import from various countries around the world. The output is sold mainly in the United States. While people like the style and quality of our products, the market is very competitive. Our pricing has to be very attractive.

The price of raw cotton rises and falls on world commodity markets as supply and demand conditions change.

## Dialogue—Presenting a Solution

**Sandra:** That is interesting. Let me guess. If the price of cotton goes up, your profits get squeezed and if the US dollar falls, you lose money also.

**Ken:** You have it exactly. If only we did not have to worry about the price of cotton going up and down and if the US dollar would remain stable, we could make a reasonable manufacturing profit. Instead, we are at the mercy of international forces over which we have absolutely no control.

**Sandra:** I understand completely. And I assure you. You are not alone. A great many companies all over the world face the same problem. Happily there is a solution. There is a whole body of financial products called derivatives. They are sophisticated tools for helping companies just like you manage the financial risks that they face every day in their businesses.

**Ken:** Well, that makes me feel a little better. At least I am not alone! How do they work?

**Sandra:** In practice, they are a bit complicated, but in principle they are really very simple. They allow you to fix the price today for something that you need in the future. For example, there is a type of derivative that fix the price you would pay for the cotton you need for the rest of the year. And there is another derivative that would allow you to fix today the amount of Hong Kong dollars that you would get for the US dollars you receive from your American customers.

**Ken:** Really! This sounds to good to be true. But there must be a catch.

**Sandra:** There is not really any catch. There are other businesses throughout the world that have opposite needs to yours. For example, the American buyers of your products benefit if the US dollar rises, but they are hurt if it falls. They have to use more dollars to pay you. They would like to eliminate that risk from their business also.

**Ken:** That makes sense.

**Sandra:** There is cost, however. There is no free lunch!

**Ken:** I figured there had to be a catch somewhere.

## Derivatives 金融衍生品

**Sandra**: Not at catch exactly—just a cost. In some cases, the cost is the profit you would have made if prices had moved in your favour. For example, when cotton prices fall, your company earns more money. If you fix the price today for the cotton you will buy in the future, you are protected if the price rises. You would have made more money if the price fell, but you are gambling on cotton prices instead of making T-shirts.

**Ken**: Well that is certainly a cost I can live with. How do I put a plan like that in place?

**Sandra**: The first thing you need to do is to sit down with your sales people and estimate the amount of each type of product that they expect to sell in each of the next 12 months. They have your production, people review the sales forecasts and calculate for you how much cotton they need in each month. When you have done all that, give me a call. We can sit down and develop a plan that will take away most if not all of your company's commodity price risk and foreign exchange risk.

Part I—Introduction 导语

## Section B—What Are Derivatives?  金融衍生品的定义

In a previous chapter we learned about securities in general and stocks and bonds in particular. Investors are suppliers—people who have cash which is surplus to their current needs and who are willing to let others use it for a certain period of time. An investor's money goes either to the business or government that needs it (primary market) or to another investor (secondary market). In either case, the investor pays over money and receives in exchange a security—stocks or bonds.

---

**Important Note**

An **asset** is something you own such as your house, car, jewelry, shares of stock, bonds, and debentures.

In a derivative transaction, the asset on which it is based does not change hands; instead a **right relating to the price** of the asset changes hands.

---

The investor has simply exchanged one asset—cash—for another asset—a stock or a bond. At any point in the future, the investor can change the stock or bond back into cash by selling it in the secondary market like a stock exchange.

### A. You are not buying an asset

Derivatives are different. When you buy a derivative, you are not buying an asset. You do not own anything. Instead you are buying a benefit, a right to do something, to take some action in the future.

Derivatives are financial securities like stocks and bonds and they trade in markets just like those for stocks and bonds. However, they have no value on their own. Their value comes entirely from the value of something else, an asset like a stock (shares of Microsoft), a bond, a currency (US dollars, Hong Kong dollars, Euros) or a commodity (oil, wheat, gold).

Barings' Singapore-based trader, Nick Leeson, lost big when he bet wrong on the direction of the Japanese stock market.

> ### Barings Bank
>
> Barings, the oldest merchant bank in the United Kingdom, banker to Her Majesty Queen Elizabeth, got into big trouble when one of its traders took unauthorized positions in options and futures contracts.
>
> Losses were close to $1 billion, exceeding the bank's entire equity capital, forcing bank's ultimate sale for one pound.
>
> This tragic story illustrates the extreme volatility of derivatives and the dangers involved in trading them.
>
> Options and futures can be used to reduce/manage/hedge risk, like insurance, but they can also be extremely speculative.
>
> Depending on how they are used, derivatives can either eliminate certain kinds of risk or they can be like playing the ponies or gambling at a casino!

**B. The price of the derivative depends on the price of asset to which it is related**

If the market price of the financial security, currency or commodity on which the derivative is based goes up, the market price of the derivative will go up. We call the instrument on which the derivative is based the underlying and its price is referred to as the underlying price.

The expression "derivative" covers any transaction where

a. there is no movement of principal and,

b. the price performance of the derivative is driven by the price movement of an underlying asset such as the price of oil or the cost of money.

## Section C—Uses of Derivatives 金融衍生品的用途

Derivatives have two main uses:

a. the management (that is, the reduction of) financial risk and,

b. speculation.

A treasurer in a risk—averse organization enters into a derivative transaction to reduce her company's risk of loss from changes in the value of a foreign currency while the chief financial officer of another company takes the other side of the same derivative because he thinks the price of the currency is going down and he can realize a profit for his organization by selling the currency today and buying it back at a lower price in the future—if he is right, of course!

### A. Derivatives are flexible

An important aspect of financial derivatives is that they are often carried off—balance sheet. This gives financial executives more flexibility in structuring their companies' assets and liabilities to minimize risk and maximize return.

For example, a mutual fund manager who has limited ability to play the currency markets because of regulatory restrictions can buy a structured note whose coupon is tied to the relationship between a particular pair of currencies.

Credit derivatives can be used to lay off and manage a company's exposure to credit events such as supplier default. Most importantly, derivative products enable the financial manager to more closely match his company's risk exposure to his view of the direction of financial markets and to his organization's risk profile.

Derivatives facilitate international trade by reducing risk.

### B. Contractual Nature

Derivatives are contracts and they have a defined term. Unlike some underlying assets, common shares for example, they do not go on forever. At some point in the future they all end. The termination date is determined before the parties enter into the transaction.

Each party to any contract receives certain rights or benefits called "consideration". No consideration, no contract. Many contracts, including many derivatives, also place obligations on each party. That means each party receives some benefit from the derivative but in turn is obligated to do something at some point (or points) during its life.

Derivatives  金融衍生品

> **Risk Management Tip**
>
> If a local manufacturer is importing raw materials and paying for them in a foreign currency, his profit will be reduced if the value of the foreign currency rises in relation to his own country's currency. He has to use more of his own currency to buy the foreign currency he needs. He can use derivatives to eliminate this risk and ensure that he earns a normal manufacturing profit.

### C. Types of derivatives

There are many types of derivatives: Three of the most common are options, futures and forwards.

Options require the payment of a premium. Futures and forwards do not. In return for paying the premium, the buyer (owner) of an option does not assume any obligations. He or she is able to decide what course of action to take during the life of the derivative. If it is not to the owner's advantage to exercise the rights he or she has under the derivative contract, he or she can simply "walk away".

On the other hand, futures and forwards place very specific obligations on each party in return for the benefits received.

Some derivatives are settled by a single payment at some point during their life. When the required payment is made, the contract ends. Other derivatives call for periodic payments to be made by the respective parties over the entire term.

### D. Liquidity

Liquidity is important when considering any tradable instrument, especially derivatives. Liquidity means how easy it is to buy or sell the instrument at a particular point in time without significantly and adversely affecting its price. Liquidity is greatest with exchange-traded products. Hundreds of thousands

> **Trading Tip**
>
> There is a price for buying, a price for selling and a price for selling quickly.

of contracts are bought and sold each day. The chance therefore of finding willing buyers and sellers at a particular time and price is very good.

Liquidity in standard OTC instruments is also good. However, as deals become more complex, liquidity declines. In fact, some deals are so complex and so "structured" that there is really no liquidity at all.

### E. Credit Risk

Credit risk is another important factor relating to derivatives. There is always the chance that the counterparty to the deal may be unable or unwilling to fulfill the obligations under the contract. Financial difficulty, bankruptcy, exchange controls are examples of situations which might arise and prevent a party to a derivative transaction from realizing the expected benefits.

---

**Definitions**

A **derivative** is a financial contract. Its value is derived from the price of an underlying asset (often simply known as the "underlying"). Changes in the derivatives value are related to the price movements of the underlying.

**Exchange-traded derivatives** are traded on the floors of organized securities exchanges and usually require a good faith or margin deposit when buying or selling a contract. Examples are interest rate, futures and options to buy and sell common shares.

**Over-the-counter derivatives** such as currency swaps are privately negotiated bilateral agreements—organized securities exchanges are not involved in either the initial transaction or subsequent trading (buying the contract from or selling it to a third party). In the currency markets, forward delivery contracts allow traders to lock in current prices when buying or selling currencies for delivery at some point in the future.

**Derivative securities** are bond-like instruments created when pools of installment loans, mortgages or leases are packaged and sold to investors.

Credit risk is lower with exchange-traded products because the clearing house (an affiliate of the exchange on which the trade took place) becomes counterparty to every trade. This eliminates the exposure to an individual buyer or seller.

### F. Leverage

Derivatives can also offer a more highly levered position than other types of trading instruments. This allows traders of these instruments to get more of a "kick" for their money.

## Section D—Words and Expressions  术语及解释

**Commodity price risk  商品价格风险**

The risk of unexpected changes in a commodity price, such as the price of oil.

**Counterparty risk  交易对手违约风险**

When counter parties are unwilling/unable to fulfill their contractual obligations.

**Currency (foreign exchange) risk  货币(外汇)风险**

The risk of unexpected changes in foreign currency exchange rates.

**Deliverable instrument  可交割的金融工具**

The asset underlying a derivative security. For a currency option, the deliverable instrument is determined by the options exchange and is either spot currency or an equivalent value in futures contracts.

**Derivative security  衍生证券**

A financial security whose price is derived from the price of another asset.

**Exchange risk  兑汇风险**

The risk that losses may result from the changes in the relative values of different currencies.

**Exchange traded  交易所交易**

A transaction where a specific instrument is bought or sold on a regulated exchange, e.g. futures.

**Exchange traded contracts  交易所交易契约**

Financial instruments listed on exchanges such as the Chicago Board of Trade.

**Financial price risk  金融价格风险**

The risk of unexpected changes in a financial price, including currency (foreign exchange) risk, interest rate risk, and commodity price risk.

**Foreign exchange (currency) risk    外汇风险**

The risk of unexpected changes in foreign currency exchange rates.

**Interest rate risk    利率风险**

The risk of unexpected changes in an interest rate.

**Long position    多头**

A position in which a particular asset (such as a spot or forward currency) has been purchased.

**Premium    盈利,升水**

The cost associated with a derivative contract, referring to the combination of intrinsic value and time value. It usually applies to options contracts. However, it also applies to off-market forward contracts.

**Settlement risk    交割风险**

The risk of non-payment of an obligation by a counterparty to a transaction, exacerbated by mismatches in payment timings.

**Short    空头交易**

More sales than purchases.

**Short position    空头**

A position in which a particular asset (such as a spot or forward currency) has been sold.

**Short selling    卖空交易**

Selling an asset that you do not own or taking a short position.

**Sold short    卖空**

Someone who has sold a commodity or currency without previously owning it. (Short sell)

**Sovereign risk    主权风险**

Sovereign risk is the additional risk assumed by investors with funds invested in foreign counties. Sovereign risk includes currency translation losses, default of foreign governments on debts, and appropriation of company assets by foreign governments.

**Speculation    投机交易**

Taking positions in financial instruments without having an underlying exposure that offsets the positions taken.

**Transaction exposure** 交易风险

Changes in the value of contractual (monetary) cash flows as a result of changes in currency values.

**Underlying** 基础工具

An asset, future, interest rate, FX rate or index upon which a derivative transaction is based.

**Volatility** 波幅

The degree to which the market price of a financial instrument moves up and down during a short period of time.

# Part II  Options 期权

*When used wisely, derivatives can form a very important part of an effective risk management strategy, protecting profits and minimizing losses.*

## Section A—The Basics 基本定义

Certain derivatives are somewhat like insurance. You may pay an insurance company a premium in order to obtain some protection against financial loss from a specific event such as a fire or accident. There are derivative products that have a payoff that depends on some event occurring. To obtain this right or benefit you must pay a premium in advance.

---

**Definitions**

- An option gives the buyer the right but not the obligation to buy or sell a standard quantity of a specific financial instrument at a specific price on or before a specific future date. A premium is due.

- An option obligates the seller to buy or sell a standard quantity of a specific financial instrument at a specific price on or before a specific future date. A premium is received in exchange for giving this commitment.

Options are available on a wide variety of financial instruments: common stocks (equity options), foreign currencies, commodities such as gold, orange juice, pork bellies, wheat, oil as well as stock, bond and economic indices and even the weather. Options can be related to the current or spot price of the underlying or they can be related to the price of the underlying for delivery at some point in the future.

## Section B—Options Are Binding Contracts  期权是契约

As is the case with all derivatives, options are binding contracts with strictly defined terms, rights, benefits, obligations and time frames.

The buyer of option pays a premium to the seller in exchange for the rights and benefits. The buyer does not have to exercise those rights if it is not advantageous to do so.

Option Contracts

If the buyer does not exercise the rights on or before the last day of the option contract, the contract ends and has no further force or effect. The buyer loses the premium that he or she has paid to seller, but that is the maximum loss that will be incurred by a buyer. The premium paid for an option is regarded as a "sunk cost". It is important to remember that the option seller keeps the premium whether or not the option is exercised.

## Section C—Equity Options  股权期权

Equity options are financial instruments, contracts, which give holders the right to buy or sell common or preferred shares (including American depositary receipts and global depositary receipts) of publicly traded companies. Equity options are traded on securities exchanges (rather than over-the-counter) and as such have standardized terms.

To the buyer or holder, an equity call option normally represents the right to buy 100 shares of underlying stock. An equity put option normally represents the right to sell 100 shares of underlying stock.

The seller of an option is obligated to perform according to the terms of the options contract: buying or selling the stock at the contracted price (the strike price) if the option is exercised by the holder.

## Important Definitions

**Writer**

The original seller of the option. The person who is obligated to sell a specific quantity of shares (call) or buy a specific quantity of shares (put) at any point during a specified time period.

**Exercise or strike price**

The price at which the holder of an option can require the writer of the option to sell shares (call) or buy shares (put).

**Exercise**

The conversion of the option into the underlying.

**Exercise notice**

Notification by the option holder that he or she is exercising his or her rights under the option.

**In the money**

A call option is in the money when the market price is **higher** than the strike price. A put option is in the money when the market price of the underlying is **lower** than the strike price. A holder can make more money by selling the underlying to the writer of the option than he or she can by selling it in market.

**Out of the money**

A call option is out of the money when the market price is lower than the strike price. A put option is out of the money when the market price is **higher** than the strike price.

**At the money**

Put and call options are at the money when the market price is exactly equal to the strike price.

**Expiry date**

The date by which the option must be exercised. Options not exercised when the expiry date has Passed and become worthless.

## Part II—Options 期权

### A. Premium

The price of an option is called its premium. The potential loss to the buyer of an option can be no greater than the premium paid for the contract, no matter what happens to the price of the underlying stock. This allows an investor to control the amount of risk assumed. The seller of the option, in return for the premium received from the buyer, assumes the risk of being assigned if the contract is exercised.

### B. Expiration

In accordance with the standardized terms of their contracts, all options expire on a certain date, called the expiration date. For conventional listed options, this can be up to nine months from the date the options are first listed for trading. An option that is not exercised by the close of business on the expiry date becomes worthless.

### C. Trading

Options are traded on the exchanges in exactly the same way as common and preferred shares. For each option there is a flow of customer orders from large financial institutions and individual investors each with an instruction to buy or sell options at a certain price.

The noise can be deafening on the floor of the Chicago Board of Trade where floor traders compete to buy and sell derivatives for their firms and their clients.

> **Important Note**
>
> Option contracts are written in integral (1, 3, 4, 10, etc.) multiples of 100 shares. One option is a contract to buy or sell 100 shares. Ten options gives the holder the right to buy (or sell) 1,000 shares of the underlying security.

In addition, the exchanges have members or professionals (called "pros") who are obligated to make competitive markets for the exchange's listed securities in a fair and orderly manner. These members trade with their own capital and their bid and ask prices supplement those coming from the public (institutional and individual). This helps to provide market liquidity, especially on days when the market is decidedly bullish or bearish and there is an imbalance of orders (more sellers than buyers or vice versa-more buyers than sellers).

From the collective bid and ask prices from pros, institutions and individual investors, the best prices are chosen, trades executed and the resulting information disseminated to the world. The investing community sets the prices for options just as it does for shares-not the exchanges.

Market trading information for options is reported in much the same way as trading information for common shares. Consider the following example.

## Section D—Buying Options  买入期权

An option is the right to buy or sell and in some cases buy and sell an underlying at a specific price for a specific period of time.

- The buyer of a call option has the right to buy a specific quantity of a specific financial instrument at a set price for a set period of time.
- The buyer of a put option has the right to sell a specific quantity of a specific financial instrument at a pre-determined price for a set period of time.
- The writer (seller) of a call option has the obligation to deliver a specific quantity of a specific financial instrument at a set price for a set period of time if called upon to do so by the holder of the option (against payment of the purchase price of course).
- The writer (seller) of a put option has the obligation to buy a specific quantity of a specific financial instrument at a set price for a set period of time if called upon to do so by the holder of the option (likewise against good delivery of the underlying).

### A. Call options

When you buy a call option, you get the right to buy (from the seller of the option) a specific quantity of the underlying at an agreed upon price for an agreed upon amount of time. At the time that you buy the option, you pay to the seller an agreed upon amount called a premium for this right.

The day on which the agreed upon time period ends is called the expiry date. At any time up to and including the expiry date, you can require the seller (call the underlying from the seller) to sell to you the agreed upon quantity of the underlying by paying to him or her the price that the two of you agreed upon.

You would buy a call when you think that the price of the underlying is going to rise.

### B. Put options

Put options, puts for short, work in reverse. They are the opposite of calls. When you buy a put, you buy the right to sell a specific quantity of the underlying at an agreed upon price for an agreed upon period of time.

You would buy a put when you think the market price of the underlying is going to fall.

### C. Straddles

Straddles combines the rights of both puts and calls. They give the buyer the right to buy the underlying at a specific price and to sell the underlying at a different price. You might buy a straddle if you think the price of the underlying will fluctuate widely but you are not sure whether it will go up or down.

## Section E—Selling Options  卖出期权

In any market, for every buyer there must be a seller. The option market is no different. When you buy a call option, someone is selling it to you. There are two possibilities:

1. You buy the option in the secondary market from another investor like yourself.
2. You buy the option from the original seller—the person who wrote the option.

### A. Writing covered call options

The writer (the original seller) of a call option is giving the buyer the right to call from him or her a certain quantity of the underlying at a specific price for a certain period of time.

Consider the following example.

You own 1,000 shares of China Petroleum and Chemical Corp. (symbol SNP) which you bought some time ago at US $ 31.50 a share. The market

> **Definition**
>
> A covered call option is one where the writer (original seller) owns the underlying shares.

price is now $36.00. You think that the price may go higher but you are very happy with the $4,500 paper profit that you have made so far and you are concerned that the price may go down eliminating part or worse, all of your gain. You know that options are traded on SNP shares. Upon checking the market, you find that there are SNP options with a strike price of US $35.00 expiring in 9 months. The last trade was US $3.50. The current market is $3.50 bid, $3.55 asked.

If you sold a call today on 1,000 SNP at the market, you would receive cash of US $3,500 ($3.50 premium per share multiplied by 1,000 shares ignoring commission). At any time during the next nine months, the buyer could require you to sell the 1,000 SNP shares you own to him or her at US $35.00 per share, US $35,000 in total (there is no commission).

The buyer would only exercise his or her right to buy the shares if the market price is above $35.00. If it is below $35.00, it would be cheaper to buy the shares in the market directly.

Suppose before the nine months has elapsed, the price of SNP shares has rise to $40.00. The buyer delivers an exercise notice to you stating that he or she wishes to exercise the option. You deliver the shares in exchange for a cheque of $35,000.

Your total proceeds from selling the shares is $38,500-$3,500 from the premium you received from selling the option plus the $35,000 you received from selling the shares themselves. Your profit on the SNP shares is $7,000-$38,500 total proceeds minus your cost of $31,500. If you had not sold the option, you could have sold the SNP shares for $40,000 thus earning a profit of $8,500. By selling the option you gave up the extra $1,500 profit.

However, the stock price may not have risen to $40.00. It might even have fallen. If the stock price stays at or below $38.50, you are farther ahead, you make more money, by selling option.

> If you own shares and write a call option on them, you are locking in a profit and reducing your portfolio risk. This is a covered call.

### B. Writing naked call options

In the previous example, the writer of the call option owned the underlying. Selling a call in this way is an effective strategy for reducing risk.

Some people write calls on shares that they do not own. These are called naked call options. This is a strategy for earning income, but it comes with high risk.

Let's see why.

You sell the same call option as in the previous example but this time you do not own any SNP shares. You receive cash of US $ 3,500 today as your premium. As before, the share price rises to US $ 40.00 and the holder of the call option delivers an exercise notice to you. You have to deliver 1,000 SNP shares to him or her at a price of $ 35.00 per share. The problem is that you do not have the SNP shares to deliver. Consequently you must go into the market and buy them. You have to pay the market price of $ 40.00 per share.

> **Definition**
>
> A naked call option is one where the writer (original seller) does not own the underlying shares.

| | |
|---|---:|
| The price you receive from the call option holder | $ 35.00 |
| The premium you received from writing the call option | $ 3.50 |
| The total proceeds you receive | $ 38.50 |
| Your cost of the shares | $ 40.00 |
| Your loss | $ 1.50 |

Your total loss on the transaction is $ 1,500 (1,000 shares multiplied by the loss per share of $ 1.50).

If the price of SNP shares stays below US $ 38.50 you make money by writing a naked call option. At $ 38.50 you break even. At any price above $ 38.50 you lose money.

> The real risk in writing naked call options is that there is no limit to how high the SNP share price can go. You have a formal legal obligation to deliver the shares at US $ 35.00 if called upon by the holder of the option no matter whether you own them or not and if you do not own them, no matter what price you have to pay to get them.

# Derivatives  金融衍生品

### Dialogue—The Travellers

**Brad**: Hello, Matt. What a pleasant surprise meeting you here today. Where are you off to?

**Matt**: Hi Brad. It's great to see you also. You know, I have been meaning to call you for some time now. It's been too long since we got together for lunch. We have a lot of catching up to do. I'm on my way to Hong Kong. There is an international conference being held there on derivatives. Our firm is expanding into that market in a big way and they are sending me to get up to date on the latest developments. How about you? Where are you headed?

**Brad**: I'm off to New York for 10 days or so. My company wants to do a public offering of shares in the United States and to try to qualify for listing on the New York Stock Exchange. I'm going to be meeting with some investment bankers there to see if we can get the process started.

**Matt**: Sounds like it should be very exciting for you. Have you been to New York before?

**Brad**: No, it's my first time. I'm really looking forward to it. Any suggestions?

**Matt**: Where are you staying?

**Brad:** My secretary has me booked in at the Waldorf Astoria. Apparently it is very comfortable and quite centrally located.

**Matt:** Yes, it's a great place. Lots of interesting bars and restaurants in the area.

**Brad:** So I'm told. I have a pretty busy schedule but I certainly plan to make time for some R & R!

**Matt:** Are you interested in art? The new Museum of Modern Art just opened recently. Apparently it is quite something to see.

**Brad:** Yes, I've heard about it. I'm definitely planning on taking it in. Anyway, I've got to run. I never leave myself enough time to get to the airport. Have a good trip.

**Matt:** Thanks, Brad. I hope your meetings are successful. Please give me a call when you get back.

## Section F—You Bought an Option and Now You Want to Get Your Money Out  套现

As a holder (buyer) of an option, there are two ways of getting your money out.
1. You can exercise the option.
   a. In the case of a call,
      - you deliver an exercise notice to the writer,
      - pay the exercise price,
      - receive the shares and,
      - sell them in the market at a higher price.

---

### Trading Tip

The only time you would exercise a call option is when the market price of the underlying is higher than the exercise (strike) price.

---

The amount of money you receive back on your call is the difference between the market price of the shares and the exercise. If this difference is larger than the premium you paid when you bought the call, you have earned a profit on the transaction. If this difference is negative, you lost money.

  b. In the case of a put,
- You deliver an exercise notice to the writer,
- you deliver the shares and,
- he or she pays you the exercise price.

2. You can sell the put or call in the secondary market.
  a. In the case of a call: If the market price of the underlying has risen since you bought the call, the market price of the call will probably be higher than your cost. You will earn a profit when you sell it.
  b. In the case of a put: If the market price of the underlying has fallen since you bought the put, the market price of the put will probably be higher than your cost. You will earn a profit when you sell it.

## Section G—You Have Written an Option (Original Seller) and You Want out of the Contract 赎回

When you write an option, you are committed under its terms until it is exercised or it expires. If you do not want that obligation any more, the only way you can get out of it is by buying the option back in the secondary market.

> **Trading Tip**
>
> This certificate is evidence of the ownership of shares in Coca-Cola Company. When you write a call option on Coca-Cola shares, you are giving the holder the right to force you to sell him or her the shares at a specific price for a specific period of time. If you do not own the shares and the holder exercises the option to buy them from you, you have to buy them in market at whatever the market price is at the time.

### A. Call options

Suppose you wrote a 9-month covered call option on 1,000 shares of Coca-Cola at a strike price of US $ 45.00. You received a premium of $ 1.00 per share, $ 1,000 in total. The market price of Coca-Cola shares at the time was $ 41.50.

Since you wrote the option, the market price of Coca-Cola has fallen to $ 39.00. The option to buy Coca-Cola shares at $ 45.00 is now less valuable so the price of the call option will have fallen also. You buy back the call in the market. Your profit is the difference between the premium you received when you sold it and the price you paid when you bought it back.

In the price of Coca-Cola shares has risen since you wrote the call, the price of the call will probably be higher than the premium you received when you sold it. In this case, when you buy it back, you will have lost money on the transaction.

### B. Put options

The same principle applies when you have written a put option and you want to unwind the contract. The only difference is that it applies in reverse.

Let us say that when the market price of IBM shares was US $ 90.00 you wrote a 9-month put option on 1,000 shares of IBM at an exercise price of US $ 90. You give to someone else the right to sell to you (and force you to buy) 1,000 shares of IBM at $ 90. You received a premium of $ 4.30 per share, $ 4,300 in total.

The market price of IBM is now $ 92.75 so the right to put the shares to you at the strike price of $ 90 is less valuable. The holder of the put option would be better off selling the shares in the market at $ 92.75 than exercising the put and selling them to you at $ 90.

You can buy back the put in the secondary market and you are relieved of your obligation under the contract. The profit you earned on the transaction is the difference between the premium you received when you wrote the option and the price you paid when you bought it back.

## Section H—Time Decay of Put and Call Options  期权买卖的时间衰减

> If the price of Coca-Cola shares has risen since you wrote the call, the price of the call will probably be higher than the premium you received when you sold it.

Notice that we said that the price of the call *will probably be higher* if the price of the underlying has risen. This is not always the case. Options have a finite life. They will expire at a definite time in the future. As we get closer and closer to that point in time, the value of a right to buy or sell a share of stock declines. There is less time for the price of the underlying to move in the direction that we want it to.

When we buy a call, we are hoping that the market price of the underlying will rise. The longer the time we have for that to happen—the longer the time until the option expires—the greater the probability is that the market price of the underlying will rise.

For example, if our call option on Coca-Cola at a strike price of $ expires in a few days and the market price of Coca-Cola shares is $, the chance that the price will rise enough so that our option "back in the money" is pretty remote.

> **Fundamental principle of options**
> 
> The value of an option declines as the expiry date approaches.

## Section I—Valuing Options  期权估价

In valuing options we start by comparing the strike price with the current market price of the underlying. A call option with strike price lower than the market price of the underlying is said to be "in-the-money". This means that there is some benefit to exercising the option.

An option's premium consists of two components: intrinsic value and time value.

## A. Intrinsic value

The amount by which an option is currently in the money is called its intrinsic value. Equity options are generally worth (will trade for) at least their intrinsic value. However, because options have a lifetime and the rights conveyed to their owners to buy or sell stock at the strike price are good into the future, options will generally trade for more than their intrinsic value. Any premium amount in excess of the intrinsic value is called time value.

## B. Time value of an option

The time value is the price the investor pays for time for the price of the underlying to rise in the case of a call and fall in the case of a put. The longer the time period is remaining until expiry, the higher the time value will be.

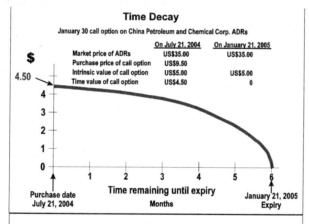

As the current date gets closer to the expiration date, the time value of an option gradually declines. On the expiration date the time value is zero.

If the price of the underlying remains constant, the price of the option will gradually decline as time passes until on the expiry date there is no time value and the premium for the option equals its intrinsic value. We call this phenomenon time decay.

The premiums paid for options at the money or out of the money represent only time value. The intrinsic value is zero.

The more out of the money an option is, the less investors will pay for it, because the price of the underlying will have to rise that much farther before the option comes into the money and has some intrinsic value.

A strike price exactly equal to the market price of the underlying is "at-the-money" and a strike price higher than the current market price of the underlying is "out-of-the-money".

## Section J—Why We Use Equity Options? 使用股权期权的原因

### A. The math

Suppose we feel that China Petroleum and Chemical Corp. (Sinopec) will benefit greatly from the booming Chinese economy. We think its profits will rise sharply during the coming months and we want to invest in the company. We have two alternatives:

1. We can buy the shares (American depositary receipts actually) directly. They are listed on the New York Stock Exchange, symbol SNP or

2. we can buy call options on the shares. They are traded on the Philadelphia Stock Exchange.

Suppose the current market price of SNP is US $ 35. The price for a 9-month option on SNP at $ 30 is $ 6.20.

| Strike price | Premium (Market price of the call) |
|---|---|
| $ 30 | $ 9.50 |
| $ 40 | $ 1.80 |

Let's compare the profit we would earn if the market price of the shares kept rising so that on the expiry date the price was $ 45. That would be the last day on which we could exercise the option so there would be no time value. The value of the option would simply be its intrinsic value—the difference between the market price of the shares and the strike price.

- If we bought the stock directly, we would have a gain of $ 10 per share. Our rate of return would be 28.5% ($ 10 profit divided by our cost of $ 35).
- If we bought the in-the-money option (strike price $ 30), we would calculate our profit as follows:

|  | Per Share |
|---|---|
| Price of the call (premium) paid to the seller | $ 9.50 |
| Price paid to the seller upon exercise of the option | $ 30.00 |
| Total cost | $ 39.50 |
| Market value of the shares | $ 45.00 |
| Profit | $ 5.50 |

In this case we would earn a profit $ 5.50 per share. This is less than the $ 10 per share we would earn if we bought the stock outright, however, we have a lot less money invested—$ 9.50 per share compared with $ 35. Therefore our rate of return is much higher: almost 60% (57.9% to be exact—$ 5.50 divided by $ 9.50).

■ If we bought the out-of-the-money option (strike price $ 40), we would calculate our profit as follows:

|  | Per Share |
|---|---|
| Price of the call (premium) paid to the seller | $ 1.80 |
| Price paid to the seller upon exercise of the option | $ 40.00 |
| Total cost | $ 41.80 |
| Market value of the shares | $ 45.00 |
| Profit | $ 3.20 |

In this case we would earn a profit $ 3.70 per share. This is less than

  a. the $ 10 per share we would earn if we bought the stock outright and
  b. the $ 5.50 per share we would earn if we had bought the in-the-money option, the $ 30 one.

However, we have even less money invested—$ 1.80 per share. In this case our rate of return is 177% ($ 3.20 divided by $ 1.80). We have almost doubled our money!

| In Summary | |
|---|---|
| Alternative | Rate of return |
| Buy the shares | 29% |
| Buy the *in-the-money* call | 58% |
| Buy the *out-of-the-money* call | 177% |

### B. The advantages

A major advantage of options is their versatility. They can be as conservative or as speculative as an investor's strategy and risk profile dictate. Options assist investors in managing investment portfolios by enable them to tailor their positions to meet a particular set of circumstances.

Options can

1. protect stock holdings from a decline in price;
2. increase income from stock holdings;
3. position investors to buy (sell) stock at a lower (higher) price;
4. reduce portfolio risk by increasing diversification;
5. position investors to take advantage of a big market move either up or down;
6. allow investors to benefit from a rise or fall in the price of the underlying without tying up the capital required to buy or sell it outright.

Easy to use, options allow the buyer the opportunity to earn a profit while limiting the downside risk (the risk of financial loss). Depending on the circumstances of the trade, the financial loss to the seller (writer) of an option may be unlimited while the profit potential is limited to the premium received.

## Section K—Words and Expressions  术语及解释

**At-the-money option  等价期权**

An option with an exercise price that is equal to the current value of the underlying asset.

**Call option  买权**

A call option is a financial contract giving the owner the right but not the obligation to buy a pre-set amount of the underlying financial instrument at a pre-set price with a pre-set maturity date.

**Counterparty risk  交易对手违约风险**

When counter parties are unwilling/unable to fulfill their contractual obligations.

**Covered call  掩护性买权**

A covered call combines a long position in a stock with a short position in a call option.

An investor constructs a covered call position by buying a security and selling a call option of the same security. A covered call is a market-neutral investment strategy.

An investor constructs a covered call position by buying the underlying security and selling a call option on that security. For example, an investor buys AT at $39 and sells a call option on AT with a strike price of $40, with expiration in 1 month. If the price the investor received for the call was $1.50, then the cost of his investment was $37.50.

An investor would use this strategy if he believed that the price of AT&T was to remain stable or go down. The risk of this strategy is if AT&T rose beyond $41.50. If this happened, the investor would no longer participate in the market rise. Since he sold the call option, its value would represent a loss as AT&T's stock price rose above the strike price of $40. This would be perfectly offset by the share he owns in AT&T. However, the $1.50 that he received for selling the call allows him to participate in the market's rise up to $41.50. In other words, the breakeven point of this option strategy is when the Stock Price = Exercise Price + Call Price. Below this price, the covered call provides a better return than merely holding the security.

**Covered call option writing  抵补销售买权**

A technique used by investors to help fund their underlying positions, typically used in the equity markets. An individual who sells a call is said to "write" the call. If this individual sells a call on a notional amount of the underlying that he has in his inventory, then the written call is said to be "covered" (by his inventory of the underlying). If the investor does not have the underlying in inventory, the investor has sold the call "naked".

**Deliverable instrument  可交割的金融工具**

The asset underlying a derivative security. For a currency option, the deliverable instrument is determined by the options exchange and is either spot currency or an equivalent value in futures contracts.

**Exchange traded  交易所交易**

A transaction where a specific instrument is bought or sold on a regulated exchange, e.g. futures.

**Exchange traded contracts**　交易所交易契约

Financial instruments listed on exchanges such as the Chicago Board of Trade.

**Exercise**　实行

The conversion of the option into the "underlying".

**Exercise price**　履约价格

The price at which the option holder has the right to buy or sell the underlying instrument.

**Expiration date**　到期日

The last date on which an option can be exercised.

**Holder**　持票人

The buyer/owner of an option.

**In-the-money option**　价内期权

An option that has value if exercised immediately. An option with an exercise price more advantageous than the current market level of the underlying.

**In-the-money spot**　价内即期汇率

An option with positive intrinsic value with respect to the prevailing market spot rate. If the option were to mature immediately, the option holder would exercise it in order to capture its economic value. For a call price to have intrinsic value, the strike must be less than the spot price. For a put price to have intrinsic value, the strike must be greater than the spot price.

**In-the-money-forward**　价内远期(合同)

An option with positive intrinsic value with respect to the prevailing market forward rate. If the option were to mature immediately, the option holder would exercise it in order to capture its economic value. For a call price to have intrinsic value, the strike must be less than the spot price. For a put price to have intrinsic value, the strike must be greater than the spot price.

**Index options**　指数期权

A call or put option contract on an index (such as a foreign stock market index).

**Interest rate swap**　利率互换

An agreement to exchange interest payments for a specific period of time on a given principal amount. The most common interest rate swap is a fixed-for-floating coupon swap. The notional principal is typically not exchanged.

**Intrinsic value**　内在价值

The value of an option if exercised immediately. One of the components of an option premium. The amount by which an option is in-the-money.

Intrinsic value is the difference between the current market price of the underlying security and the striking price of a related option. When the intrinsic value is positive, the option is said to be in the money. For instance, when ABC, Inc. call options traded at 12 1/2 and the stock traded at 13 3/8, the calls had intrinsic value of 7/8 and were in the money. For a put to have intrinsic value, the current market price of the underlying security must be below the striking price. If the intrinsic value is negative, the call is said to be out of the money.

**Naked option**　无担保期权

An option position taken without having the underlying.

**Naked option writing**　沽出未抵押期权

The act of selling options without having any offsetting exposure in the underlying cash instrument.

**Notice of exercise**　执行通知

Notification by telex, fax or phone which must be given irrevocably by the buyer to the seller of the option prior or at the time of expiry.

**Option**　期权

An agreement between two parties that gives the Holder (buyer), the right but not the obligation to buy or sell a specific instrument at a specified price on or before a specific future date. On exercise the Seller (writer) of the option must deliver or take delivery of the underlying instrument at the specified price. The right but not the obligation to buy (sell) some underlying cash instrument at a pre-determined rate on a pre-determined expiration date in a pre-set notional amount.

**Out-of-the-money option**　价外期权

An option with an exercise price more disadvantageous than the current market level of the underlying. An out-of-the-money option has time value but no intrinsic value. An option that has no value if exercised immediately.

**Out-of-the-money spot**　价外即期汇率

An option with no intrinsic value with respect to the prevailing market spot rate. If the option were to mature immediately, the option holder would let it expire. For a call price to have intrinsic value, the strike must be less than the spot price. For a put price to have intrinsic value, the strike must be greater than the spot price.

**Over the counter (OTC)** 柜台买卖

A bilateral transaction between a client and a bank, negotiated privately between the parties. Any transaction that takes place between two counterparties and does not involve an exchange is said to be an over-the-counter transaction.

**Premium** 盈利,升水

The cost associated with a derivative contract, referring to the combination of intrinsic value and time value. It usually applies to options contracts. However, it also applies to off-market forward contracts.

The cost of the option contract. It is made up of two components, intrinsic value and time value.

**Put option** 卖权

An option that gives the holder (buyer), the right but not the obligation to sell the underlying instrument at a pre-agreed strike rate (exercise rate) on or before a specific future date.

**Strike price (exercise price)** 履约价格

The price at which the option holder has the right to buy-or-sell the underlying instrument.

**Time value of an option** 期权的时间价值

The difference between the value of an option and the option's intrinsic value.

The amount (if any), by which the premium of an option exceeds the intrinsic value.

**Traded option** 可交易期权

An option contract bought or sold on a regulated exchange.

**Volatility** 波幅

The degree to which the market price of a financial instrument moves up and down during a short period of time.

**Writer** 出权人

The Seller of an option.

Part III—Futures and Forwards 期货及远期

# Part III
## Futures and Forwards 期货及远期

*Financial futures are the fastest way to make and lose lots of money. Both the potential profits and losses are open-ended.*

Wheat, gold, coffee and orange solids are examples of commodities that are actively traded.

## Section A—The Basics  基础知识

Financial futures and forward contracts are legally binding agreements to make or take delivery of specific financial instrument at an agreed upon future date at an agreed upon price. The commonly traded instruments are currencies (US dollars, Euros, British pounds, Hong Kong dollars) and commodities (gold, oil, wheat, soybeans).

## Section B—Futures Contracts  期货合同

A financial futures contracts have standard terms. This means that they are for standard quantities of the underlying and they expire on set dates. Futures are exchange-traded instruments and thus have secondary markets. The price is determined through open outcry on the floor of an organized exchange or by screen based trading. A futures contract can be (and generally is) traded many times during its life (like bonds and unlike bank loans).

---

### Example

Coffee futures trade on the New York Board of Trade. Each contract is for 37,500 pounds (about 17,000 kilograms). Contract months are March, May, July, September, December. This means a trader can buy or sell one or more contracts for the delivery of 37,500 pounds of coffee in any one of those months. The spot price (April) is US1.33 per pound. The July forward price $ 1.25. This means that a trader could enter into a contract today (April) to buy 37,500 pounds of coffee at US $ 1.25 per pound for delivery in July. Because the forward price is lower than the spot price, the market is expecting the price of coffee to fall.

---

### A. Producers and consumers

Futures contracts are bought and sold by producers and consumers to reduce their risk of losses from changes in commodity prices. For example, in the spring when a farmer is planting his crops, he wants to be sure he can sell it at a profit in the fall. He can enter into a futures contract that gives him the right *and the obligation* to sell a specific quantity of wheat in September at a price set in April. He is guaranteed to receive the set price no matter what happens to the market price of wheat in the meantime.

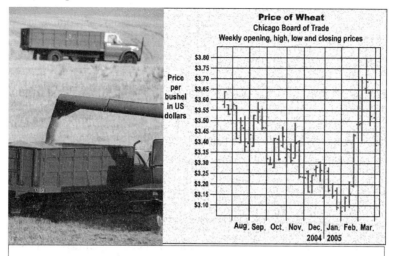

Prices of commodities can rise and fall quickly and by large amounts.

---

**This Is Really Important!**

In options contracts, **only the seller** is legally committed to buy or sell the underlying. The buyer only does so if it is advantageous for him or her to do so.

In futures and forwards contracts, **both buyer and seller** are legally committed to buy or sell the underlying at the maturity date of the contract.

---

The farmer gives up the profit he would have made if the price of wheat in September is higher than the price set in the contract. This is the price (the cost to him) of totally eliminating the risk that the price of wheat will be lower in September than the contract price.

Another example would be a company like Starbucks. Its customers consume large quantities of coffee every day all over the world. Starbucks makes a good profit from this business. However, the price of coffee beans fluctuates widely from time to time. If the price of raw coffee suddenly rose sharply, Starbuck's customers would not be very happy if they suddenly found that the price of their morning mocha latte had doubled! Starbucks most likely avoids this problem by buying coffee forward in the futures market.

## Derivatives  金融衍生品

> **Definition**
>
> **Hedgers** have a business interest in the underlying currency or commodity and is using futures trading to minimize, eliminate or control currency risk, for example, **MNCs**, **banks**, exporters/importers, etc..

Starbucks estimates its needs for coffee at set times in the future and buys that quantity of coffee for delivery at those times. Thus it knows for sure in advance what its raw material costs will be and what it will have to charge its customers in order to make a normal profit on its normal business.

This strategy is called hedging and used widely by producers of commodities and the businesses that use those commodities as raw materials. The producers sell part or all of their production forward. This means that they sell today a specific quantity of their production to be delivered at some future date at a price set today.

The users buy part or all of their raw material requirements forward. This means that they buy today a specific quantity of their needs to be delivered to them at a price set today.

### B. Speculators

Futures contracts have standard terms and are traded actively on exchanges. The price of a particular contract will move up or down as supply and demand conditions for the underlying change. For example, a frost in Florida will reduce the supply of oranges used to make orange juice. When supply of anything falls (and demand stays the same), the price goes up. By reducing the supply of oranges, the frost will cause the price of oranges to rise. There are fewer oranges available. The people who need them—the producers of orange juice—will have to pay more to get them.

> **Definition**
>
> **Speculators** have no business interest in the underlying commodity or currency. They are betting, speculating on the price of the underlying changing in their favour.

Orange juice futures are contracts for the delivery of a specific quantity of orange juice in the future. If the price of oranges rises, the price of the futures contract will rise. Remember, the futures contract gives the holder the right to buy orange juice at the old, lower price.

This kind of market is very attractive to people called speculators. They try to make money by anticipating the upward and downward price movements of underlying like commodities and currencies. If they think that the price of gold will rise in the future, they can enter into a futures contract. If they are right and the gold price rises, they can sell the contract and earn a profit.

### C. Leverage

The real advantage to speculators (they may prefer to be called traders), is that they can control a very large quantity of the underlying with very little cash. This means that a small movement in price can result in a very big profit *or loss*.

For example, a trader today buys one July coffee contract. The price is US1.25 per pound. This means that in July when the contract matures, he is required to buy 37,500 pounds of coffee at a price of US $ 1.25 per pound—US $ 46,875 in total. He has to deposit US $ 3,500 with his broker as margin.

If the price of coffee for delivery in July rises by just one percent (one and one-quarter cents, $ 0.0125), the value of the contract he holds rises to $ 47,344.

|  | Original price | New price | Dollar change |
| --- | --- | --- | --- |
| Price per pound | $ 1.2500 | $ 1.2625 | $ 0.0125 |
| Value of the contract | $ 46,875 | $ 47,344 | $ 468.7500 |

The price of coffee rose a little more than one cent a pound. The value of the trader's contract rose $ 469. The trader deposited $ 3,500 as margin with his broker when he bought the contract. This is the amount of cash that he has invested in the deal. If he sold out right now, he would earn $ 469 and get his $ 3,500 margin deposit back. His rate of return on his investment is 13.4%.

Coffee forwards trade actively. The price regularly fluctuates within a trading range of two to three cents. Therefore within minutes or even seconds of buying a forward contract, a trader could be up or down several hundred dollars on just one contract.

### D. Settlement

Futures contracts are rarely settled by delivery of the underlying. In almost all cases, the buyers and sellers enter into reversing trades some time before the maturity date. For example, a trader may have bought 10 July coffee forward contracts. On settlement day he is required to buy 375,000 pounds of coffee. Most traders do not want to do this. They have no place to store that amount of coffee.

---

**Don't Let This Happen to You!**

The joke is often told about the novice trader in commodities who is stunned when answers the doorbell. There is a big truck in his driveway loaded to the brim with potatoes and the driver is asking him where he would like them dumped!

---

Instead, at some time before the settlement date, the trader will enter into 10 contracts to sell coffee in July. Since the contracts are for the quantity of coffee to be delivered on the same date, the exchange cancels them out. The trader has unwound his position and is now flat. He has no exposure to the price of coffee.

---

**Evening Television News Report**

**Ron:** Good evening, ladies and gentlemen. I'm Ron Howard reporting from Shanghai with your nightly business news. In our top story tonight, a sudden frost has hit the rich coffee-producing region of central Brazil. The unexpectedly harsh weather has apparently devastated this season's crop. Our reporter, Betty Williamson, has the details on this breaking story from Rio de Janeiro. Betty, over to you.

**Betty:** Thank you, Ron. It was just yesterday morning that a major coffee producer here was telling me how optimistic he was about this season's production. In less than a month he expected to be harvesting his best crop ever. World coffee prices were high so he was expecting his company to have an excellent year.

All that has suddenly changed. Last night cold air swept in from the Atlantic Ocean causing temperatures throughout the region to plunge to minus 7 degrees Celsius. There was a heavy frost on the trees and even some snow on the ground. Most of the trees were heavily damaged.

Producers expect that total coffee production will be down over 90% from last year. This is clearly a very serious blow to Brazil's surging economy.

Growth in GDP was widely predicted to top 6% this year. The actual number is likely to come in much lower than that.

This is Betty Williamson reporting to you from Rio de Janeiro. Back to you, Ron, in the studio.

**Ron:** Thank you, Betty, for your most informative report. We are very fortunate to have with us tonight in our studio, Dr. Benjamin Carter, Professor of Finance at Qing Hua University in Beijing. Dr. Carter, clearly this catastrophe in Brazil will have world-wide ramifications. Can you please explain to our viewers some of the effects it will have.

**Dr. Carter:** Brazil is one of the world's largest producers of coffee. A large percentage of that production is exported. Brazil has been running a substantial trade surplus for some time now fueled not only by exports of coffee but also increasing international demand for its manufactured goods. This development is going to sharply reduce the trade surplus and may even cause it to turn negative, a deficit, until adjustments can occur elsewhere in the economy.

The Brazilian currency, the real, has been very strong lately largely because of the trade surplus and the strong domestic economy. Losing most of the coffee crop is going to sharply reduce economic growth. Moreover, the central government may have to increase foreign borrowings to balance its budget and provide subsidies to other industries to offset the loss of the coffee production and keep employment generally high.

# Derivatives 金融衍生品

The much lower foreign currency earnings and the increases foreign borrowing will put significant downward pressure on the real. I definitely expect we will see a sharp fall off in the value of the real when markets open in the morning. For traders, however, the major impact will be on coffee prices on the world's commodity markets. Such a big reduction in the supply of coffee will cause spot and futures prices to rise dramatically.

## Dialogue-Hedging

**Andrew:** Andrew Morgan speaking. How may I help you?

**Steve:** Good morning, Mr. Morgan. My name is Steve Phillips. Your name was given to me by Bob Smith, an Account Executive in your downtown office. Bob has been handling my personal financial affairs for many years.

**Andrew:** Yes, I know Bob very well. He and I are old friends. How can I help you?

**Steve:** I am Treasurer of High Quality Foods here in Shanghai. We import large quantities of raw coffee especially from producers in Brazil. We roast the coffee, add flavourings and supply it to upscale coffee houses, restaurants and specialty restaurants throughout southern China.

**Andrew:** That is very interesting. I imagine that you are calling because of the problem with the coffee crop in Brazil.

**Steve:** That's right. We have a nice, profitable operation here. When coffee prices are stable, we make a reasonable manufacturing profit and are able to supply our customers with top quality beans at a price that allows them to make an attractive return. The frost has caused coffee prices to skyrocket. There is no way we can pass along that increase to our customers. I want to know if there is some way that we can protect ourselves from the risk of fluctuating commodity prices.

**Andrew:** There is indeed. The process is called hedging. It is a very effective tool for managing risk. I would like to suggest that you drop into our office. I can tell you in detail how it works and show you first hand our trading center where the strategy can be implemented. Would it be convenient for you to come in tomorrow around 2?

**Steve:** That sounds excellent. Thank you very much. I will look forward to seeing you tomorrow at 2:00 pm.

## Section C—Forward Contracts  远期合同

Forward contracts are private, customized contracts between two parties, usually a bank and its clients (multi-national corporations, exporters, importers, etc.). Forward contracts are structured to specifically meet each client's particular needs. There is no secondary market for forward contracts since they are private arrangements with no standardized terms. It is like bank loans which are tailored specially for each borrower and bonds which are standardized.

Forward contracts are usually settled at maturity. That is, the underlying is actually delivered.

## Section D—Margins  保证金

### A. Initial margin

The initial investment required to establish a futures position is usually 3% to 5% of the contract value. To buy one UK pound contract, you would have to put up about \$4,000 (\$100,000 × 4%). You would also have to keep a "maintenance margin" usually about 75% of the initial margin. In this case, you could never let your account go below \$3,000 (75% of \$4,000). If you cannot make a margin call, your contract is liquidated by the broker.

### B. Maintenance margin

At the end of the day every trader's account is "marked to market". This means that paper profits are added and paper losses are subtracted. For example, one soybean contract is for 5,000 bushels. If the price falls by 10 cents per bushel, the value of the contract falls by 5,000 multiplied by 10 cents or \$500. If a trader has 2 soybean contracts, \$1,000 will be deducted from his margin account. The trader must maintain a margin of \$1.350 for each contract he holds. If after deducting the \$1,000 loss, there is less than \$2,700 (2 contracts multiplied by \$1,350) in his account, he must deposit enough money to bring the account balance back to \$2,700.

## Dialogue—The Margin Call

**Rick:** Rick Lee speaking.

**Brian:** Brian Thorpe from Shanghai International Securities.

**Rick:** Yes, Brian. What can I do for you?

**Brian:** You are long 5 July soybean contracts. The price fell the limit yesterday and it is down sharply again this morning. I am afraid we are going to have to ask you for more margin.

**Rick:** Oh no!!! I just put up another $10,000 last week and now you tell me I need even more!

**Brian:** I'm afraid so.

**Rick:** How much this time?

**Brian:** $12,500 will put you back on side.

**Rick:** I'm not sure I can raise that amount. What other options do I have?

**Brian:** The only other thing you can do is sell out your position.

**Rick:** If I do that, I will take a big loss!

**Brian:** Nevertheless, that might be your best course. No telling how low the price will go before we have a correction. Remember the saying, "Let your profits run, but cut your losses."

**Rick:** What happens if I don't do anything?

**Brian:** The firm will sell out your position at market.

**Rick:** I don't have much choice then, do I?

**Brian:** No, unfortunately not. Trading commodity futures can be a risky business.

**Rick:** How much time do I have?

**Brian:** We'll need your cheque by the close of business today or first thing tomorrow morning latest. The firm will start closing out positions before lunchtime.

**Rick:** Can I get back to you in an hour?

**Brian:** That'll be fine.

Part Ⅲ—Futures and Forwards  期货及远期

## Section E—Long and Short  多头及空头交易

When a trader or investor owns a financial instrument—shares of stock, bonds, commodities, currencies or derivatives-he or she is said to be long that particular asset. If the price goes up, he or she makes money. If it goes down, a loss is incurred. Generally speaking, we buy financial assets—we go long—when we think the price will rise.

Sometimes, however, we feel that the price will fall and we would like to make money from this idea.

In effect what we want to do is sell something that we do not yet own. This is called short selling. We are said to go short the particular currency or commodity, etc..

A wide variety of currencies can be bought and sold for delivery now—spot market—or later—futures market.

The buyer, however, does not care whether we own the financial instrument or not. He or she just wants to receive whatever it is he or she bought—100 ounces of gold, for example, in exchange for paying the purchase price.

If we have sold 100 ounces of gold and we do not own it, we can get around this problem by borrowing the gold from someone else, usually an investment dealer or a bank.

The investment dealer loans us the gold and we deliver it to our buyer in exchange for his cheque. We are now short 100 ounces of gold. Our buyer is long 100 ounces of gold.

We, of course, are hoping that the price of gold will fall. If it does, we buy it back in the market and return it to the investment dealer from which we borrowed it. Our profit is the difference between the price we received for the gold when we sold it short and the price we paid when we bought it back.

The price could rise, however. Our friendly investment dealer does not really care about the rising price of gold. It simply wants the 100 ounces of gold that we borrowed returned to it at some point in the future. This highlights the risk in short selling. We have to return gold, not money, in repaying the loan. If the price of gold doubles, that is the price we have to pay to buy it back. With short selling the potential loss is unlimited because there is no limit to how high the price can go.

---

### Trading Tip

Be careful when selling short. The potential loss is unlimited. At some point we have to buy back the stock, bond, commodity or currency that we borrowed. There is no upper limit to the market price we may have to pay at that time. There are many true stories of very wealthy financiers being forced into bankruptcy because they sold large quantities of shares short and then had to pay astronomical prices to buy them back!

---

## Section F—Foreign Currencies　外汇

When we buy shares of stock, bonds and commodities, the price is measured in terms of a currency. When we buy a currency, however, the price cannot be measured in terms of itself. Instead, it is measured in terms of another currency. For example, the price of the US dollar can be expressed in any of the following ways:

| **Currency** | **Symbol** | **Units required to buy US $ 1.00** |
|---|---|---|
| Chinese yuan | CNY | 8.2767 |
| Canadian dollar | CAD | 1.2183 |
| Euro | EUR | 0.7766 |
| Pounds sterling | GBP | 0.5315 |

**What This Means**

This means that it takes 8.2767 yuan to buy one US dollar.

We can also say that one US dollar is worth 1.21 Canadian dollars.

Foreign currencies can be bought and sold for immediate delivery. This is the spot market and the price is called the spot price. They can also be bought and sold for delivery at some agreed upon time in the future at a price set today. This is the forward market and the price is the forward price.

## Section G—Futures and Forward Contracts—Similarities and Differences
## 期货合同与远期合同的相同与不同之处

Futures and forward contracts are similar in the following ways:

1. Both are derivative securities for future delivery/receipt. The parties agree today on price and quantity for settlement in the future—1 week to 10 years.

2. Both are used to hedge currency risk, interest rate risk or commodity price risk.

And they differ in these ways:

1. Forward contracts are private, customized contracts between a bank and its clients (multi-national corporations, exporters, importers, etc.) depending on the client's needs. There is no secondary market for forward contracts since they are private contractual agreements like most bank loans and unlike bonds.

2. Forward contracts are settled at expiration. Futures contracts are continually settled (mark to market).

3. Profits/losses for a futures contract accumulate on a daily basis unlike a forward contract where profits/losses are realized all at once at contract expiration.

4. Most (90%) of forward contracts are settled with delivery/receipt of the asset. Most futures contracts (99%) are settled with cash, not the commodity, currency or other asset.

5. Futures markets have daily price limits. If the settlement price changes by the daily price limit, trading is stopped until the next day.

### Dialogue—The Traders

**Kim:** That was a wild market this morning, eh?

**John:** I'll say. I imagine there will be more than a few guys crying in their beer tonight. Can you believe soybeans down the limit two days in a row! That crop report from the US Department of Agriculture sure changed things.

**Kim:** You bet it did. It looks like it will be a much better year for the farmers than anyone predicted. The market is way over supplied.

**John:** Long weekend coming up. What have you got planned?

## Derivatives  金融衍生品

**Kim:** I'm going to take the family camping up in the mountains, maybe do a little fishing. I sure could use some relaxing time. How about you?

**John:** I know what you mean. I'm sure ready for a break. My girlfriend's folks have invited us to spend the weekend with them. They have a nice place in the country, a couple of hours drive from here. And her mother is a great cook! I expect to come back a few pounds heavier!

**Kim:** Sounds like a lot of fun. By the way, how do you like your new Buick? It's about time I got rid of my old clunker and I haven't made up my mind yet what I should buy.

**John:** We like it very much. The ride is great, there's lots of room for the kids and the dog and plenty of power for the straightaway. Have you got something in mind?

**Kim:** Well, I really like the new Jaguar, but I just don't know if I'm ready to spring for that much money. It's been a good year and all we should get is nice bonuses, but I guess I'm a little conservative when it comes to my own money.

**John:** They really are beautiful machines. My father-in-law has one. He absolutely loves it!

**Kim:** I took one for a test drive last week. I couldn't believe how well it handled! It's a sports car disguised as a family sedan! I thought I would go back and have another look tonight. Do you want to come along?

**John:** Sure. I'd love to. Are you planning on leaving right from work?

**Kim:** Yes. I drove in this morning instead of taking the train.

**John:** That'll be a lot of fun.

**Kim:** Well, I guess we better get back to the floor or neither one of us will have jobs! I can't very well buy a new car if I'm not working!

**John:** Quite right. Have a good afternoon. See you at 5.

Part III —Futures and Forwards  期货及远期

The traders, and the new Jaguar.

## Section H—Words and Expressions  术语及解释

**Appreciation**  升值

An increase in a currency value relative to another currency in a floating exchange rate system.

**Arbitrage**  套汇

The process of purchasing and selling foreign exchange, stocks, bonds and other commodities in several markets intending to make profit from the difference in price.

**Commodity price risk**  商品价格风险

The risk of unexpected changes in a commodity price, such as the price of oil.

**Convertible currency**  可自由兑换货币

A currency that can be traded for other currencies at will.

**Counterparty risk**  交易对手违约风险

When counter parties are unwilling/unable to fulfill their contractual obligations.

However, the $1.50 that he received for selling the call allows him to participate in the market's rise up.

**Cross rate**  交叉汇率

The exchange rate for one non US dollar currency against another non US dollar currency, e.g. DEM/JPY.

**Currency (foreign exchange) risk**  货币(外汇)风险

The risk of unexpected changes in foreign currency exchange rates.

**Currency cross-hedge**  货币交叉避险

A hedge of currency risk using a currency that is correlated with the currency in which the underlying exposure is denominated.

**Currency of reference**  被报价币

The currency that is being bought or sold. It is most convenient to place the currency of reference in the denominator of a foreign exchange quote.

**Currency option**  货币期权

A contract giving the option holder the right to buy or sell an underlying currency at a specified price and on a specified date. The option writer (seller) holds the obligation to fulfill the other side of the contract.

**Deliverable instrument**　可交割的金融工具

The asset underlying a derivative security. For a currency option, the deliverable instrument is determined by the options exchange and is either spot currency or an equivalent value in futures contracts.

**Devaluation**　汇率的法定贬值

A decrease in a currency value relative to another currency in a fixed exchange rate system. The official lowering of the value of one country's currency in terms of one or more foreign currencies.

**Euro**　欧元

The single currency of the European Economic and Monetary Union (EMU) introduced in January 1999. EMU members are Austria, Belgium, Finland, France, Germany, Ireland, Italy, Luxembourg, Netherlands, Portugal and Spain.

**Eurodollars**　欧洲美元

Dollar-denominated deposits held in a country other than the United States.

**Exchange rate**　汇率

The price of one currency in terms of another, i.e. the number of units of one currency that may be exchanged for one unit of another currency.

**Exchange risk**　兑汇风险

The risk that losses may result from the changes in the relative values of different currencies.

**Exchange traded**　交易所交易

A transaction where a specific instrument is bought or sold on a regulated exchange, e.g. futures.

**Exchange traded contracts**　交易所交易契约

Financial instruments listed on exchanges such as the Chicago Board of Trade.

**External market**　境外市场

A market for financial securities that are placed outside the borders of the country issuing that currency.

**Financial price risk**　金融价格风险

The risk of unexpected changes in a financial price, including currency (foreign exchange) risk, interest rate risk, and commodity price risk.

**Fixed exchange rate system**　固定汇率制度

An exchange rate system in which governments stand ready to buy and sell currency at official exchange rates.

**Fixed forward contract**　定期远期契约

Currency is bought or sold at a given future date.

**Floating rate note（FRN）**　浮息票据

A bond linked to LIBOR.

**Foreign exchange**　外汇

Currency of another country, or a financial instrument that facilitates payment from one currency to another.

**Foreign exchange broker**　外汇经纪人

Brokers serving as matchmakers in the foreign exchange market that do not put their own money at risk.

**Foreign exchange dealer**　外汇经销商

A financial institution making a market in foreign exchange.

**Foreign exchange（currency）risk**　外汇风险

The risk of unexpected changes in foreign currency exchange rates.

**Forward contract**　远期合同

An over-the-counter obligation to buy or sell a financial instrument or to make a payment at some point in the future, the details of which were settled privately between the two counterparties. Forward contracts generally are arranged to have zero mark-to-market value at inception, although they may be off-market. Examples include forward foreign exchange contracts in which one party is obligated to buy foreign exchange from another party at a fixed rate for delivery on a pre-set date. Off-market forward contracts are used often in structured combinations, with the value on the forward contract offsetting the value of the other instrument(s).

A commitment to exchange a specified amount of one currency for a specified amount of another currency on a specified future date.

**Forward discount**　远期贴水

A currency whose nominal value in the forward market is lower than in the spot market (Contrast with forward premium).

**Forward market**  远期市场

A market for forward contracts in which trades are made for future delivery according to an agreed-upon delivery date, exchange rate, and amount.

**Forward parity**  远期平价

When the forward rate is an unbiased predictor of future spot exchange rates.

**Forward premium**  远期升水

A currency whose nominal value in the forward market is higher than in the spot market. (Contrast with forward discount.)

**Freely floating exchange rate system**  自由浮动汇率制

An exchange rate system in which currency values are allowed to fluctuate according to supply and demand forces in the market without direct interference by government authorities.

**Fundamental analysis**  基本分析

A method of predicting exchange rates using the relationships of exchange rates to fundamental economic variables such as GNP growth, money supply, and trade balances.

**Futures contract**  期货合同

A commitment to exchange a specified amount of one currency for a specified amount of another currency at a specified time in the future. Futures contracts are periodically mark-to-market, so that changes in value are settled throughout the life of the contract. Exchange-traded currency futures are mark-to-market on a daily basis.

An exchange-traded obligation to buy or sell a financial instrument or to make a payment at one of the exchange's fixed delivery dates, the details of which are transparent publicly on the trading floor and for which contract settlement takes place through the exchange's clearinghouse.

**Hedge**  套期交易

A transaction that offsets an exposure to fluctuations in financial prices of some other contract or business risk. It may consist of cash instruments or derivatives.

A transaction that reduces or mitigates risk.

A position or operation that offsets an underlying exposure. For example, a forward currency hedge uses a forward currency contract to offset the exposure of an underlying position in a foreign currency. Hedges reduce the total variability of the combined position.

**Hedging**　套期保值

Reducing the risk of a cash position by using the futures instruments to offset the price movement of the cash asset.

**Herstatt risk**　赫思塔特风险

The failure to settle one side of an FX trade by value date. Named after bank where this failure occurred in 1974.

**Index futures**　指数合同

A futures contract that allows investors to buy or sell an index (such as a foreign stock index) in the futures market.

**Index options**　指数期权

A call or put option contract on an index (such as a foreign stock market index).

**Interest rate risk**　利率风险

The risk of unexpected changes in an interest rate.

**International monetary system**　国际货币体系

The global network of governmental and commercial institutions within which currency exchange rates are determined.

**London interbank offer rate (LIBOR)**　伦敦银行同业拆放利率

This is the rate that the most credit-worthy international banks dealing in Euro-dollars charge each other for large loans. The offer rate that a Euromarket bank demands in order to place a deposit at (or, equivalently, make a loan to) another Euromarket bank in London. It is also the benchmark used to price many Capital Market and Derivative transactions.

**Long position**　多头

A position in which a particular asset (such as a spot or forward currency) has been purchased.

**Mark-to-market**　逐日结算制

A process whereby existing positions are revalued on a daily basis. The process by which changes in the value of futures contracts are settled daily.

**Mark to market accounting**　逐日结算会计原则

A method of accounting most suited for financial instruments in which contracts are revalued at regular intervals using prevailing market prices. This is known as taking a "snapshot" of the market.

**Net position** 净持仓量

A currency position after aggregating and canceling all offsetting transactions in each currency, maturity and security.

**Over the counter (OTC)** 柜台买卖

A bilateral transaction between a client and a bank, negotiated privately between the parties. Any transaction that takes place between two counterparties and does not involve an exchange is said to be an over-the-counter transaction.

**Prime rate** 最优惠利率

The prime rate is a loan rate charged by banks to their best or "prime" customers. The rate is determined by general trends in interest rates. As rates decline, the prime rate will also move lower. However, it does not typically move on a day-by-day basis. Prime rate changes are usually led by major money center banks. Normally, the prime rate will move in steps and then remain constant until a major rate change has been made. This usually happens when the central bank makes major changes in monetary policy.

**Purchasing power parity (law of one price)** 购买力平价

The principle that equivalent assets sell for the same price. Purchasing power parity is enforced in the currency markets by financial market arbitrage.

**Settlement risk** 交割风险

The risk of non-payment of an obligation by a counterparty to a transaction, exacerbated by mismatches in payment timings.

**Short** 空头交易

More sales than purchases.

**Short position** 空头

A position in which a particular asset (such as a spot or forward currency) has been sold.

**Short selling** 卖空交易

Selling an asset that you do not own, or taking a short position.

**Sold short** 卖空

Someone who has sold a commodity without previously owning it. (Short sell)

**Sovereign risk** 主权风险

Sovereign risk is the additional risk assumed by investors with funds invested in foreign counties. Sovereign risk includes currency translation losses, default of foreign governments on debts, and appropriation of company assets by foreign governments.

**Speculation** 投机交易

Taking positions in financial instruments without having an underlying exposure that offsets the positions taken.

**Spot** 现货

The price in the cash market for delivery using the standard market convention. In the foreign exchange market, spot is delivered for value two days from the transaction date or for the next day in the case of the Canadian dollar exchanged against the US dollar.

**Spot exchange rate** 即期汇率

Exchange rate today for settlement in two days.

**Spot market** 现货市场

A market in which trades are made for immediate delivery (within two business days for most spot currencies).

**Spot foreign exchange** 现汇

A transaction to exchange one currency for another at a rate agreed today (the Spot rate), for settlement in two business days time.

**Spread** 价差

The difference between buying and selling rates.

The difference in price or yield between two assets that differ by type of financial instrument, maturity, strike or some other factor. A credit spread is the difference in yield between a corporate bond and the corresponding government bond. A yield curve spread is the spread between two government bonds of differing maturity.

**Stock index futures** 股票指数期货

A futures contract on a stock index.

**Structured notes** 结构票据

Fixed income instruments with embedded derivative products.

**Technical analysis**　技术分析

Any method of forecasting future exchange rates based on the history of exchange rates.

**Trading desk（dealing desk）**　交易柜台

The desk at an international bank that trades spot and forward foreign exchange.

**Transaction exposure**　交易风险

Changes in the value of contractual（monetary）cash flows as a result of changes in currency values.

**Trillion**　万亿

One thousand billion（12 zeroes）.

**Underlying**　基础工具

An asset, future, interest rate, FX rate or index upon which a derivative transaction is based.

**Value date**　计息日

Date on which a foreign exchange contract is executed, i.e. seller delivers.

**Volatility**　波幅

The degree to which the market price of a financial instrument moves up and down during a short period of time.

**Yard**　十亿

One thousand million（billion）.

**Derivatives** 金融衍生品

# Exercises
练习

## Listening Comprehension Exercises 听力综合练习

### A. Dialogue—What's New?

Have three classmates read out loud the dialogue among Ken, Brian and Sandra (To get maximum benefit from the exercise you should keep your own book closed). Listen carefully and answer the following questions:

1. What business is Ken in?
2. What does Ken want help with?
3. What did Brian suggest?
4. Who is Sandra?
5. What did Ken, Brian and Sandra agree to do?

### B. Evening News Report

With your book closed, have someone read aloud the Evening News Report. Answer the following questions:

1. What unexpected event occurred in Brazil?
2. What effect will it have on the supply of coffee?
3. Who is Dr. Carter?
4. What does he think will happen?
5. What is the name of the Brazilian currency?
6. If you were purchasing manager for Starbucks, what would the effect of this development be on your company's business? How could you protect against this risk?

### C. Dialogue—Hedging

With your book closed, have two classmates read the dialogue out loud. Answer the following questions:

1. What is Steve's position in the company?
2. What business is Steve's company in?
3. What are other examples of businesses where the product of one is the raw material of the other and the price risk for both can be eliminated by hedging?

**D. Dialogue—The Margin Call**

1. Why did Brian call Rick?
2. What is the business relationship between Brian and Rick?
3. What is the problem Rick is facing and why?
4. What is the process that is done every day?
5. What options does Rick have?
6. What can Brian's firm do?
7. What would you do if you were Rick?
8. What could Rick do if the price of the soybeans had gone up instead of down?

## Speaking Exercises  对话练习

**A. Dialogue—Hedging**

With a partner practice reading the dialogue out loud. Work hard at developing a smooth style and then complete the following exercises:

1. One partner explains to the other what is meant by commodity price risk.
2. The other partner explains to the first what is meant by foreign exchange risk.
3. Jointly develop a strategy that will protect Steve's business from exposure to commodity and exchange rate risk.

Tip: You will need to hedge both the commodity and the currency.

4. What are some other businesses that would likely face problems similar to those facing Steve?

**B. Selling Short**

Choose a partner. You are an investment banker. One of your good clients has called you. He wants to sell gold short. He has never sold anything short before. What do you say to him?

Tip: You should explain the risks to him and make sure that short selling matches his risk profile—it is a suitable strategy given his particular income, net worth and family circumstances.

**C. Evening News Report**

Discuss with a partner about Dr. Carter's opinion on the effect of the frost on the value of the Brazilian real and the market price of coffee.

**D. Derivatives**

1. What types of derivatives can make international trade less risky? Discuss with a partner how these particular derivatives can make international trading less risky.

2. Explain to a partner how derivatives differ from stocks and bonds.

3. Have your partner explain to you how derivatives are the same as stocks and bonds.

**E. Futures, forwards and options**

1. Explain to a partner the difference between forwards and options. Which one is the most risky and why?

2. Explain to a prospective client what the risk of selling a call is.

3. You entered into a futures contract to buy corn as a speculator (you are not a farmer and you are not managing a business that uses corn as a raw material). Explain to your wife how you will avoid having a truck loaded with 5,000 bushels of corn suddenly appear in your driveway.

4. Explain to a partner the main characteristics of forwards.

5. Have your partner explain to you the main characteristics of futures.

6. Discuss with your partner how futures and forwards are different. What businesses would use forwards and why? Who would buy, sell and trade futures and why? Who would use both forwards and futures?

## Skill-building Exercises—Writing and Speaking 说写练习

Look at the picture below.

1. What are the two people in the picture looking at?

2. Who do you think he is talking to on his cell phone?

3. Why do you think the two people in the picture are so happy?

4. Write a dialogue of the cell phone conversation.

5. Write a dialogue between the man and the woman in picture after the cell phone call has ended.

6. Practice reading your dialogue with a partner.

7. Exchange your dialogue with your classmates.

## Skill-building Exercises—Vocabulary 词汇练习

**A. Complete the following sentences.**

1. An investment contract based on an underlying investment is called a _____.

2. The cost associated with a derivative contract; the combination of intrinsic value and time value is the _____.

3. How easy it is to buy or sell a financial instrument at a particular point in time without significantly and adversely affecting its price is referred to as _____.

4. A _____ option conveys the right but not the obligation to buy.

5. A _____ option conveys the right but not the obligation to sell.

6. _____ are responsible for providing liquidity in options.

7. An order to buy or sell options at the best available price is _____ order.

8. An order to buy or sell options at a certain price is a _____ order.

Answers: 1. (derivative) 2. (premium) 3. (marketability) 4. (call) 5. (put) 6. (market makers) 7. (market) 8. (limit)

Derivatives 金融衍生品

**B. Match the definitions below with the words in the list that follows:**

1. The price of one currency in terms of another;. the number of units of one currency that may be exchanged for one unit of another currency. _____

2. Selling an asset that you do not own, with the expectation of a decline in its price. _____

3. A position in which a particular asset (shares, currency, commodities) has been purchased. _____

4. A transaction intending to reduce risk of loss from price fluctuations. _____

5. A product used for commerce that is traded on an organized exchange. _____

6. An over-the-counter obligation to buy or sell a financial instrument or to make a payment at some point in the future, the details of which were settled privately between the two counterparties. _____

7. A process whereby existing positions are revalued on a daily basis. A method of accounting in which contracts are revalued at regular intervals using prevailing market prices; also known as taking a snapshot of the market. _____

8. A market in which trades are made for immediate delivery. _____

9. Exchange-traded contracts that give the holder the right to buy or sell a certain commodity, currency or financial instrument at a specified price at a specified period of time. _____

10. A financial contract giving the owner the right but not the obligation to buy a pre-set amount of the underlying financial instrument (shares, currency, commodities) at a pre-set price with a pre-set maturity date. Investors buy these when they think the price of the underlying is going up. _____

11. An option with an exercise price that is equal to the current value of the underlying asset. _____

12. The last date on which an option can be exercised. _____

13. The amount by which the premium of an option exceeds the intrinsic value. _____

14. The conversion of an option into the underlying. _____

15. A financial contract giving the owner the right but not the obligation to sell a pre-set amount of the underlying financial instrument at a pre-set price with a pre-set maturity

date. _____

16. The buyer/owner of an option. _____

17. The amount by which the price of a call option exceeds the price at which it may be exercised. _____

18. An asset, future, interest rate, FX rate or index upon which a derivative transaction is based. _____

19. The Seller of an option. _____

20. The price at which the option holder has the right to buy/sell the underlying instrument. _____

| | | |
|---|---|---|
| 1. Intrinsic value | 13. Premium | 24. Underlying |
| 2. Exercise | 14. Expiration date | 25. Spot |
| 3. Writer | 15. Call option | 26. Mark-to-market |
| 4. At-the-money | 16. Long | 27. Exchange rate |
| 5. Mark-to-market | 17. Put option | 28. Spot market |
| 6. Exchange rate | 18. Short selling | 29. Forward contract |
| 7. Spot market | 19. Exercise price (Strike price) | 30. Commodity |
| 8. Forward contract | | 31. Hedge |
| 9. Intrinsic value | 20. Futures | 32. Long |
| 10. Time value | 21. Underlying | 33. Short selling |
| 11. Commodity | 22. Holder | 34. Futures |
| 12. Hedge | 23. Derivative | 35. Derivative |

## Test Your Knowledge  知识测试

1. What are some risks you would face as a homeowner that insurance could protect you against?

2. What is the breakeven point for an option?

3. A call option gives its owner _____
   a. ownership in the underlying corporation.
   b. ownership in the underlying corporation plus voting rights.
   c. a right to buy shares of the underlying stock.
   d. an obligation to buy shares of the underlying stocks.

4. The writer of a call option _____
   a. Has the right to buy shares of the underlying stock.
   b. has the obligation to buy shares.
   c. has the right to sell the shares.
   d. has the obligation to sell the shares.

5. What happens to the premium when an option is exercised. Is it returned to the buyer or does the writer (seller) keep it?

6. What do we mean when we say that a call option is in the money?

7. A call option's intrinsic value is _____
   a. the amount by which the option is currently out of the money.
   b. the amount by which the option is currently in the money.
   c. equal only to options current market value.
   d. equal only to the amount of unrealized profit over the options initial purchase or sale.

8. A put option's time value is _____
   a. the amount by which the options strike price is either greater or less than the current underlying stock price.
   b. always the same as the total premium paid for or received from the option in the market place.
   c. inversely proportionating to the amount of time until the option's expiration.
   d. any premium in excess of the option's intrinsic value.

9. You have purchased June 60 call for 2.75. If you exercise this contract, what is you net purchase price per share.

10. Why would an investor buy a put?

11. A call option is in-the-money if _____
    a. its strike price is the same as the current market price of the underlying security.
    b. the expiry date has not yet been reached.
    c. its strike price is below the current market price of the underlying security.
    d. its strike price is above the current market price of the underlying security.

12. A put option is in-the-money if _____
    a. its strike price is below the current market price of the underlying security.
    b. its strike price is above the current market price of the underlying security.
    c. its strike price is the same as the current market price of the underlying security.

d. the expiry date has not yet been reached.

13. You have just finished planting a large field of wheat. The price of wheat is high at the moment. You would like to be sure about that price in the fall when you harvest your crop so you decide to sell your production forward. You enter into a 2 forward contracts to deliver wheat in September. Each contract is for 5,000 bushels. The price you will quote when you deliver the wheat is US $ 3.65 per bushel. You have eliminated your commodity price risk. If your farm is in China, what other risks do you run?

    Tip: There are two separate and distinct risks. You can protect yourself against one of them. There is not much you can do about the other one.

14. What are examples of importers who face commodity price risk? What types of businesses might encounter the reverse problem?

15. What factors could cause the price of wheat to rise on world markets? What factors could cause it to fall?

16. You are a farmer. Your main crop is soybeans. It is spring and you want to make sure you can make a reasonable profit. What can you do to reduce your risk?

17. What are some risks businesses face over which they generally have no control?

18. What do we mean when we say that derivatives are contracts?

19. What could cause the price of a derivative to rise?

20. What are the two uses of derivatives?

21. Look at the picture below and answer the questions that follow.

a. What kind of firm do you think the man in the picture works for?
b. What do you think his position is or what do you think he does at the firm?
c. Why do you think he appears so upset, concerned, sad?
d. What should he do now?

**Answers:** 3. c  4. b  7. b  8. d  11. c  12. b

# Case Study—The Impacts of Subprime Mortgage Crisis
# 案例分析——次贷危机的影响

On March 13, 2007, the New York Stock Exchange delisted New Century Financial Corporation which was the second-Lbiggest subprime mortgage lender in the Usited States. Later the company's bankruptcy marked the formal outbreak of the subprime Mortgage Crisis. On March 16, 2008, JP Morgan Chase announced the acquisition of the verge of Bear Stearns-Lthe fifth – largest U. S. investment bank. The subprime mortgage crisis became the global financial crisis. Government pumped in cash, but the crisis deepened and broadened, crippling industries and crushing hopes with a invisible force since the Great Depression of the 1930s.

The subprime mortgage crisis is an ongoing real estate and financial crisis triggered by a dramatic rise in mortgage delinquencies and foreclosures in the United States, with major adverse consequences for banks and financial markets around the globe. The crisis, which has its roots in the closing years of the 20th century, became apparent in 2007 and has exposed pervasive weaknesses in financial industry regulation and the global financial system.

Approximately 80% of U. S. mortgages issued in recent years to subprime borrowers were adjustable-Lrate mortgages. After U. S. house prices peaked in mid-L2006 and began their steep decline thereafter, refinancing became more difficult. As adjustable-Lrate mortgages began to reset at higher rates, mortgage delinquencies soared. Securities backed with subprime mortgages, widely held by financial firms, lost most of theirvalue. The result has been a large decline in the capital of many banks and U. S. government sponsored enterprises, tightening credit around the world.

The global crisis has posed several challenges to East Asia. First, Japan and East Asia need to make greater effort to develop a more mature internal market for final goods and services. Intra-Lregional trade already accounts for 56% and this ratio is comparable to that of the European Union(62%). Nevertheless, the extent of trade integration is more self complete in the European Union that in East Asia in the sense that Europe is able to offer internal markets for both intermediate goods and final ones. By contrast, East Asia has internal markets mainly for intermediate goods, given the growing production and trade networks fostered through regional FDI activities that began in the 1980s. However, East Asia continues to depend heavily on the United States and Europe as markets for their final products. The sluggish increase in domestic demand in Japan, as well as the high levels of savings relative to investments in East Asia, has contributed to this phenomenon. The further impact of US subprime mortgage crisis on China's economy and monetary policy cannot be underestimated, central bank Lyovernor Zhou Xiaochuan warned on $6^{th}$, March, 2008.

subprime mortgage crisis 次贷危机
mortgage 抵押
global financial crisis 全球金融

Derivatives 金融衍生品

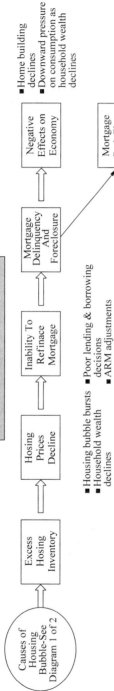

# Sample Examination Questions 模拟试题

**Vocabulary**

1. Use the following words or phrases in a sentence.

    a. premium

    b. put

    c. exercise price

    d. intrinsic value

    e. call

2. Define the following words and phrases and provide a Chinese translation.

    a. exchange traded

    b. underlying

    c. option

    d. forward

    e. OTC

    f. binding

    g. covered call

    h. time decay

    i. at the money

    j. speculator

**Understanding**

1. What kinds of risks can derivatives help protect against?
2. What are derivatives?
3. Explain how a derivative differs from a common share or bar of gold.
4. How are forwards and futures different? How are they the same?
5. What is the difference between exercise price and strike price?

6. What is the advantage of a straddle? Are there any disadvantages and if so, what are they?

7. You have bought a put option. You decide not to hold it any longer. How can you get your money out?

8. What determines the price of options?

9. In what circumstances does the holder of a put option make money?

10. Why might Starbucks enter into a futures contract and what would it likely cover?

11. Explain margin call and what kinds of things can happen if a trader receives one.

12. What is the difference between long and short?

13. Why might a trader go short a particular security or commodity?

# Insurance
# 保 险

The time to buy insurance is when you don't need it.

## Introduction 导语

Insurance is designed to protect you from loss, grow your assets or help you save money for the future. It is a critical part of ensuring your financial well-being.

Insurance 保险

# The Shanghai Times

Shanghai, China     March 25, 2....     Evening edition

Tomorrow's weather
Mostly sunny
High 14°C
Low 8°C
Winds light

## Rush hour pile up kills 3, injures 20
### Major arteries tied up for hours

**Central bank ups key interest rate to 6%**

Beijing-A tragic accident during rush hour this morning left three people dead and hospitalized at least 20 others, many with life threatening injuries. An intercity bus, a family van and several cars were involved. Traffic was at a standstill for several hours as rescue crews worked feverishly to free victims trapped inside crushed vehicles. Authorities blamed the accident on poor weather conditions. A heavy rain was falling at the time, the roadway was very slippery and visibility was reduced to just a few meters. Beijing; In a surprise move yesterday, the Governor of the central bank announced that effective immediately, the rate it charges commercial banks will rise from 5½% to 6%.

The Governor stated that the unexpectedly large rise was necessary to curb what he called excessive speculation in certain markets that was creating unacceptable inflationary pressures.

### Commercial banks' response immediate

China's big four state banks responded quickly by raising the rates they charge their customers on mortgage loans for apartments and houses.

The move is designed to raise home buyers' borrowing costs in order to cool the country's hot property market.

Banks also raised the down payment, borrowers must provide to 30% of the purchase price from 20% and have tightened income restrictions for loan qualification.

In a recent forum, the Central bank governor encouraged commercial banks to adopt market oriented interest rates and base the rate they charge customers on the perceived risk.

Insurance 保险

## Dialogue—Calling Home (Cell Phone Conversation)

**Husband:** Maybe you saw the report on TV-there was a very serious accident this morning and I was involved.

**Wife:** Are you all right? What happened?

**Husband:** I am really shaken up, a few scrapes and bruises, but nothing really serious. Unfortunately, many other people were not so lucky.

**Wife:** Thank goodness! How did it happen?

**Husband:** The road was really slippery and it was raining so hard that we could hardly see.

**Wife:** What about our van? Is it badly damaged? Can it be fixed?

**Husband:** I am sorry to say that it has been totally destroyed. It caught fire after I got to safety and I am afraid that a burned out shell is all that remains.

**Wife:** That is terrible! What are we going to do about the van? Can we afford to buy a new one? How will you get to work?

**Husband:** You may remember that I met with our insurance agent last month. He reviewed our coverage and suggested that we make some changes to our policy.

**Wife:** What did he recommend?

**Husband:** He suggested that we add a rider that would pay the cost of renting a replacement vehicle for us to use if something happened to our van-stolen, damaged in an accident. The insurance company would cover us for two weeks to give us time to have our van repaired or to buy a new one.

**Wife:** And did you take his recommendation?

**Husband:** Yes, I certainly did. It did not increase our premium very much and I thought it made sense.

**Wife:** That is good news. At least get to work, but how can we buy a new van? We borrowed all that money from the bank. We still have to pay it back and now we do not even have a van!

**Husband:** That is why we have insurance. We pay a small amount of money called the deductible and the insurance company pays us an amount of money equal to the market value of the vehicle. The market value of our van is higher than the amount we owe the bank, we will have the money to repay the bank loan and have enough left over for a down payment on a nice new one. Start thinking about what kind you might like!

**Wife:** That is really incredible. I had no idea that insurance could be so helpful to us. It always seemed like we were paying out money every month and not getting anything in return. Now I see what a wonderful product insurance is. If we did not have it, we would be in terrible state right now!

## Section A—What Insurance Is and Why We Need It? 什么是保险？为什么需要保险？

On any given day, a few people will suffer a catastrophic loss. Somebody's house will burn down. A family's bread winner will die. A motorist will go through a stop sign and seriously injure a pedestrian.

For most of us, the occurrence of any one of these events is likely to mean financial disaster for us and our family.

- If our house burns down, where would we ever find the money to rebuild and to replace our belongings?

- If the family bread winner is no longer around, how will the remaining family

# Insurance  保险

members get the money they need to buy food, clothing and make rent or mortgage payments?

- If we injure someone, we are responsible. The person may sue us and the court may award damages against us that are so high that it takes most of our income for the rest of our lives to make the payments?

> **Definition**
>
> Risk:
> The possibility that some unexpected event will occur that will cause us to suffer a financial loss.

Clearly these risks are too great for most of us to take. This is where insurance comes in.

## Section B—How Insurance Works?  保险的作用

**Insurance spreads the risk of financial loss among a great many people.**

Each person pays a small monthly fee called a premium to an insurance company to protect against financial loss should a specific incident occur. In return, the insurance company promises to pay a specific amount of money to him or her should that specific event occur.

### A. Many people share the risk

The insurance company collects the small amounts of money from many people and adds them together to create a large pool of funds. This pool of money is what the insurance company uses to make the very large payments to the people who suffer catastrophic losses. The risk of loss is spread over a large number of people.

### B. Losses do not happen all at once

There is another factor that is important. Events that are covered by insurance do not all happen on the first day of the year. They are spread out more or less evenly over the whole year. This means that the insurance company collects the money from the many before it has to pay it out to the few.

> **Important Note**
>
> Insurance companies are one of the most important suppliers (sellers) of money in the financial marketplace.

Insurance companies invest this pool of money in

the money and capital markets. They make mortgage loans and buy bonds, stocks and money market instruments. The interest, dividends and capital gains that they earn on these investments are added to the pool of money from the premiums.

This means that there is more money available to pay the few than just what was collected from the many. Therefore, the premiums the many pay are lower than they would otherwise be. Investment income of insurance companies means lower premium payments by people buying insurance.

## Section C—The Fundamentals？ 基础知识

Insurance is a formal, legally binding contract between the insurance company and the individual (or organization) buying the insurance. This contract is called a policy and the purchaser of the insurance is called a policyholder, also called the owner of the insurance policy.

The owner is usually the insured person, but it may also be a relative of the insured, a partnership or a corporation. All rights, benefits and privileges under insurance policies are controlled by their owners. Ownership may be assigned or transferred by the owner to someone else.

### Definitions

- **Insurance**: A formal arrangement for reducing risk by transferring the risks of many individuals, companies, etc. to a single insurer. In exchange for payments from the policyholder (called premiums), the insurer agrees to pay the policy holder a sum of money upon the occurrence of a specific event.
- **Insured**: The person, group or property for which an insurance policy is issued.
- **Coverage**: Another word for insurance. Insurers use the term coverage to mean either the currency amounts of insurance purchased (¥2,000,000 of liability coverage) or the type of loss covered (coverage for theft).
- **Policy**: The printed document issued to the policyholder by the company stating the terms of the insurance contract.

## Insurance 保险

> - **Face Value**: The amount of the insurance policy coverage in force on a given policy. In a life insurance policy, it is called the death benefit.
> - **Premium**: The amount of money charged by the insurer to provide the insurance coverage.
> - **Beneficiary**: person (or organization) to whom insurance proceeds are to be paid in the event of the insured's death.
> - **Loss payee**: person (or organization) to whom insurance proceeds are to be paid in the event of loss or damage to property.
> - **Insurable interest**: an economic interest in the preservation from loss, destruction or financial impairment of whatever is being insured.

### A. Types of insurance

There are many forms of insurance. These are the main ones:

- Life insurance

   Money paid in the event of the death of the insured.

- Health insurance

   Money paid for doctors, nurses, medications, hospital care in case the insured becomes sick or injured.

- Accident insurance

   Money paid in the event the insured loses one or more body parts or is killed in an accident.

- Property insurance

   Money paid in the event that property is lost, damaged or stolen.

- Liability insurance

   Money paid in the event that the insured cause damage to someone else's person or property.

When an event occurs that is covered by an insurance policy (house fire for example), the insurance company pays the amount specified in the policy for the loss related to that type of event.

The person (or organization) to whom the insurance proceeds are to be paid in the event of a loss is called the "beneficiary" in the case of life insurance and the "loss payee" in the case of property insurance.

**B. Insurable interest**

One of the most important points to remember is that the client must have an insurable interest. Otherwise a contract of insurance will not be issued. This means that the person (or organization) to whom the insurance proceeds are to be paid if and when the specific event occurs must suffer a financial loss in proportion to the amount of insurance.

---

**Insurable Interest**

We may be very distraught if a really close friend should die. However, if we do not depend on that person for financial support, we have no insurable interest in his or her life. Therefore an insurer would not issue a policy of insurance on that person's life naming us as the beneficiary.

---

Generally, an insurable interest must be demonstrated when a policy is issued and in the case of property insurance, must exist at the time of a loss. Once a life insurance policy has been issued, the insurer must pay the policy benefit, whether or not an insurable interest continues to exist.

---

**Example**

A wife would have an insurable interest in her husband's life. If he were to die, she would suffer financially. If the couple were to divorce and no alimony payments were required to be made by the husband, the wife would no longer have an "insurable interest" in her former husband's life. However, if he should die before he changed the beneficiary (to his new wife, for example), his former wife would be entitled to collect the insurance proceeds.

---

**C. What a typical insurance policy contains**

An insurance policy sets out in great detail, the terms and conditions of the contract including

**Insurance** 保险

- The amount of each premium payment to be made by the policyholder.
- When and how often premium payments are to be made.
- The risks covered-what events the insurance will pay for.
- How much the insurance company will pay in respect of each occurrence of an event that is covered by the policy.
- What the policyholder must do (or not do) in order to keep the insurance in force.

While we generally think of buying insurance as buying protection against financial loss, insurance can also play important roles in saving for the future and for estate planning (organizing your affairs to leave the most possible money to the people you most want to leave it to).

**D. The event has occurred. Now what happens?**

**Filing a claim**

We (policyholder or beneficiary) notify our insurance company and tell its representative that

a) an event that is covered by our insurance policy has occurred and

b) we have suffered a financial loss.

---

### Insurance Tip

The insurance company is only required to pay the amount of money provided for in the policy. If the actual loss exceeds this amount, the excess will not be covered by insurance and the policyholder will lose. Make sure the amount of insurance you buy is high enough to avoid any unpleasant surprises!

---

The company's representative, called a claims adjuster, will ask us some details about the event and the amount of the loss. Most likely we will be asked to fill out a claim form which will provide the insurance company with the details it requires and by which we swear that the information is true and correct in all respects.

Depending on the nature of the event, the insurance company may send a representative to visit us to confirm the amount of our loss and settle on the amount we will be paid. In most cases we will be asked to provide documents to support our claim such as police reports, death certificates, medical reports, original receipts.

Once the claims adjuster is satisfied that the event actually did occur and we have settled with him or her on the amount of the loss, we can expect to receive a cheque for the portion covered by the insurance company, usually within a few days.

---

**Claim Form**

**Policyholder information**
　　Name of insured _____
　　Address of insured _____
　　Phone numbers  Home _____  Work _____  Cellular _____

**Loss information**
　　Date the loss occurred _____
　　Police Department and report number _____
　　Fire Department and report number _____
　　Brief description of the loss _____
　　Location of the loss _____
　　Description of injuries _____

**Other parties involved**
　　Name _____
　　Address _____
　　Phone numbers _____
　　Personal ID number _____
　　Insurer _____

---

　　This is a typical claim form showing the type of information you would be expected to provide to the insurance company's claims adjuster—the person who will be reviewing your information and making a decision on whether or not to accept your claim—to pay you the money you ask to cover your loss.

## Insurance 保险

### Dialogue—Filing a Claim

**Operator**: Shanghai Property and Casualty Company. How may I direct your call?
**David**: Claims Department, please.
**Operator**: Thank you. Transferring your call now.
**Roger**: Claims Department, Roger speaking.
**David**: Good morning, Roger. My name is David Hewitt. Unfortunately I was involved in a serious accident yesterday and my van was totally destroyed. I would like to file a claim, please.
**Roger**: Certainly. May I have your policy number please?
**David**: Yes. I have my policy here in front of me. The number is AD 4389-0137.
**Roger**: Please give me a moment to pull it up on the screen. Yes, here it is. The vehicle is a 2002 Toyota. Please tell me what happened.
**David**: I was on my way to work yesterday morning when a car in front of me started skidding. The driver lost control and the car veered into the next lane right in front of a big bus. The bus driver slammed on his brakes. I think the back end of the bus swung around and suddenly there were cars flying everywhere. The next thing I remember is somebody pulling me out of my van. Moments later the van caught fire.

**Roger:** Was anyone else in the van with you?

**David:** No. I was alone.

**Roger:** Did you go to the hospital?

**David:** No. I got some scrapes and bruises that were treated at the scene. The seat belt and air bag did their jobs.

**Roger:** I am glad to hear that. Nevertheless, we would like to have you thoroughly checked out by a doctor just to make sure there are no hidden injuries. Please make an appointment with a doctor of your choice for a full physical examination. Have the doctor send us a full report along with the bill.

**David:** Thank you very much. I will take care of that right away.

**Roger:** Where is the van now?

**David:** I am not sure. The police had it towed away somewhere.

**Roger:** Can you please find out and let me know. Also I will need a copy of the police report. Can you please make arrangements to get a copy to me as soon as possible?

**David:** Yes, of course. Is there anything else?

**Roger:** No, that is all the information that I need for now. We will send someone around to look at the van. Once I have his appraisal and the report from the doctor and the police confirming the facts, we will have a cheque in your hands within 24 hours. Your claim number is H04893. Please use it in any correspondence with us.

**David:** Thank you very much for your efficient service.

**Roger:** You are most welcome. We are here to help.

---

### Insurance Tip

Keep receipts and serial numbers for important purchases (TV, digital camera, household appliances) in a safe place so you can easily prove your loss should the need ever arise. Pictures are also very helpful.

Insurance 保险

The claims department of an insurance company can be a busy place.

## Section D—Words and Expressions  术语及解释

**Agent**  保险代理人

An individual who sells insurance and who provides ongoing services such as advice and guidance about insurance matters to policyholders.

**At risk**  担风险

Exposed to the possibility of loss.

**Auto insurance**  汽车保险

Auto insurance pays for the expenses incurred for repairing or replacing the policyholder's vehicle if it is in an accident, damaged by vandals or stolen. It also protects the owner from financial loss (liability) if the vehicle is involved in an accident and someone else's property is damaged or another people are killed or injured.

**Beneficiary**  受益人

An individual, company, organization, etc. entitled to receive benefits under a life insurance policy.

**Benefit**  受益

A payment or entitlement under an insurance policy.

**Cancellation**  注销

Termination of an insurance policy by an insured or an insurance company before its expiration date.

**Carrier**  保险公司

The company that issues and assumes the risk of an insurance policy.

**Casualty insurance**  意外事故保险

Insurance coverage for loss or liability arising from a sudden, unexpected event such as an accident.

**Casualty loss**  意外损失

Financial loss or loss of property arising from a sudden, unexpected event such as an accident.

**Claim**  索赔

Notification to an insurance company requesting an amount of payment due under the terms of the policy.

## Insurance 保险

**Claims adjuster** 理赔清算人
Insurance company employee who evaluates claims by policyholders and determines the amount that the insurance company will pay.

**Coverage** 保险范围及总额
Another word for insurance.

**Declarations** 声明事项
Section of an insurance policy that shows who is insured, what property is covered, when and where coverage is effective and how much coverage applies.

**Endorsement** 批单
An attachment to an insurance policy which adds specified events and contingencies to those contained in the main body of the policy. Also called a rider.

**Exclusion** 除外事项
Property, perils, people or situations that are not covered by the insurance policy.

**Face amount** 投保金额
The amount of insurance provided by the terms of an insurance contract, usually found on the first page of the policy. In a life insurance policy, the death benefit.

**Health insurance** 健康保险
Insurance against loss by illness or bodily injury. Health insurance provides coverage for medicine, visits to the doctor or emergency room, hospital stays and other medical expenses. Policies differ in what they cover, the size of the deductible and/or co-payment, limits of coverage and the options for treatment available to the policy holder.

**Insurable interest** 可保权益
The beneficiary who would suffer loss if the event insured against occurs; without an insurable interest, an insurance company will not issue a policy.

**Insurance** 保险
A promise of compensation for specific potential future losses in exchange for a periodic payment. Insurance is designed to protect the financial well-being of an individual, company or other entity in the case of unexpected loss. Some forms of insurance are required by law, while others are optional. Agreeing to the terms of an insurance policy creates a contract between the insured and the insurer. In exchange for payments from the insured (called premiums), the insurer agrees to pay the policyholder a sum of money upon the occurrence of a specific event. In most cases, the policyholder pays part of the loss (called the deductible), and the insurer pays the rest. Examples include car

insurance, health insurance, disability insurance, life insurance, and business insurance.

**Insurance contract**　承保范围

The application, the policy and any other documents attached to the policy, including any amending agreements that may be issued, constituting the entire contract.

**Liability insurance**　责任险

Insurance coverage to protect against claims that one's negligence or inappropriate action resulted in bodily injury or property damage.

**Life Insurance**　人寿险

Insurance to be paid to one or more beneficiaries when the insured dies.

**Limit of Liability**　责任限制

The maximum amount the insurer will pay for a particular loss.

**Loss Payee**　留置权人

Party besides the insured (such as a lending institution) that has an insurable interest in the property insured. Also called a lienholder.

**Peril**　危险事故

Something that endangers people or property or involves risk.

**Policy**　保险单

A contract of insurance, describing the term, coverage, premiums and deductibles.

**Policyholder**　保单持有人

The person who owns an insurance policy. This is usually the insured person, but it may also be a relative of the insured, a partnership or a corporation.

**Premium**　保险费

The periodic payment made on an insurance policy.

**Property Damage**　财产损毁

Physical injury to, destruction of or loss of use of property.

**Property insurance**　财产保险

Insurance that pays for loss or damage to property.

**Provisions**　保险条款

Statements contained in an insurance policy which explain the benefits, conditions and other features of the insurance contract.

**Rider**　批单

An attachment to an insurance policy which adds specified events and contingencies to those contained in the main body of the policy. Also called an endorsement.

**Risk**　风险

The quantifiable likelihood of loss.

**Term**　保期　保险期限

Period for which the policy runs. In life insurance, this is to the end of the term period for term insurance.

# Part II  The Insurance Market  保险市场

*The insurance industry is comprised of various types of organizations ranging from relatively small regional companies to giant international financial powerhouses.*

## Section A—Who Supplies Insurance?  谁提供保险?

Most insurance is provided by corporations. They may privately-held, part of large, broadly-based, fully diversified financial services organization or publicly traded on national stock exchanges. Some are owned by policyholders themselves. Others are owned by government. In recent years, many commercial banks have set up their own insurance companies in order to participate in this attractive and growing market.

## Section B—Who Buys Insurance?  谁购买保险?

Individuals, families, businesses, organizations and governments all buy insurance.

## Section C—Where Do We Buy Insurance?  何处购买保险?

1. Directly with an insurance company
   a) At bank or insurance company offices.
   b) From home-based insurance company employees working either on a salary or commission.
   c) Through the Internet.

2. Indirectly through an Intermediary
    a) Insurance brokers-independent insurance specialists who are not tied to any company; they will shop the market looking for the best deal for their clients.
    b) Insurance agents-independent insurance specialists who represent one insurance company.

---

### Definitions

**Insurance agent:**
Individual who is licensed to sell insurance for one or more specific insurance companies.

**Independent broker:**
An independent agent who represents the buyer, rather than the insurance company, and tries to find the buyer the best policy by comparison shopping.

---

## Section D—What Do We Pay for Insurance? 保险的成本(保费)

### The Premium:

The premium is the amount the insurance company charges the insured for assuming the risk of loss. The insurance company calculates the premium by determining the likelihood of that a particular loss will occur and then applying that probability to the amount to be paid out if the event triggering the loss does occur.

Insurance companies have had many years experience with very large numbers of people of all ages. Analysis of this information has allowed insurers to predict with great accuracy how many events of a certain type will occur in a year-for example, how many auto accidents will occur this year, where someone is badly injured, how many 47-year old male smokers will die this year.

The people who make a business studying this data are called actuaries and the statistical tables they create and use are called actuarial tables.

Insurance 保险

| SAMPLE MORTALITY TABLE | | | | |
|---|---|---|---|---|
| | Male | | Female | |
| Exact age | Death probability | Life expectancy | Death probability | Life expectancy |
| 25 | 0.001331 | 50.4 | 0.000492 | 55.3 |
| 26 | 0.001291 | 49.5 | 0.000504 | 54.3 |
| 27 | 0.001269 | 48.5 | 0.000523 | 53.4 |
| 28 | 0.001275 | 47.6 | 0.000549 | 52.4 |
| 29 | 0.001306 | 46.7 | 0.000584 | 51.4 |
| 30 | 0.001346 | 45.7 | 0.000624 | 50.4 |
| 31 | 0.001391 | 44.8 | 0.000671 | 49.5 |
| 32 | 0.001455 | 43.8 | 0.000724 | 48.5 |
| 33 | 0.001538 | 42.9 | 0.000788 | 47.5 |
| 34 | 0.001641 | 42.0 | 0.000862 | 46.6 |
| 35 | 0.001761 | 41.0 | 0.000943 | 45.6 |
| 36 | 0.001895 | 40.1 | 0.001031 | 44.7 |
| 37 | 0.002044 | 39.2 | 0.001127 | 43.7 |

Insurers use tables like these to calculate the probability that a particular event will occur during a particular year.

For example, a 30-year-old-man can expect to live for another 45.7 years. Of all the 30-year-old men alive today, some will live more than 45.7 years, some will live less than 45.7 years, but on average they will live 45.7 years.

The table also tells us how many people of a certain age can be expected to die during the year. If you are a 33-year-old woman, the probability that you will die during the year is 0.000788. This means that out of 1,000,000 33-year-old women alive today, 788 will die during the year.

## Section E—How Do We Buy Insurance? 如何购买保险

**A. The main parts to an insurance transaction—there are three:**

- The risk—What kind of event or events are to be covered? In other words, in what circumstances will the insurer make a payment to the insured?
- The insured—Who is being covered? In other words, who is being protected from suffering a financial loss should a specific event occur?

- The insurer—Who is providing the coverage? In other words, who is assuming the risk and making the payment if the specified event should occur?

**B. How does the process begin?**

For most of us, buying insurance comes about in one of two ways:

**Case 1-The initiative comes from the prospective buyer:**

a) We recognize that we run the risk of suffering a very damaging financial loss if a certain event should occur—we are involved in a car accident for example.

The three parts to an insurance transaction: risk, insurer and insured.

b) We make a decision to lay off, transfer this risk to someone else—an insurer.

c) We select a company or individual that we want to do business with. We describe what risk we want protection against and how much protection we feel we need.

**Case 2-The initiative comes from the seller (insurance company representative):**

We are approached by an independent insurance agent, broker or other insurance company representative either on a cold call or as a referral from a friend or relative.

**The First Meeting:**

The insurance representative will concentrate on understanding the prospective client's situation, needs and objectives. This process is called a "needs analysis".

Attention would be focused first on what difficulties the prospective client and family members (if any) would face if one or more particular events were to occur. These are the risks that need to be covered.

> **Definition**
>
> **Insured:**
> - The person, group, or property for which an insurance policy is issued.
> - The condition of having insurance.

Next would come a detailed evaluation of the client's personal situation and finally an exploration of goals and objectives. What is the client trying to achieve financially and how can insurance help in the realization of that dream?

The representative would then structure an insurance package that would best meet the client's objectives and provide the appropriate level of protection for the identified risks.

### Did you know?

96% of life insurance is sold at the kitchen table!

### Financial Planning

The process of formulating long-term financial goals and developing strategies to meet them. These are the steps:

1. collecting and analyzing information concerning a person's or a family's personal and financial situation in order to identify needs and determine net worth;

2. establishing specific financial objectives; and

3. formulating, implementing and continuously monitoring a financial plan to achieve those objectives.

### Estate Planning

The process of developing and maintaining a plan that will preserve your accumulated wealth and ensure an effective and beneficial distribution of your assets to your heirs. Developing your plan should include:

1. creating and conserving an estate;

2. maximizing its value when you pass away;

3. creating adequate liquidity for settling the estate; and

4. establishing a proper plan for distributing the estate to your heirs.

An estate plan:

a. tells others how to handle your affairs and finances after you die;

b. helps to distribute your assets at death;

c. helps to ensure your estate is divided according to your wishes;

d. help to minimize taxes, so more of your estate is left for your heirs.

### Will

A written document executed in the form required by law by which a person makes a disposition of personal assets and property to take effect upon his or her death.

**After the meeting:**

The insurance representative will write up an insurance proposal containing a description of the risks to be covered, the amount of protection needed, the form of insurance desired and detailed personal information about the prospective client.

### Marketing Tip

A top insurance agent is a professional who

- listens well,
- explains products thoroughly,
- doesn't appear to be "pushing" a particular product or company, and
- works hard at developing a good report with a prospective client.

If the insurance representative is an independent broker, he or she will send the proposal to several insurance companies in order to obtain the lowest price. If the representative works for an agent of a particular company, he or she will forward the proposal to that company's underwriting department.

The insurance company's underwriting department will review the details of the proposal.

### Definition:

Underwriting: The process of insuring someone or something.

If it considers the risk acceptable, it will provide a quote to the representative-what the premium would be for the coverage desired.

The representative will report the good news to the prospective client. If the price quoted is acceptable, the client will make whatever payment is required and a policy of insurance will be issued.

### A Career in Insurance Underwriting

*Want a job that will provide challenge and risk? Try insurance underwriting.*

**Underwriter:**
- The company receiving premiums and accepting responsibility for fulfilling the policy contract.
- The company employee who decides whether the company should assume a particular risk; or the agent who sells the policy.

"Underwriting is a key position," says Todd, Director of Product Marketing for an insurance industry trade association. "If an underwriter makes a mistake, it can affect 20,000 policies. If the company loses ¥4,000 on each policy, the underwriter has made an ¥80 million mistake."

### More Than Crunching Numbers

So who are these professionals that protect company finances? Underwriters use math and analytical skills to determine what insurance companies should charge policyholders.

Typically, underwriters start and stay within a trade line—property, health or life insurance—and work with group or individual plans. New underwriters begin by doing routine work like collecting customer data and analyzing customer applications.

"As you become more skilled, you'll be exposed to more and more complex cases," says Barbara, Director of Underwriting for an international insurance group. Junior underwriters typically have either business experience that relates to underwriting or a college degree in finance or economics. Liberal arts graduates can become underwriters if they've taken business, accounting and math classes.

However, underwriters need more than subject-matter knowledge and a math background. The best underwriters are outgoing and analytical, Barbara says. "You have to be curious and have a strong personality so that when you're challenged on how you underwrote, you're able to articulate how you developed your rates and how you designed the plans. You have to be able to explain the plan so clients understand why one feature might be better than another."

### A Peek at the Paychecks

What kind of compensation will this hard work earn you? In 2002, there were about 102,000 underwriters working in the United States, earning a median salary of $45,590, according to US Bureau of Labor Statistics data. The middle 50 percent earned between $35,190 and $60,890 a year, while the highest 10 percent earned more than $79,400.

### Moving Up the Ranks

David, an insurance company vice president, took a common career path in insurance underwriting. He was an underwriter for two years, then a senior underwriter and then a supervisor. "I went to work in product development for a couple of years, then came back as a regional underwriting manager," he says. "From there, I went into operations." Continuing education and certification gave his career a critical boost. "Having aspirations for other positions within the company got me started with the Chartered Property Casualty Underwriters Designation," David says. "It's not an easy designation to earn. It took me five years—two exams a year—and I was studying about an hour a day for those five years."

## Section F—Words and Expressions  术语及解释

**Actuary  保险精算师**

A specialist in the mathematics of risk, especially as it relates to insurance calculations such as premiums, reserves, dividends, and insurance and annuity rates. They work for insurance companies to evaluate applications based on risk.

**Estate planning  产权计划**

The process of developing and maintaining a plan that will preserve your accumulated wealth and ensure an effective and beneficial distribution of your assets to your heirs. Developing your plan may include: a) creating and conserving an estate; b) maximizing its value when you pass away; c) creating adequate liquidity for settling the estate; and d) establishing a proper plan for distributing the estate to your heirs.

**Financial planning** 财务计划

The process of formulating and meeting long-term financial goals. The steps to establishing a plan may include: 1) collecting and analyzing information concerning a person's or a family's personal and financial situation in order to identify needs and determine net worth; 2) establishing specific financial objectives; and 3) formulating, implementing, and continuously monitoring a financial plan to achieve those objectives.

**Independent broker** 独立保险经纪人

An independent agent who represents the buyer, rather than the insurance company, and tries to find the buyer the best policy by comparison shopping.

**Insurance agent** 保险代理人

An individual who is licensed to sell insurance for one or more specific insurance companies.

**Insured** 被保险人

The party who is being insured. In life insurance, it is the person, if he or she dies, the insurance company will pay out a death benefit to a designated beneficiary.

**Insurer** 承保人

A party that provides insurance coverage, typically through a contract of insurance.

**Mortality rate** 死亡率

The number of deaths in a group of people, usually expressed as deaths per thousand.

**Mortality tables** 死亡率表

Tables used to predict the life expectancy and the death rates for people of different ages and various types (smoker, non-smoker; male, female).

**Underwriter** 核保人

Company receiving premiums and accepting responsibility for fulfilling the policy contract. Also, company employee who decides whether the company should assume a particular risk.

# Part III  Life Insurance  人寿保险

*The key objective of life insurance is to leave your family and loved ones without any financial worries. It is a crucial part of an effective financial management strategy.*

## Section A—Introduction  导语

Life insurance is primarily designed to provide surviving family members with the cash needed to replace the earnings of the family breadwinner should that person premature. It can also be used as a part of a savings program and for estate planning purposes. Used properly, life insurance is an important part of an effective financial management strategy.

---

**Life Insurance**

Guarantees the payment of a pre-specified amount of money upon your death and is paid tax-free to the beneficiaries chosen by you. Life insurance is unique in its ability to create financial certainty in a changing world.

---

**A. Uses of life insurance**

Life insurance is typically used to provide funds

- to pay final expenses,
- to retire outstanding debts (bank loans, mortgages, credit cards),
- for dependents' living costs and the children's education,
- to allow remaining partners or shareholders in a privately-held business to buy out the insured's interest without having to sell or liquidate the business,
- to pay taxes in order to preserve family assets (farms, businesses, real estate) for the next generation, and
- to endow charities.

---

**Insurance Tip**

It is a good idea to arrange for enough insurance to fully repay any outstanding credit card balances and advances under personal lines of credit.

---

When an individual uses insurance to provide a lump-sum payment of cash to his or her beneficiaries, they will have an alternate income source to meet their daily living needs.

### B. Who should get the money?

Most insurance professionals recommend that the insurance be made payable to specifically named individuals called beneficiaries. In this way insurance is paid directly, bypassing many legal issues that can arise when a person dies. Family members get the cash they need to cover daily living costs while other matters are being settled. The people who the insured thought might be helped by the money, can in fact get it immediately.

### C. The main types of life insurance

Life insurance can be divided into two general types:
a) Insurance that offers just protection in the event of the death of the policyholder.
b) Insurance that has both a savings and protection component.

## Section B—Life Insurance That Provides Protection Only 只提供保障的寿险

**Term insurance**

Called term insurance, this is the simplest and cheapest form of life insurance. Term policies offer insurance protection for a specified period of time (term)—typically, 1, 5, 10, 15, 20 or 30 years or until a specific age (such as 65).

---

**Important Note**

Term life insurance is typically purchased by individuals who need insurance coverage for a temporary period of time or who need a large amount of life insurance at the lowest possible cost.

---

Premiums may increase each year. We call this type annually renewable term insurance. If the premiums remain the same for several years, the insurance is called level term.

Should the insured die at any time during the term, the insurer will pay the face amount of the policy.

At the end of the contract term the insurance coverage ends. If the individual wants to continue to be insured, a new policy must be written. The premium for the renewal will almost certainly be higher. As a person grows older, more and more people in his or her age group can be expected to die so the expected payout by the insurer is higher. The insurer offsets this higher payout by charging higher premiums.

Some term insurance policies contain a "guaranteed renewable" clause. This means that when the policy ends, the insured can renew it even if his or her health has deteriorated to a point where insurance would be difficult if not impossible to obtain. No medical exam is required. If the insured does renew the policy, the premium will be higher because that he or she will be older. A higher percentage of people in that age bracket will die so the insurer's risk is greater.

If the term insurance does not contain the guaranteed renewable clause, the policyholder will most likely have to undergo a medical exam. At that point the insurer has the option of not renewing the policy. If the medical exam reveals a health risk, the insurer may decide not to renew the policy or may renew it but at a substantially higher premium.

Guaranteed Insurability

Term insurance covers a person for a fixed number of years-1 year, 5 years, for example-when that period of time is up, the insurance coverage ends. If you want to renew the insurance for another period of time or even convert it to whole life, some companies will make you take a full medical exam to make sure that you are still healthy. If you have developed some health problem, lung cancer, for example, you may not be able to renew your insurance. Therefore, it is a good idea to add a guaranteed insurability rider to your term insurance policy. Then no matter what the condition of your health when you come to renew, you will be assured of having your insurance continue.

Insurance 保险

> Insurance Tip
>
> Term insurance is usually recommended to meet the needs of families with young children. It is ideal for protecting against the risk of a family losing one of its key income earners.

## Section C—Life Insurance That Provides Both Protection and Savings 提供保障兼储蓄功能的寿险

**Permanent or whole life insurance**

Permanent life insurance policies offer protection as long as the policyholder lives and continues to pay premiums on a timely basis. This kind of insurance not only provides a death benefit (protection), but also has a method of building up a cash value as premiums are paid. Consequently, premiums charged for these policies are generally much higher than those charged for term insurance.

The insured can borrow the cash value from the insurer at any time-interest is payable and any outstanding loans are deducted from the face amount payable upon the insured's death.

The policyholder may choose at any time to receive the policy's cash value by surrendering the policy. Any outstanding loan balance and accrued loan interest would be deducted.

The unknown in a whole life policy is the dividend which varies from year to year depending on the performance of the company. If its investment portfolio is doing well and the mortality rate is not higher than projected, premiums are paid back to the policy holder in the form of dividends.

With whole life policies, the premiums are usually level over the life of the policy. The premiums do not rise as time passes and the insured grows older. Premiums are payable either until the insured dies or in some policies, reaches a certain age, 90 for example. Some insurers offer single payment life insurance policies which require just one initial lump sum payment.

## Section D—Some Additional Features of Life Insurance Policies 其他种类的寿险

Many life insurance policies whether term or permanent provide additional payments if the insured should die as a result of an accident. The face value is doubled (and in some policies, tripled) if this should happen. This is referred to as "accidental death benefit", "double (or triple) indemnity".

## Section E—What Does It Cost? 决定保险费的因素

Regardless of the form, the premiums for life insurance depend on several factors:
- The age of the insured when the policy is taken out. The older the person is, the higher the premium will be.
- The term of the policy. The longer the insurer can expect to collect the premiums, the lower they will be.
- The occupation of the insured. Some occupations are considered high risk (airline pilots, high rise construction workers, for example) so the premium is higher.
- The health of the insured. And particularly whether or not the insured smokes.
- The gender of the insured. Women live longer than men so the premiums they pay are lower.

The older the person is when the insurance is taken out, the higher will be the mortality rate. In other words, the older you are, the higher will be the percentage of people in your age bracket that will die during the year. This means that the insurer's expected payout will be higher. This higher amount is recouped from the policyholders in that age bracket by way of higher premiums.

Premiums are often higher for people in occupations considered high risk and for people who are considered to have health issues. For example, the premiums paid by smokers are generally much higher than those paid by non-smokers. Females pay less than males of the same age and health profile because experience has shown that the life expectancy of females is several years longer than that of males.

Insurance  保险

Wise use of life insurance can protect your family. It will ensure that your lifestyle can continue should something happen to you. It is comforting to know that there will be adequate funds available to cover education, medical and other expenses.

## Section F—The Pay Out  赔付

Life insurance proceeds can be paid out in a variety of ways. The policy may be structured to provide a lump sum payment to the beneficiary upon the death of the insured.

Alternatively, the policy may provide for a series of payments to be made over time. This is called an annuity and may take one of several forms. It can be payable for as long as the beneficiary lives. Or it can be a Term-Certain Annuity. Also known as a fixed-term annuity, this type of annuity is based on a specific payment period chosen at the time the insurance policy is purchased. The most common choices are 5, 10, 15 and 20 years. If the beneficiary dies prior to the end of the term, the remaining payments will be made to his or her heirs.

> Permanent insurance is designed to last throughout a person's life to provide for long-term needs.

## Section G—Words and Expressions  术语及解释

**Accidental death & dismemberment**  意外死亡和伤残

This insurance is purchased as protection against accidental death or dismemberment (i.e. loss of an arm, a leg, eye or other body part).

**Annually renewable term**  每年可续保险

A form of renewable term insurance that provides coverage for one year and allows the policy owner to renew his or her coverage each year, without evidence of insurability.

**Annuitant**  年金领受者

The person receiving the income from an annuity.

**Annuity**  年金

A contract that provides regular income payments for either a specified period or for the lifetime of the annuitant.

**Benefit**  受益金额

The amount payable by the insurance company to the beneficiary of a policy.

**Cash surrender value (CSV)**  解约现金价值

The amount available in cash upon the surrender of a life insurance policy.

**Evidence of insurability**  可保证明

Any statement or proof of a person's physical condition, occupation, etc., affecting acceptance of the applicant for insurance.

**Final expenses**  寿终费用

Expenses incurred at the time of a person's death. These include funeral costs, court expenses associated with probating his or her will, current bills or debt, and taxes. Depending on their circumstances, the survivors may also want to pay the outstanding balances of mortgage and loans.

**Level term insurance**　定额定期保险

Term coverage on which the face value and premiums remain unchanged from the date the policy comes into force to the date the policy expires.

**Life expectancy**　平均寿命

The average number of years remaining for a person of a given age to live as shown on the mortality or annuity table used as a reference.

**Medical expenses**　医疗费

Reasonable charges for medical, surgical, x-ray, dental, ambulance, hospital, professional nursing, prosthetic devices, and funeral expenses. (The insurance company defines what is reasonable.)

**Medical**　医疗报告

A document completed by a physician or another approved examiner and submitted to an insurer to supply medical evidence of insurability (or lack of insurability) or in relation to a claim.

**Permanent insurance**　终身寿险

Life insurance designed to provide protection until the life insured's death.

**Term insurance**　定期寿险

Protection during limited number of years; expiring without value if the insured does not die during the stated period.

**Whole life**　终身寿险中的一种

Life insurance which provides coverage for an individual's whole life, rather than a specified term. A savings component, called cash value or loan value, builds over time and can be used for wealth accumulation. Whole life is the most basic form of cash value life insurance. The insurance company essentially makes all of the decisions regarding the policy. Regular premiums both pay insurance costs and cause equity to accrue in a savings account. A fixed death benefit is paid to the beneficiary along with the balance of the savings account. Premiums are fixed throughout the life of the policy even though the breakdown between insurance and savings swings toward the insurance over time. Management fees also eat up a portion of the premiums. The insurance company will invest money primarily in fixed-income securities, meaning that the savings investment will be subject to interest rate and inflation risk.

**Will** 遗嘱

A written document executed in the form required by law by which a person makes a disposition of personal assets and property to take effect upon his or her death.

# Part IV

## Personal Property and Liability Insurance
## 个人财产及责任险

*For most of us, our houses are the largest purchase we will ever make in our lives. Protect that investment through a carefully structured insurance policy.*

## Section A—Introduction  导语

### A. Houses, villas and town homes

Whether you own a cottage, a castle or something in between, you will want to protect your investment in case it is damaged or destroyed. Since you are the owner, you are at risk in the event of a loss. If your house is destroyed by fire, you will need money to pay back the bank holding the mortgage and to rebuild. Insurance will give you the funds that you need.

### B. Apartment living

Apartment living has one very important difference when it comes to insurance. Your actions have a much greater chance of affecting others when you live in an apartment building than if you live in a house because you are much closer to your neighbours. A fire in your apartment could easily spread to over apartments, possibly even destroying the entire building. If you are judged to be at fault, a court could make you pay for all of the damage—the cost of rebuilding, for example.

Water damage is another example. Suppose you go out and forget to turn off the tap in the bathtub. The water overflows and eventually runs down into the apartment below you. The occupants are not home so they are not aware of what is happening. When they return they find to their dismay that their expensive carpet has been destroyed. They will expect you to pay for it and a court would probably agree.

Insurance 保险

### Rental apartments

When you rent an apartment, your investment is limited to the cost of your personal possessions. Therefore the insurance you need is limited to coverage for your belonging and protection in the event you or your family members cause injury to others or damage to the building or to other people's possessions.

### Condominium apartments

Condominium living combines the insurance requirements of both houses and apartments. You own the apartment so you have a substantial investment to protect and probably a mortgage to pay back.

You live close to your neighbours so you are at a much greater risk of causing injury or damage to others than if you lived in a home.

#### Important Note

As a condominium owner you have shared responsibilities with other owners. Your condominium owner's policy helps you meet obligations that arise from this sharing.

#### Dialogue

Hello, Tony. Hello, Monica. I understand that the two of you have taken a very important step.

Yes, Jim. We will be closing the purchase of an apartment early next week. We want to make sure that we have the proper insurance coverage in place.

A very wise decision. Apartment ownership—what we would call owning a condominium—combines the convenience of apartment living with the advantages of real estate ownership. It does, however, present some unique insurance challenges. Generally speaking, the building itself is owned and operated by a condominium association, a home-owner association or a co-operative. In many instances, the association entity assumes responsibility for insuring certain types of damage to the dwelling structure. In other cases, the condominium/association does not insure the structure. We'll look at each one in detail.

Similarly, you are at a much greater risk of suffering the actions of others that cause injury or damage to you or your family members.

It is important to carefully design an insurance policy that meets your special needs.

---

### Potential Problem

Suppose someone is seriously injured on common property, perhaps at the swimming pool, and the court awards a judgment that's higher than the amount of liability coverage provided by the condominium association policy. You, along with all the other unit owners can be held jointly and severally liable for the shortfall. If the injured party is successful in getting a judgment against you, you could lose your apartment, your personal property and even have a portion of your earnings garnished.

Should this unfortunate situation arise, your condominium owner's policy would pay your legal fees and any damages awarded against you.

---

## Section B—Insuring the Building 房屋保险

### A. Houses and condominium apartments

The basic insurance you should have is the same for both types of accommodation. The policy should cover the cost of paying for damage to the structure. Remember, land does not burn so you do not need to insure the value of the land in the value of your home-just the cost of replacing the bricks and mortar.

### B. Condominium apartments

Condominium apartments are typically managed by an association of owners. Your association may insure the building and common elements under a single package policy, commonly called an association master policy.

The association insures the basic apartment building including the walls, roof, floors, elevators and so on, but leaves to you the responsibility of insuring appliances, carpeting, cabinets, wall coverings, bathroom fixtures and other items in your unit.

Insurance 保险

> **Example**
>
> You decided to install a better quality carpet when you bought your apartment. The association insurance would cover only the value of the original carpet. Your homeowner's policy would make up the difference in case of loss.

You will need a policy that does the following:

1. Complements the association policy by covering things it does not-things that are considered your responsibility, and

2. Protects you from loss
   a. if the association insurance does not pay the full amount of your loss for the following reasons:
      i. inadequate or lapsed coverage;
      ii. the master policy deductible
   b. from damage to your unit by the actions or negligence of other apartment owners for which you are not reimbursed by the association or its insurer;
   c. from your liability for damage caused to the basic building and other units by your actions or negligence or the actions or negligence of others considered to be under your care-your children, other family members, guests, etc.

3. Covers the value of building additions or alterations made by you at your expense and value you have added.

## Section C—Protecting Yourself Against Liability for Damage Caused to Others  第三者损失赔偿责任险

**Liability Coverage**

Personal liability coverage protects you if others make a claim or bring suit against you for bodily injury or property damage for which you or a member of your family are responsible, either in your home or elsewhere and to which coverage applies. In addition to settlement costs, this coverage may pay defence costs and court costs-even if a suit brought against you is groundless. It is important, however, that you select liability limits high enough to protect your assets.

> **Example**
>
> Let us say you are barbequing on your balcony and sparks from your fire land on someone else's balcony and start a fire. You would be responsible to pay for that unit owner's loss and also for any damage caused to the building itself.

The medical payments part of your policy's liability coverage is divided into two categories. The first pays medical bills of others injured in your home even though you may not be responsible for their injury. The second pays medical expenses up to the limits in the policy for people who are on your premises with your permission and accidentally injured. The coverage also extends to people accidentally injured by your activities. However, the coverage does not pay for medical expenses for you or members of your family that live with you.

## Section D—Insuring the Contents (of Your Home)  家庭财产保险

### Personal Property Coverage

You have a large investment in your personal property. Therefore, you need enough coverage to compensate you if you suffer a loss. Unfortunately many people are underinsured in terms of their personal property. One of the best ways to make sure that you have adequate coverage is to complete a detailed inventory of your possessions along with purchase dates, prices and serial numbers where applicable.

## Insurance 保险

| Item number | Quantity | Brand Name | Manufacturer | Series, model or style no. | Identification Description of item (name, type) | Date purchased (or age) | Cost | Replacement cost | Actual cash value, market value or resale value |
|---|---|---|---|---|---|---|---|---|---|
| | | | | | | | | | |

**INVENTORY**

Name of insured / Policy number / Date
Location / Carrier

Remarks / Total

It is very important to keep detailed records of your possessions. A form like the one above is a useful way of keeping track of what you own. It may seem like a lot of work, but you will be really glad that you did it if your home is ever destroyed by fire. Having your claim processed will be much simpler and you will well on your way to getting your life back together.

Once you have completed your inventory listing, put a copy in a safe place outside your home—your bank safety deposit box for example. Taking photographs or videos are a great addition to your inventory record. Actual receipts will speed up your settlement of your claim if you should ever have a loss so save them along with your inventory listing outside your home.

# Part IV—Personal Property and Liability Insurance 个人财产及责任险

### Insurance Tips

Consider adding an inflation-guard feature to your policy. It automatically increases coverage for your belongings as general price levels rise.

Buy replacement cost coverage rather than depreciated or market value coverage. It is a bit more expensive but it puts you back in the same position you were in before the loss occurred.

You may have paid a lot of money for fine furniture. Unfortunately the market value for used furniture, even very good quality, is a relatively small fraction of the original purchase price. With market value coverage, the insurance company would only pay what you could get by selling the furniture to a second hand store. With replacement cost coverage, you can buy the same kind of furniture as you had and the insurance company will pay whatever the purchase price turns out to be—up to the limits of the policy, of course.

### Dialogue

**Marsha:** Did you see the memo Roger sent around about the new flexible working hours?

**Lori:** Yes, I did. It's going to be great. I always have a struggle dropping my daughter off at day care and then fighting the traffic to get here by 9. Now it won't matter. What do you think about it? Will you find it helpful?

**Marsha:** I think it's super. I like to come in early. Now I can finish by 3 in the afternoon and have plenty of time for shopping or even hit the beach!

**Lori:** Everyone I talked to is really happy about it. I've always thought that this is a great company to work for. Now it's just gotten better!

**Marsha:** I agree. I've been here for 3 years now and I just love it. I wouldn't want to work anywhere else.

### Insurance  保险

> **Tip**
>
> Buy separate insurance coverage for expensive items like jewelry.

## Section E—What Is not Covered  家庭财产保险中不包括的项目

Certain high value items called scheduled property are treated differently from a homeowner's normal personal property. These items include the following:

- Money, banknotes, coins
- Securities
- Jewellery
- Furs
- Gold and silverware
- Paintings and other objects of art
- Rugs and tapestries
- Firearms
- Computers and related data processing equipment
- Business equipment
- Boats and trailers

> Own any of these? Make sure to have them appraised and insured separately!

## Part IV—Personal Property and Liability Insurance 个人财产及责任险

All homeowners' policies put limits on the amounts the insurance company will pay for, loss or damage to any of these types of items. If the replacement value of any items you have in any of these categories exceeds the maximum value for that particular category, you will need to have a rider to your policy to cover the extra value. For one-of-a-kind items like jewellery and paintings, it is important to have them appraised.

**Additional Living Expenses**

Many policies cover the actual loss incurred for necessary increased expenses over and above what you normally spend for food, shelter and related items for the shortest time required to repair or replace the premises or for your household to settle elsewhere up to 24 months. For example, if your home is uninhabitable because of fire or other damage, the insurance will cover the cost of staying in a hotel and eating your meals in a restaurant for a reasonable period of time.

**Home Business Insurance**

Perhaps you will be operating a business from your home. In that case you will probably want to arrange special coverage for home-based businesses. This protects you from loss of business equipment such as computers, fax machines, photocopiers-things that would not normally be considered personal property under a homeowners' policy. It also covers loss of profits in the event something happens that causes you to shut down your business for a while and increased costs you incur in relocating.

---

### A Final Note

Condominium living is very popular and the insurance industry has responded by providing a broad selection of coverages and policies. It is important to understand that conditions in condominium association by laws and other governing regulations vary widely and are often written in formal, hard to understand legalese. Read it carefully and do not be afraid to ask for help from a trusted lawyer or insurance advisor. You want to make sure that your policy covers any gaps in the condominium master policy. This is the way you will avoid any unpleasant surprises down the road.

# Insurance 保险

## Dialogue—The "To Do" List

**Man:** It's going to be raining pretty hard all day today according to weather report, I just heard on the radio.

**Wife:** That's too bad. I guess we won't be working in the garden after all.

**Man:** No, it doesn't look that way. I have a suggestion, however.

**Wife:** What's that?

**Man:** You know how we have been putting off doing an inventory of all our stuff for insurance purposes in case we have a fire or robbery?

**Wife:** We keep saying that we must do it, but we never seem to get around to it. I'm sure we will wish we had done it if we ever have a problem.

**Man:** Well, today is the perfect opportunity. We can't very well work outside and it's not very nice to go anywhere.

**Wife:** You're quite right. And with the kids away at summer camp, we can work away at it without being interrupted all the time.

**Man:** I'm so glad you agree. Let's get at it!

## Section F—Words and Expressions   术语及解释

**Appraisal**   估价

A professional opinion, usually written, of the market value of a property, such as a home, business, or other asset whose market price is not easily determined. Usually required when a property is sold, taxed, insured or financed.

**Appraiser**   估价人

A person qualified by education, training and experience to provide appraisals. Also called an evaluator.

**Actual Cash Value（ACV）**   实际现金价值

The fair or reasonable cash price for which the property could be sold in the market in the ordinary course of business and not at forced sale.

**Condominium**   居住者自有产权的公寓

An apartment complex in which individuals own their own apartments and share joint ownership of common elements such as the lobby, parking garage, sports facilities with other unit owners.

**Deductible**   自负额

The amount of a loss that a policyholder has to pay out-of-pocket before the insurance company is required to make any payment.

**Family member**   家庭成员

A person related to the named insured or his or her spouse by blood, marriage or adoption and who lives in the named insured's household.

**Inventory**   财产目录

A written record of personal property owned, along with price paid and current value, used for tax or insurance purposes.

**Liability**   责任

Something for which a person is responsible or legally required to make up for any loss or damage.

**Renter's insurance**   租房人保险

A type of home insurance that protects the holder against accidents, damages, and losses that occur in a rented residence. Renter's insurance provides coverage both for the insured's belongings and for liability that may result from an accident in the insured's home. Many policies cover replacement cost, meaning that the insured will receive the money necessary to purchase a new item that is equivalent to the damaged one instead of a portion of that cost adjusted for depreciation.

**Replacement cost insurance**　重置成本保险

Insurance which replaces lost, stolen or destroyed property by paying current market prices rather than depreciated value.

# Part V　Automobile Insurance　汽车保险

*By ensuring that you are able to pay for losses or harm that your actions may cause to others, you affirm your responsibility to your community.*

## Section A—Types of Automobile Insurance　车险的种类

Auto insurance can be divided into two broad categories:

A. Property damage—that is loss you suffer as a result of the loss of your vehicle.

B. Public liability—that means losses you suffer and costs you incur as a result of damage or injury you cause to other people and their property.

### Be Wise

Protect yourself, your family and your community. Make sure you carry enough auto insurance.

## Section B—Who Is at Fault?  谁承担过失

Operating an automobile can sometimes lead to unfortunate occurrences-accidents. In most cases, someone was responsible for causing the accident. It could be carelessness, inattention, recklessness, driving under the influence of drugs or alcohol or just a simple mistake. However, if you are judged to have been responsible for causing the accident, being at fault, you would be required to pay large sums of money to the injured parties. Costs can include:

- medical bills (ambulance, doctors, nurses, medications, hospital care),
- damage to other vehicles,
- damage to property (light poles knocked over, guard rails broken, hedges and fences destroyed),
- pain and suffering, and
- lost wages.

---

### Example

Suppose an accident occurs in which someone who normally earns a very high salary, a business executive for example, is injured so severely that he is unable to return to work. If the court decides that you (or one of your family members) caused an accident, you could be required to pay an amount equal to what the executive could reasonably be expected to earn over his lifetime!

---

If someone is injured in an auto accident, he or she may experience a lot of pain and suffering. There is no way to take that away so courts do the only thing possible—they make whoever caused the pain and suffering to pay a substantial sum of money as a penalty and as a way of compensating the victim for having endured it.

Taking everything together, a serious auto accident can be an extremely costly experience. Insurance takes that risk away. Of course, if you are not at fault, then the other driver is responsible for making payments to you and your passengers. Hopefully he or she will have lots of insurance.

## Section C—Protecting Yourself Against Liability for Damage Caused to Others  公共责任保险

This insurance is called public liability coverage, it protects you in the event that you (or someone in your family) are judged to have been responsible for having caused an accident. In addition to paying for damage and injury to persons and property, it pays your legal costs if you have to go to court. In many places the law requires drivers to carry this type of insurance.

If you cause a serious accident, the costs of going to court will be very high. Good lawyers are expensive and juries are prone to awarding large amounts of money to victims to compensate them for the pain and suffering they have endured. Protect yourself by making sure your insurance coverage is sufficient to cover any eventuality. You will be glad you did!

### Insurance Tip

If you cause a serious accident, the amount you may have to pay can be extremely high. It is important that you purchase a sufficiently large amount of public liability insurance to fully protect yourself in the event should the unthinkable things occur.

## Section D—Covering Medical Costs  投保医疗费用

**Personal Injury Protection**
Covers you, your passengers or pedestrians for medical expenses or lost wages.

**Medical Payments Coverage**

Guarantees immediate medical payments for you, your passengers and other parties involved in the accident, regardless of who is at fault. Termed "good faith" coverage, the objective is to ensure that the injured people get the necessary medical attention immediately leaving the issues of fault, liability and insurance to be dealt with later.

## Section E—Protecting Your Vehicle  车险是汽车的保障

**Loss or damage to your car or its contents (property)**

**Collision**

Pays to fix your car after an accident (collision) with another vehicle or other stationary objects such as a guard rail, curb or light pole.

**Comprehensive**

Provides coverage for damage to your car caused by something other than hail, windstorm, earthquake, glass breakage, vandalism or theft.

---

Insurance Tip

**Understand your policy**

Before a loss occurs, sit down and carefully read your insurance policy. Call your agent or company if you have any questions about what is or is not covered.

---

**Parked auto collision**

If your car is parked and unoccupied and it is damaged by a hit-and-run driver, this coverage pays for the cost of repairing it. Most companies waive the deductible in this event.

**Personal property coverage**

Pays for personal property belonging to your family (such as coats, cameras, etc.) that is damaged or stolen while in your car.

**Coverage for electronics**

Coverage furnished for electronics that are permanently installed in your vehicle, such as televisions, telephones, fax machines and DVD players and for factory—installed electronics and computer equipment.

**Air bag replacement coverage**

Pays for the cost of reinstalling a factory-installed air bag even if one is activated without being involved in an accident.

## Section F—Other Kinds of Coverage That Are Readily Available
其他种类的车险

**Rental car coverage**

Pays for a rental car while damage to your auto is being repaired. Many companies pay for the cost of renting a car that is similar to your own. For example, if you drive a BMW, your insurance will pay for the cost of renting a similar BMW.

**Uninsured motorist coverage**

Pays your costs and damages if you or your passengers are injured by a driver with inadequate insurance or worse, no insurance at all.

**Emergency travel expense coverage**

If you are stranded somewhere away from your primary residence because of damage to a vehicle, this coverage pays for emergency travel expenses like hotels and meals.

**Towing and labour**

Pays when you need a tow due to a mechanical breakdown on the road.

## Section G—You've Had an Accident, Now What? 车险的索赔步骤

**Step 1: Exchange information**

If you are involved in an accident, get the other driver's name, address, phone number, insurance carrier, policy number and insurer's phone number. Be prepared to give the same information about yourself to the other driver.

**Step 2: Identify witnesses**

Ask witnesses of the accident for their names and phone numbers in case their account of the accident is needed.

**Step 3: Identify exactly what damage has been done to the vehicles.**

If you have a camera, take lots of pictures-damaged areas, injuries, road conditions.

**Step 4: File an accident report**

Contact local law enforcement officers to have an accident report prepared.

**Step 5: Notify your insurer**

Contact your insurance company about the accident as soon as possible. An insurance adjuster will review the accident report to determine who caused the accident. If the accident was not your fault, you can have either your insurance company or the at-fault driver's insurance company handle the repair or replacement of your vehicle.

---

Insurance Tip

If you are not "at fault", use the other driver's company. You will not have a claim on your automobile policy and you will not have to pay a deductible.

---

**Step 6: Write it down**

While the scene is still fresh in your mind, write down exactly what happened. Draw diagrams.

**Step 7: Do not release insurers too early**

Do not relieve your insurance company of its responsibility until the damages are settled to your satisfaction. Get your insurance company to handle the claim instead of trying to do it yourself if the other party's insurance company claims that its policyholder was not "at fault" or if it offers you a settlement that you feel is much too low.

**Step 8: Consider these settlement factors**

If you were injured in accident caused by another driver—the "at fault" or "liable" party, you may be entitled to a monetary settlement for injuries you sustained. However, it can take several days for some injuries to become apparent. Do not agree to a settlement until you are sure there are no hidden injuries, back or neck problems caused by whiplash, for example.

The insurance company is responsible to pay for the reasonable cost of repairs to your vehicle. An insurance adjuster will assess the damage. Usually, insurance companies and auto body shops negotiate disagreements about what should be repaired. If you disagree with their conclusions, you have the right to obtain another appraisal at any auto body shop.

### Insurance 保险

> If your car is damaged in an accident but you can still drive it, you will likely be required to take it to three auto body shops for an estimate of the cost of fixing it.
>
> If the car cannot be driven, the insurance company will send an adjuster around to look at it to assess the damage.

## Section H—How Much Will Auto Insurance Cost? 车险的成本

Drivers are grouped according to the level of risk each one poses—that is, the amount paid out by insurers in each category of policyholders. Insurance companies group drivers in the following way:

- **Sex**: Men have more accidents on the road than women.
- **Age**: Drivers under 25 (and for some insurers, under 30) are considered more likely to have an accident.
- **Marital Status**: Married drivers tend to have fewer accidents than single drivers.
- **Personal Driving Record**: Years of driving experience, accidents, speeding tickets and drunk-driving offenses are all factors in determining how much of a risk you pose as a motorist.
- **How You Use Your Vehicle**: If you commute by car during rush hours, you are at greater risk of having an accident than if you only drive for errands and recreation on the weekends. Drivers who use their own vehicles for business also are considered to be at a greater risk.
- **Type of Vehicle**: The value, size, weight, age of your vehicle, even the cost of replacement parts are essential to determining the price of your insurance. Larger, heavier vehicles are considered at lower risk than smaller, lighter ones. More expensive cars are costlier to have repaired than economy models so the premium is higher.

## Part V—Automobile Insurance 汽车保险

### Dialogue—Stuck in Traffic

**Husband**: Hi, Honey. It's me. Unfortunately I'm stuck in traffic. There has apparently been a big accident up ahead. We are just not moving.
**Wife**: That's too bad. Where are you?
**Husband**: I'm on the Garden City Expressway near the sports stadium. I was on my way to drop off some samples at a new client's office and then I was going to pick up Billy from kindergarten. It looks like I could be stuck here for a while. I'm afraid that I won't be able to get there on time to pick him up before they close. They really hate it when parents are late and we've been late a couple of times this month already. Is there any chance you could get away early and pick him up?
**Wife**: Things are fairly slow here today. I should be able to get Marge to cover for me. I'll check with her and call you back. I don't expect there will be any problem though. How was your day otherwise?
**Husband**: Everything was good. Peter Grimes, one of our salesmen is moving to Beijing to open a new office. Some of his accounts here are being allocated to the rest of us. I should pick up some nice new business. Peter laid a solid groundwork based on excellent service. I know his clients have been very pleased.
**Wife**: That is excellent news! I'm sure Peter will be sorely missed, but it is a great opportunity for you and the others. Do you know much about the accounts yet? Do they have good growth potential?
**Husband**: I have not had much chance to study them in detail, but I think the prospects are good.
**Wife**: I'm glad to hear that. Anything else interesting?
**Husband**: No, that's pretty much it. Just as long as you can pick up Billy.
**Wife**: Should be fine. Call you shortly.

## Insurance  保险

The cost of your insurance policy is based on the average cost of covering actual losses, spread out over your particular "rating group" as a whole. While you may never have an accident or have your car stolen and therefore will never need to be compensated, others in your category may not be so lucky. Your premium will help to pay for their losses just as their premiums would help to pay for yours.

For example, if you are a 23-year-old man and you park your new sports car on a downtown street in a large city, you will likely pay more for insurance than a 37-year-old woman who parks her four-wheel-drive in the suburbs, simply because, based on average losses, you have a greater chance of having an accident or being the victim of auto theft.

---

### Insurance Tips

- The more bells and whistles (riders) that you add to your policy, the more it will cost you. For example, do you really need emergency travel expense coverage? Ensure that the riders you are adding are worth the cost.
- The deductible is the amount of the loss that you pay. The insurance company pays the amount above that up to the limit set out in the policy. Most losses are for small amounts. The higher you set the deductible, the less likely it is that you will file a claim and the less the insurance company can expect to pay out. Insurance companies reward you for this by lowering the premium.
- If you are driving an old car which is not worth very much, it may not make sense to carry collision insurance on it. The premium you would have to pay over time will probably be less than the amount you would lose if the car were damaged or even destroyed in an accident.

---

## Section I—Words and Expressions  术语及解释

**Accident**  意外事故

An event or repeated exposure to conditions that unexpectedly causes injury or damage during the policy period.

**Bodily injury**  人身伤害

Bodily harm, including death that results from an accident.

**Bodily injury coverage**　伤害保险

　　An insurance policy that pays for injuries caused to other individuals in the event of a motor vehicle accident.

**Business use**　商务用

　　The use of a vehicle in a business or occupation.

**Collision**　碰撞

　　The impact of a vehicle with another object or vehicle or the upset of a vehicle.

**Collision coverage**　碰撞保险

　　Covers damage to a covered auto caused by collision with another object or vehicle.

**Comprehensive coverage**　综合保障险

　　Insurance designed to pay for the repair or replacement of the policy owner's car in the event of damage not resulting from an accident. Comprehensive coverage usually requires the payment of a deductible when a claim is made.

**Financial responsibility laws**　财务责任法

　　Some jurisdictions have laws that require owners or operators of autos to provide evidence that they have funds to pay for automobile losses for which they might become liable. This usually means having insurance.

**Legal liability**　法律责任

　　Legal obligation imposed on a party for its negligence, failure to fulfill contractual obligations or violation of law.

**Liability coverage**　责任保险

　　Covers damage for Bodily Injury or Property Damage for which an insured becomes legally responsible because of an auto accident.

**Medical payment coverage**　医疗费保险

　　Pays medical expenses incurred in an auto accident for the insured and passengers in the insured's car.

**Negligence**　过失

　　The failure to use the degree of care that is required to protect others from harm.

**Personal injury protection insurance**　人身伤害保险

　　Type of auto insurance that provides coverage for basic medical expenses incurred by the insured in an accident regardless of who was at fault.

| Insurance 保险 |
| --- |

**Punitive damages**　惩罚性赔偿

Damages awarded to a victim that are meant to punish the defendant for his or her actions rather than reimburse the victim for loss.

**Underinsured motorist coverage**　保险不足驾驶人保险

An automobile policy option which covers one for property damage and bodily injury caused by another motorist whose coverage is insufficient to cover the damages one has suffered. This policy compensates the injured party for the difference between the injury suffered and the liability covered by the insurance of the driver at fault.

**Uninsured motorist coverage**　无保险驾驶人保险

An automobile policy option which covers one for property damage and bodily injury caused by another motorist who does not carry liability insurance.

# Exercises

## Listening Comprehension Exercises 听力综合练习

**A.** *The Shanghai Times*—Front Page

With your book closed, have someone read aloud all of the articles on the front page of *The Shanghai Times* and answer the following questions:

1. Where did the accident occur?
2. How many people died and how many were injured in the accident?
3. What was the weather like at the time of the accident?
4. What was the surprise action taken by the Governor of the central bank?
5. Why did he feel that the action was necessary?

**B.** Dialogue—Filing A Claim

With your book closed, have two people read aloud the dialogue about filing a claim and answer the following questions:

1. When would someone file a claim?
2. Who is a claim filed with?
3. Who handles the claim for the company?
4. What kind of information do you have to provide?

**C.** Text—The First Meeting

With your book closed, have someone read aloud the paragraphs describing the first meeting (Part II—The Insurance Market).

1. Explain in your own words what would happen at the first meeting between an insurance salesman and a prospective client in order for both parties to get the most benefit out

## Insurance 保险

of the meeting and from the insurance if the client decides to make the purchase.

2. Why are these steps so important to both parties?

**D. A Career in Underwriting**

With your book closed, have someone read out loud the article—A Career in Insurance Underwriting (Part II-The Insurance Market) and answer the following questions:

1. Who or what is an underwriter?
2. What kind of training is necessary?
3. Would you like a career in underwriting? Why or why not?

# Speaking Exercises 对话练习

**A. Dialogue—Calling Home**

Choose a partner. One takes the role of the husband, the other takes the role of the wife. Read your dialogue out loud. Work hard at developing a smooth style.

Husband: Explain in your own words what happened.

Wife: Tell your husband in your own words how insurance can be helpful to you both after what has happened.

**B. Dialogue—Filing A Claim**

You have just experienced a loss that you think should be covered by insurance. Write a dialogue for two persons in which you want to get paid for your loss by your insurance company.

**C. The Telephone Call**

Look at the man in the picture at the right. Who do you think he might be talking to? Write a dialogue for two people that is suggested by the picture. For example, he could be an insurance salesman on the way to meet an important client. Or he could be a businessman calling his insurance agent to ask some questions about the insurance coverage for the restaurant he owns.

**D. The Insurance Salesman**

The man in the picture below is waiting to meet for the first time with a businessman or woman. It looks like he is going over in his mind what he will say to the prospective client.

Write down the points you think he should cover in the meeting. Prepare a short oral presentation. Practice your presentation with a friend or family member.

**E. *The Shanghai Times*—Front Page**

Choose a partner. One takes the role of the husband, the other takes the role of the wife. You are considering buying a new apartment. Discuss how the action taken by the central bank and the response by commercial banks will affect your decision on whether or not to buy a new house.

**F. The Conversation**

Pretend that you are the woman in the picture below. You cannot help overhearing the conversation between the two men behind you. They have been discussing insurance and you have found what they are saying is very interesting.

Write a dialogue of what the two men are talking about.

## Insurance 保险

## Building Vocabulary Exercises  词汇练习

**A. Complete the following sentences.**

1. A specialist in the mathematics of risk is called a _____.

2. Tables used to predict life expectancy and death rates are called _____.

3. A written document a person uses to state what is to happen to his or her possessions when he or she dies is called a _____.

4. A person who receives the money from the insurance company when an insured person dies is called a _____.

5. Insurance that protects you against inflation is called _____.

6. A series of payments made over a long period of time is called an _____.

7. A contract of insurance is called a _____.

8. The amount the insurance company charges for assuming the risk of loss is called the _____.

9. A formal notice to the insurance company that a loss has occurred is called a _____.

**Answers:** 1. (actuary) 2. (mortality tables) 3. (will) 4. (beneficiary) 5. (replacement cost coverage) 6. (annuity) 7. (policy) 8. (premium) 9. (claim)

**B. Match the definitions below with the words in the list that follows:**

1. Insurance that provides coverage for your entire life. People you name collect a death benefit if you die while covered. Part of your payments to the insurance company building up savings over time. _____

2. An additional insurance benefit paid to your heirs if you should die or lose one or more body parts, such as arms, hands, legs or feet or sight in one or both eyes as a result of an accident. _____

3. A statistician who calculates risk. Professional odds-makers who study life expectancy or mortality rates for insurance purposes. _____

4. Property insurance where only the items specifically excluded from the policy are not covered. _____

5. Term life insurance which can be changed into any permanent or whole life policy without evidence of insurability. _____

6. The portion of the cost or loss insured against, which the insured must pay before the policy benefits become payable. _____

7. A form of life insurance issued for a specific period of years. _____

8. The payment a policy owner is required to make to keep an insurance policy in force. _____

9. An agreement attached to a policy that either expands or waives the conditions or coverage. _____

10. A contract between you and an insurance company. You agree to pay a specified amount to the company for the policy coverage and in return the company agrees to pay a sum of money to people you choose in the event of your death. _____

11. The option in a life insurance policy that doubles or triples the benefits of the policy if the death is ruled accidentally. This option is also referred to as double or triple indemnity. _____

12. Term life insurance policies which may be renewed at the rate for the attained age without evidence of insurability. _____

13. Coverage that pays the cost of buying new items in place of those lost, damaged or stolen that are covered by insurance rather than just your original cost less wear and tear or

## Insurance 保险

depreciation. _____

14. A term life insurance policy that is renewed each year and which has both an insurance component and an investment component. The investment component invests excess premiums and generates returns to the policyholder. _____

15. Whole life insurance that provides coverage for your entire life and builds up savings over time. Under this type of insurance you can invest your savings in one of several mutual funds, which often are managed by the insurance company. _____

16. A party who receives a legal benefit. An individual who becomes entitled to one or more payments upon the death of the policy holder. _____

1. Beneficiary
2. Whole life
3. Actuaries
4. Life insurance
5. Accidental death and dismemberment benefit
6. Variable life insurance
7. All risk coverage
8. Convertible term
9. Insurance premium
10. Renewable term
11. Insurance riders
12. Term Insurance
13. Replacement value insurance
14. Insurance deductible
15. Accidental death benefit
16. Universal life insurance

## Test Your Knowledge 知识测试

1. What are some risks you would face as a homeowner that insurance could protect you against?

2. When we speak of "inventory" in the context of insurance, what do we mean and why is it important?

3. List the main types of insurance.

4. Refer to the dialogue "Filing a Claim". Discuss with a partner why Roger asked David to go to a doctor for a complete physical examination.

5. In the dialogue "Calling Home", the husband told his wife that he had added something to his basic automobile insurance policy. What kind of coverage did he add and what is formal insurance term used to describe something added to an insurance policy?

6. Give an example of a relationship that would create an insurable interest and explain why.

7. Discuss with a partner why insurance companies insist on there be an insurable interest before they will issue an insurance policy.

8. Give examples of situations where term insurance would be appropriate.

9. Should you insure your 6-year-old child?

10. List some reasons that individuals buy life insurance.

11. Explain the difference between term life insurance and whole life insurance.

12. What are some factors that affect the cost of life insurance?

## Insurance 保险

# Sample Examination Questions 模拟试题

**Vocabulary**

1. Use the following words or phrases in a sentence.

    a. breadwinner

    b. policyholder

    c. beneficiary

    d. life insurance

    e. car accident

    f. underwriter

    g. mortgage insurance

    h. inventory

    i. rider

    j. at fault

2. Define the following words and phrases and provide a Chinese translation.

    a. premium

    b. risk

    c. coverage

    d. loss

    e. insurable interest

    f. collision

    g. face amount

    h. accidental death and dismemberment

    i. comprehensive

**Understanding**

1. Who buys insurance?
2. Who sells insurance?
3. What are the main types of insurance?

4. What is the role of the claims adjuster?
5. What is the difference between an insurance agent and an insurance broker?
6. Explain the importance of financial planning.
7. What is the purpose of life insurance?
8. What is the difference between term life insurance and whole life insurance?
9. How is the insurance premium determined?
10. Why do smokers generally pay higher insurance premiums than non-smokers?
11. What is a will and why is it important?
12. What special insurance do people who live in apartments need?
13. What can happen if you cause damage or injury to someone or his or her property when you do not have insurance?
14. Why is it important to have an inventory of your personal possessions?
15. Does a person affect the amount he or she pays for life insurance? Why or why not?
16. What is the difference between whole life insurance and permanent insurance?
17. What is replacement cost coverage and what are its advantages?
18. What kinds of things can automobile insurance cover?

金融英语

# Elective Course A  Ethics

选修内容A  金融职业伦理

*What I did was honest when I did it. Now, as a result of changed conditions, what I did may or may not be honest.*

## 1. Ethical Behaviour

Ethics is the moral standard of what is right behaviour and what is wrong behaviour. Ethical behaviour reflects established customs that vary throughout the world and that are subject to change from time to time. In our diversified global workplace, people have different values. This often leads to different behaviour patterns, which some people view as ethical while others do not.

Doing the right thing is considered ethical behaviour while doing the wrong thing is considered unethical. But what is right and wrong? In the business world, for example, the difference between right and wrong is not always clear. Many types of unethical behaviour are illegal, but not all. For example, giving someone a gift is ethical and legal. Giving a gift as a condition of obtaining business (a bribe) is considered unethical by many and is illegal in some parts of the world. Whether a gift is a gift or a bribe is not always clear.

In our daily lives we face decisions in which we can make ethical or unethical choices. We make those choice based on what we have learned from our parents, teachers, friends, leaders and coworkers. Our combined past experiences make up what we refer to as our conscience, which in turn helps us to know right from wrong.

## 2. Politics

Politics is the art of manoeuvring within a group to achieve one's aims and objectives. These can either personal goals—earn more money, get a promotion—or they can be organizational (corporate) goals—take an important customer away from a competitor, get the company's stock price up.

In order to achieve our goals we usually need the help of other people. Power is the ability to get other people to do the things we want, to influence other people's behaviour. Politics is the network of interactions by which power is acquired, transferred and exercised upon others. It is the process of gaining and using power. Political behaviour can be ethical or unethical.

Ethical politics includes behaviour that benefits both the individual and the organization. Ethical politics creates a win-win situation. On the other hand, unethical politics includes behaviour that benefits the individual and hurts the organization. Unethical politics creates a win-lose situation. Unethical politics also includes management behaviour that helps the organization but hurts the individual. Behaviour that helps the individual but does not hurt the organization is also considered ethical. Creating a win-win situation for all stakeholders-increases the firm's financial performance.

A good code of ethics establishes guidelines that clearly describe ethical and unethical behaviour. Most organizations consider ethics codes to be important and many have developed codes of ethics.

## 3. Good Ethics Means Good Business

Good business and good ethics are synonymous. Ethics is at the heart and center of business and profits and ethics are intrinsically related. At first, one may be richly rewarded for knifing people in the back, but retaliation follows, trust is lost and productivity declines. It is difficult to get ahead when people do not like you. Unethical behaviour and stress appear to be linked.

Suppose that you are a supervisor in the Production Department. In order to make the product you need materials and supplies which the Purchasing Department orders. If you do not get all the materials you need on time, you may have difficulty reaching your production quota. If your department consistently fails to meet its quota, you may find your opportunities for promotion limited, or worse, you may be disciplined or fired. If you engage in unethical political behaviour, your working relationship with the people in the Purchasing Department may be poor. As a result, you may not get the materials you need when you need them.

---

### Dialogue

**Bob:** I'm sorry the Peterson account was not assigned to you. You deserved it. Roger's claim of being more qualified to handle the job is not true. I'm really surprised that our boss, Ted, believed Roger's claim.

**Sally:** I agree. Nobody likes Roger because he always has to get his own way. I cannot stand the way Roger puts down co-workers and members of other departments to force them to give him his own way. Roger has pulled the old emergency routine so many times now that purchasing and maintenance ignore his requests. This hurts our department.

**Bob:** You are right. Roger only thinks of himself. He never considers other people or what is best for the company. I have overheard Ted telling him he has to be a team player if he wants to get ahead.

**Sally:** The way he tries to beat everyone out all the time is sickening. He will do anything to get ahead. But the way he behaves, he will never climb the corporate ladder.

To be ethically successful, organizations must audit the ethical behaviour of their employees and confront and discipline employees who are unethical. Top managers need to lead by ethical example, they need to be honest with employees and they need to build trust.

## 4. Ethics and Decision-making

If, after making a decision, you are proud to tell all the relevant parties your decision, the decision is probably ethical. If you are embarrassed to tell others your decision or you keep rationalizing the decision, it may not be ethical. Do unto others as you want them to do unto you. Don't do anything to anyone that you would not want them to do to you.

Before making a decision, making a statement or taking action of any kind, ask yourself these questions. Is it the truth? Is it fair to all concerned? Will it build goodwill and better friendship? Will it be beneficial to all concerned? Is it the right thing to do, say?

People using unethical politics tend to lie, cheat and break the rules. In time people recognize unethical people and distrust them. Generally people who use ethical politics are more productive in the long run than people who use unethical politics. People who use unethical politics may get short-run performance results, but in the long run, performance will be lower.

This   or this?

### Career Management Tip

Are you president of your company? Do you want your company's sales, profits and stock price to go through the roof? Then create an environment where ethical politics, cooperative effort and working as a team are encouraged and rewarded.

Are you at an early stage in your career? Do you have your eye on a management level position? Then practice ethical politics. Use every opportunity you can to develop "win-win" situations. Unethical behaviour can get you fired, which will stop your performance within an organization and can also result in your going to prison.

### Managers and Senior Staff Fired for Unethical Practices

BOSTON-A dozen Prudential Securities employees have been asked to resign following investigations of market timing of mutual funds.

*The Wall Street Journal* said the employees include the managers of Prudential's downtown Boston office and its office in Garden City on New York's Long Island.

The action followed an internal company review of the firm's 12,000 brokers and 700 offices.

The Journal said Prudential's practices have come under investigation during the past month by Massachusetts and New York securities regulators, the Securities and Exchange Commission and the National Association of Securities Dealers.

Investigators are reportedly determining whether brokers improperly allowed hedge funds to buy and sell mutual funds rapidly—a practice known as market timing.

While not illegal, the practice is considered improper if a mutual fund's prospectus says it discourages market timing—as many do—because such trading can hurt the returns of long-term shareholders.

## 4. Ethics and Decision-making

### Dialogue—The Problem Hits Home

**Joe:** Good morning, Tony. How are things going?

**Tony:** Hi, Joe. Ok I guess. Things are pretty rough around here, eh?

**Joe:** Yes, they sure are. Did you hear the news? The company is letting another 2,500 people go this month.

**Tony:** Yes, I heard. I am really worried. When they cut 3,000 jobs last fall I was afraid that I might get the axe. Fortunately I managed to survive. Now I am not so sure. Our office is not doing very well. So many of our customers have gone over to other brokers. We have really tried hard to keep them, but most are extremely upset over the way we treated them for years.

**Joe:** I know what you mean. Our group is having trouble also. I've had my résumé posted for some time and I have applied to many other companies, but it seems like people from Marsh are not thought of very highly anymore.

**Tony:** I'm afraid you're right. Things don't look very good for us. That's for sure!

**Joe:** How are Marge and the kids taking it?

**Tony:** Well, they're obviously pretty upset and awfully worried. We took out a large loan last summer to finish the basement. If I lose my job, we won't be able to make the payments and will probably end up losing the house. It's amazing how fast things can change. I still remember Christmas 2003. The incentive fees we earned from the insurance companies reached record highs which meant we got great bonuses.

**Joe:** Those were the days. I took my family to a Hyatt resort hotel in Hawaii. We had a fabulous time. I don't imagine we'll be doing that for a long time to come!

**Tony:** So true.

**Joe:** Do you have a big position in company stock?

**Tony:** No, not much fortunately. How about you?

**Joe:** I put a lot of shares in my retirement fund—you know, support the company you work for. Not only is the stock down 40%, but they just announced that they are cutting the dividend in half. Even if I don't lose my job, Betty will have to go back to work. We don't have that many years left to try to build our savings back up before retirement. And we were counting on the dividend income to help pay the college tuition costs for Jamie.

**Tony:** Things are pretty bad all right, but look on the bright side. At least we're not going to jail, not yet anyway! You heard about those three guys from the downtown office?

**Joe:** Yes, I did and they probably won't be all before this thing is finished.

**Tony:** Well, I better get back to work. Have to make the best of a back situation until something better comes along.

**Joe:** Yes, it's been good talking to you. See you later.

**Tony:** Bye for now. Good luck.

**Joe:** Thanks! you, too.

**Tony:** Thanks.

## Dialogue—The E-mail

**Robert:** Hello, Martin. I'm glad I bumped into you. I wanted to talk to you about that E-mail that Frank sent around. Did you see it?

**Martin:** Yes, I did. It makes me very nervous also. He wants us to clean out our files. I thought that we are under a court order to keep everything.

**Robert:** That is my understanding also. It seems to me that we are taking big risk by destroying evidence, even if it may incriminate us later on.

## 4. Ethics and Decision-making

**Martin:** I agree. But you know Frank. He had that problem in Texas a few years ago and he doesn't want to go through it again.

**Robert:** You are right. What are you going to do? I don't know for sure. I thought I would talk to a lawyer about it myself and see what he recommends.

**Martin:** That's a good idea. Do you mind letting me know what you find out?

**Robert:** Of course not. I'll give you a call as soon as I have any information.

**Martin:** Thanks a lot. I really appreciate it. Say, are you free for lunch sometime this week. It has been a while since we got together?

**Robert:** Friday is open. How is that for you?

**Martin:** Friday's fine. How about I meet you at O'Malley's Pub at 12:15?

**Robert:** Sounds great.

**Martin:** Excellent. I'll give you a call Friday morning to confirm.

Elective Course A Ethics 选修内容 A 金融职业伦理

## Case Study
# Lincoln Savings and Loan Association

## Background

**Savings and loan associations**

Savings and Loan Associations (also called "thrift institutions" or simply "thrifts") in the United States are financial intermediaries like banks. Their main business purpose is to take deposits from the public and make loans to people to buy homes. Deposits up to US $60,000 are guaranteed by the United States government. This means that if a savings and loan association goes bankrupt and cannot pay back the money it owes to its depositors, the federal government will—up to $60,000 per account.

**Regulation**

The industry was heavily regulated. S & Ls, as they are called, could only make residential mortgage loans and invest in government securities. The interest rates they could charge on their loans and pay to their depositors were fixed by law at relatively low levels.

Nevertheless, despite the low interest rates, deposit accounts at savings and loan associations were attractive to many people. They provided a very secure investment because of the government guarantee. Most people deposited much less than the $60,000 limit on the guarantee. The deposits were very liquid. They could be withdrawn (converted to cash) at any time. And there were few attractive alternative investments for small amounts of money.

**Changing times**

During the 1970s, however, conditions changed substantially. Largely driven by the quadrupling of the oil price in 1973, the rate of inflation rose dramatically. Interest rates rose to levels well above the amounts savings and loan associations could legally pay. A wide variety of investment vehicles became available to small investors. For example, mutual funds promising much higher returns than those on S & L deposits were aggressively marketed by independent sales agents all across the country.

The savings and loan associations could not compete in these new market conditions.

Case Study: Lincoln Savings and Loan Association

They either had to be deregulated or the entire industry would die.

**Deregulation**

Faced with this dilemma, the government chose deregulation. First, the interest rate caps on loans and deposits were removed. Second, the range of assets savings and loan associations could buy and the type of liabilities they could incur were broadened considerably. For example, S & Ls were permitted to invest up to 40% of their assets in commercial real estate loans and up to 11% of their assets in business loans. While might real estate loans had to be secured, the business loans could be unsecured. In addition to offering savings deposits to the public paying market rates of interest, they could sell unsecured debentures to the public through their branches. Unlike the deposits, the debentures were not guaranteed by the federal government.

One other important change also occurred. The federal government insurance on individual deposits with all types of financial institutions including savings and loan associations was increased from $ 60,000 to $ 100,000.

**The new look**

Savings and Loan Institutions were therefore permitted to take on much riskier investments in the knowledge that each depositor's money was insured by the government up to $ 100,000. Many traditionally conservative S & Ls changed overnight to become aggressive, high-flying, risk-taking, financial institutions. The end result was one of the most expensive and far-reaching government bailouts ever.

## Lincoln Savings and Loan Association

Lincoln Savings and Loan was one of the most spectacular examples of the result of the deregulation of the industry. Lincoln was a savings and loan association that was based in Phoenix, Arizona. In 1984, it was acquired by American Continental Corporation (ACC), a real estate development company, which had been founded in 1978 by Charles H. Keating, Jr., a flamboyant businessman whose extravagant lifestyle and outrageous spending habits were legendary.

Before its acquisition by ACC, Lincoln had been a traditional thrift. It gathered its deposits through a 29-branch network and made long-term mortgage loans on single family homes. Charles Keating's involvement with Lincoln quickly changed all that.

He installed himself as Chairman and completely replaced Lincoln's management. He implemented a program of aggressively increasing deposits through the existing branch network and by nationwide marketing. The interest rates offered were ½% to 1% above those available at competitors. The money flooded in.

Keating also changed Lincoln's lending and investment policies. Large construction loans, large loans for the acquisition and development of real estate, large scale direct real estate investments and substantial investments in debt and equity securities were emphasized.

## Roland's Diary

The following are extracts from the diary of Roland Fleming written during a critical period in Lincoln's history.

**July 23, 1986**

The American economy is booming. The stock market is soaring. I'm working for one of the most dynamic and profitable financial institutions in the United States. I'm only 25 and I just got a job where I earn more than $100,000 a year!

When I graduated, I wasn't interested in working for a bank. However, that interview with Lincoln Savings and Loan for the job as assistant loan officer really changed my mind. Lincoln Savings and Loan is going places and I'm going with it!

Lincoln's chairman is one of the most dynamic and exciting people I've ever met. He believes in promoting young people fast. His son is president of Lincoln. He got the job when he was only 26!

I started as a loan officer. However, in the last three years, I have been fast tracked. In my new position as Special Projects Manager, I am responsible for coordinating the company's real estate activities. They constitute an important part of Lincoln's assets. In many situations, I will be working closely with Mr. Keating.

When ACC acquired Lincoln, Lincoln's main business was in residential mortgage loans. These were safe investments but certainly not very exciting. Mr. Keating changed all that. By using his expertise in real estate development and his contacts from ACC, he has shifted Lincoln's main activity to land development projects. He isn't even risking the depositors' money since all deposits up to $100,000 are insured by the government. In the last two years, the real estate transactions have provided the main source of Lincoln's profits and I am right in the middle. It's going to be an exciting few years!

**December 20, 1986**

It's now almost six months since I took this job and started keeping this journal and boy, has it been a roller coaster ride. I have been just as busy as I thought I would be and the real estate transactions have been coming thick and fast. The most recent innovation that Mr. Keating has instituted in Lincoln is the sale of ACC bonds in Lincoln's branches. It seems an obvious extension of Lincoln's services to provide investment opportunities to our customers other than the usual savings accounts and CDs.

I'm looking forward to the holidays to get a break—life has been hectic. I'll be having an ice fishing trip in Minnesota with Uncle Harry and my dad. Since he retired, Uncle Harry has become a fishing fanatic, although what he sees in sitting for hours in a wooden hut in the middle of a frozen lake, staring into a hole in the ice, I do not know!

**March 26, 1987**

Mr. Keating reviewed Lincoln's operating results with me. He wants to push another real estate transaction through the books before the end of the March $31^{st}$-quarter-end to boost the company's profits. I suggested we try to sell one of the Hidden Valley parcels. We just received an independent appraisal of $8.5 million. for 1,000 acres there. Lincoln's original cost was $2.9 million. The company would realize a substantial profit if Mr. Keating can make a deal. Mr. Keating thinks he can swing it with the help of his friend Ernie Garcia who is a real estate developer. If we push this one through, it will mean a big bonus for me.

**March 31, 1987**

The Hidden Valley transaction went through today, just under the wire on the very last day of the quarter. Mr. Keating is a magician!

Ernie Garcia introduced Mr. Keating to one of his friends, Fernando Acosta, who owns West Continental Mortgage Company (Westcon), a Tucson, Arizona, mortgage broker.

Wescon bought the 1,000-acre Hidden Valley parcel for $14 million—an $11.1 million profit!

Uncle Harry called today to say that he had followed my advice and bought some ACC bonds. Given how well Lincoln is doing with all these real estate deals, he really can't go wrong. It's a far smarter investment than the certificates of deposits (CDs) he has been investing in. He might even be able to go fishing in Europe with the extra income.

**April 15, 1987**

Wescon (Mr. Acosta's company) was given an unsecured $3.5 million loan by ECG Holdings Ltd. (Mr. Garcia s company) at the end of March, just before the Hidden Valley-Wescon transaction went through. The $3.5 million is the down payment that Wescon used for the transaction. The remaining purchase price was paid by Wescon by issuing a note to Lincoln for $10.5 million. The note is very unusual. I hope Wescon can make the payments on it.

**April 22, 1987**

I'm beginning to be concerned about the Hidden Valley-Wescon transaction. I did some checking on Wescon and its net worth is less than $50,000. How is it going to meet its payments on a note of $10.5 million? If Wescon can't meet these payments, I'm not sure we should have taken credit for the profit on the sale of the 1,000 acres in Hidden Valley. If the Wescon notes aren't worth $10.5 million, then we didn't receive $14 million for the parcel and then surely the profit on the transaction must be less than $11.1 million.

**April 30, 1987**

I've just talked to my friend Greg Grovel. He took the public accounting route after college and now has his own practice. He wants to do consulting work for Lincoln, particularly in relation to our real estate transactions. I asked him about the revenue recognition issue for the Hidden Valley-Wescon transaction and also about valuing Wescon's note. He said he would prepare a memo for me. He has an interest in helping us out. We can give him a lot of work.

**May 9, 1987**

Just got the memo from Greg. His interpretation is that the Hidden Valley-Wescon transaction satisfies the rules and therefore there isn't a problem in recognizing the revenue. I'm really relieved. The auditors are due in next week and the Wescon deal is just one of several, similar transactions we have planned for this year. Our income statement would have looked really sick if we'd had to exclude them all from our revenue. I'm still a bit concerned about Wescon's ability to repay the note, but maybe I shouldn't be concerned. Uncle Harry's ACC bonds should be OK as long as the real estate transactions are valid.

**June 2, 1987**

Discovered an interesting thing today. Lincoln made a loan commitment of $30 million to ECG Holdings (Ernie Garcia's company) at the end of March and $19.6 million was immediately withdrawn in cash. Mr. Keating must really think Ernie Garcia is going places if he can get that size of a loan from Lincoln.

**April 25, 1988**

Just back from a weekend fishing with Uncle Harry. We spent some time talking about the latest ACC bond issue. We went over the prospectus and I helped Uncle Harry understand the financial statements. I was able to explain to Uncle Harry how much my work had contributed to Lincoln's profit for 1987.

There were eight transactions involving parcels from Hidden Valley (including the Wescon deal). In total, they contributed $103 million to revenue and $62 million to pretax profit. These deals were all structured like the Wescon transaction with a down payment of 25% from the buyer and notes receivable for the balance.

At the same time as the sales took place, Lincoln made substantial loans for other purposes to each buyer—over $200 million in total. Those loans really helped swing the deals.

Uncle Harry is determined to put all his savings into ACC bonds. I didn't try to talk him out of it, but I did explain to him that the ACC bonds are not federally insured like his CDs. I didn't push the point too hard. Lincoln is doing so well that the insurance probably doesn't matter.

I do worry, though, that prospectus shows that the market value of ACC's investments is far below what the company paid for them. Given the stock market crash of October last year; that's probably not surprising. I don't suppose it matters much though because the company is doing so well in other areas.

**May 25, 1989**

I haven't written in this journal for over a year and looking back on what I wrote then, I can't believe how naive I was. I really thought Keating was a god and could do no wrong!

Lincoln finally was seized by the federal regulators last month, although the writing was on the wall long before that. I had suspicions two years ago, but because I was so dazzled by Keating, I convinced myself that there wasn't a problem. If only I had followed my instincts...

Although I'm out of a job (and given that I worked for Lincoln, finding a new one isn't easy), my biggest worry is Uncle Harry. He put all of his savings in the ACC bonds after I told him they were OK. He has lost everything and Dad says he is really depressed. He worked so hard to save for his retirement and to think that he lost it all because of me! How could I have been so gullible and stupid?

## Elective Course A Ethics 选修内容 A 金融职业伦理

> $ 200,000,000
> American Continental Corporation
> Subordinate Debentures
> (Issuable in Series)

**Minimum Purchase:** $ 1,000

American Continental Corporation (the "Company") is offering directly to the public up to $ 200,000,000 aggregate principal amount of its Subordinate Debentures (the "Debentures"). The Company intends to offer the Debentures for sale directly to the public from time to time pursuant to this Prospectus. Based upon market conditions the Company periodically will establish series of Debentures which will conform to the description of the Debentures set forth in this Prospectus. At December 31, 1987, the Company had issued $ 92,627,000 aggregate principal amount of Debentures in 118 series.

The Debentures will be offered to the public primarily through the selling efforts of full-time employees of the Company and its affiliates other than Lincoln Savings and Loan Association ("Lincoln Savings") at each of Lincoln Savings' branches in California and at the Company's offices in Phoenix, Arizona. In addition, subject to the receipt of applicable state regulatory approvals, the Company may send notice of the offering of one or more series of Debentures or a copy of this Prospectus and the Prospectus Supplement(s) relating to such series, to holders of other securities of the Company and its subsidiaries in the states where such holders reside. See "Plan of Distribution".

Unless otherwise stated in a Prospectus Supplement, interest on each series of Debentures will be payable on the $28^{th}$ day of each calendar month, with respect to interest accrued through the last day of the preceding calendar month. Each Debenture will bear interest from the date on which payment of the purchase price is received by the Company. The Debentures will be redeemable on the dates and at the prices, set forth in the Prospectus Supplement relating to such series.

The Debentures will be subordinated to all Senior Indebtedness (as defined) of the Company. The Indenture under which the Debentures are to be issued does not limit the amount of Senior Indebtedness the Company may incur. At December 31, 1987, the Company had outstanding approximately $ 150,134,000 of Senior Indebtedness. Unless otherwise stated in a Prospectus Supplement, the Debentures will be sold in minimum denominations of $ 1,000. See "Description of Debentures".

Because the Debentures are being offered by the Company directly to the public without a firm underwriting commitment, no assurance can be given as to the amount of Debentures that will be sold and the Company is not required to sell any minimum aggregate principal amount of Debentures or of any series of Debentures. It is unlikely that a market for the Debentures will exist after the offering. Accordingly, it will be difficult to resell the Debentures particularly because it is anticipated that various series will bear different interest rates and have different maturity dates. For a description of certain risks and other factors, see "Special Factors".

**THESE SECURITIES HAVE NOT BEEN APPROVED OR DISAPPROVED BY THE SECURITIES AND EXCHANGE COMMISSION, NOR HAS THE COMMISSION PASSED UPON THE ACCURACY OR ADEQUACY OF THIS PROSPECTUS, ANY REPRESENTATION TO THE CONTRARY IS A CRIMINAL OFFENSE.**

**THE DEBENTURES BEING OFFERED ARE THE SOLE OBLIGATION OF THE COMPANY AND ARE NOT BEING OFFERED AS SAVINGS ACCOUNTS OR DEPOSITS AND ARE NOT INSURED BY THE FEDERAL SAVINGS AND LOAN INSURANCE CORPORATION.**

|  | Maximum Price to Public (1) | Underwriting Discount | Maximum Proceeds to Company (1) (2) |
|---|---|---|---|
| Per Debenture | 100% | -0- | 100% |
| Maximum Aggregate Offering Price | $ 200,000,000 | -0- | $ 200,000,000 |

(1) In no case shall the Maximum Price to Public of all series of Debentures exceed the amount set forth under Maximum Aggregate Offering Price.

(2) Before deducting expenses payable by the Company, estimated to be $ 195,000 plus $ 25,000 per series. See "Use of Proceeds."

(3) There is no minimum amount of Debentures required to be sold by the Company.

This Prospectus does not contain complete information with respect to each series of Debentures proposed to be sold. A Prospectus Supplement with respect to each series of Debentures offered hereunder will set forth with regard to such series. (i) the maximum aggregate principal amount, interest rate and maturity date of the Debentures of such series and (ii) the redemption provisions with respect to such series. Debentures of any series may not be sold and offers to buy may not be accepted unless the purchasers have received both this prospectus and the Prospectus Supplement relating to such series.

*The date of the Prospectus is April 1988.*

**Questions for Discussion**

1. How would you define ethical conduct?
2. Is ethical behavior necessary in society? Why or why not?
3. Why do some people act unethically?
4. What is fraudulent financial reporting?
5. What probably motivated ACC/Lincoln's management to misstate its financial statements?
6. What conditions were present which allowed the fraudulent reporting to occur?
7. What could or should have prevented or detected it?
8. Why might an auditor be willing to certify a company's financial statements when there is solid evidence of questionable transactions?

# Elective Course B  Money Laundering
## 选修内容B  反洗钱

The world's third largest business, money laundering is the lifeblood of drug dealers, fraudsters, smugglers, arms dealers, terrorists and tax-evaders.

## 1. Money Laundering and Crime

Organized criminals in general and drug traffickers in particular generate huge amounts of cash. These people must make their illegally acquired wealth appear legitimate in order to derive the maximum benefit from their illegal activities.

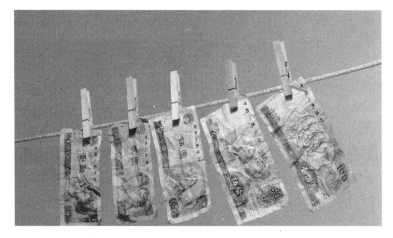

Money laundering is the process by which large amounts of illegally obtained money (from drug trafficking, terrorist activity or other serious crime) is given the appearance of having originated from a legitimate source. When the process succeeds, the individuals involved are free to use the money for personal consumption (buying luxurious homes, fancy cars, and world travel) and investing in stocks, bonds, real estate and businesses.

## 2. Benefits of Laundering Money

Various people from all walks of life become involved in money laundering. Why?

- Avoid prosecution for the crime that produced the money in the first place.
- Increase personal income by re-investing the proceeds of the crime.
- Avoid seizure of accumulated wealth—the laws of some countries permit the authorities to seize cash and assets (cars, houses, jewelry, yachts) that can be shown to have been purchased with the proceeds of a crime.
- Appear as a legitimate businessman or woman.

> Money laundering is a serious and on-going problem that causes significant difficulties in all parts of the world.

■ Evade taxes on legitimate income (earnings from a business, for example) or the income earned from committing a crime.

## 3. Some History

The term may have originated from Mafia ownership of laundromats in the United States. Gangsters there were earning huge sums in cash from extortion, prostitution, gambling and bootleg liquor. They needed to show a legitimate source for these monies.

The major headache that gangsters faced was that the money was in cash, often in small denomination coins. If the coins were put into the bank, questions would be asked. Moreover, the storage of large amounts of money in low value coins was a storage nightmare. To overcome these problems, they entered two new businesses: one was slot machine gambling and the other was coin-operated laundries—so, it is said, that the term "money laundry" was born.

One of the ways in which they were able to do this was by purchasing outwardly legitimate businesses and to mix their illicit earnings with the legitimate earnings they received from these businesses. Laundromats were chosen by these gangsters because they were cash businesses.

The term also perfectly describes what takes place—illegal or dirty money is put through a cycle of transactions—washed—so that it comes out the other end as legal or clean money. In other words, the source of illegally obtained funds is obscured through a succession of transfers and deals in order that those same funds can eventually be made to appear as legitimate income.

Meyer Lansky, a financial genius affectionately called "the Mob's Accountant", was determined not to be convicted of tax evasion the way Mob boss, Al Capone, was. So he set about searching for ways to hide money for himself and his cronies. He soon discovered the benefits of numbered Swiss bank accounts. For select customers, many Swiss private banks were willing to establish accounts that could be identified only by number. At the time Swiss

# Elective Course B Money Laundering 选修内容 B 反洗钱

banking laws were extremely tight. Banks were absolutely forbidden to disclose any information to authorities about the true ownership of the numbered accounts. Only one or two of the top officers of the bank had access to the information that could connect a particular account to its real owner.

Money from any source could be deposited into these accounts with complete anonymity. There was absolutely no way that the money could ever be traced back to the owner or its source—legitimate or otherwise—could be determined.

One of the most influential money launderers ever, Meyer Lansky developed the loan-back technique. Under this arrangement, the banks in Switzerland holding funds deposited by the Mafia would in turn loan the money to legitimate businesses owned by Mafia bosses. The money came back into the United States as loans from reputable Swiss banks to ordinary businesses. There was no way of proving that the money that the Mafia was using to finance legitimate businesses originally came from criminal activities. Furthermore, no income tax was paid on those profits. The Mafia paid taxes on the earnings from legitimate businesses in which they invested, of course, but after deducting the interest they paid to the Swiss banks on the loans.

Coin-operated laundries (laundromats) are good vehicles for concealing the source of large amount of coins and small-denomination banknotes. The illegitimate proceeds can easily be commingled with the cash received from customers and deposited in the bank in the normal course of business.

### 3. Some History

#### A Word of Advice

Al Capone, one of America's most notorious gangsters, was convicted and sent to prison not for murdering countless people, but for not paying income taxes on the earnings from his criminal activities such as rum-running (selling liquor when it was against the law), prostitution, extortion, gambling, etc.

Suppose you rob a bank—a crime—and are caught, but the police never find the money. If you voluntarily pay income tax on the money you stole, you will be charged just with robbing the bank. If the police do not get the money back and you do not report it as income and pay tax on it, you will be prosecuted for two distinct crimes: robbing a bank and tax evasion.

If done successfully, money laundering allows the criminals to:
- maintain control over the proceeds of their crimes, and
- provide a legitimate cover for their source of income.

Money laundering plays a fundamental role in facilitating the ambitions of the drug traffickers, the terrorists, the organized criminals, the insider traders, the tax evaders as well as the many others who need to avoid the kind of attention from the authorities that sudden wealth brings from illegal activities. By engaging in this type of activity they hope to place the proceeds beyond the reach of any asset forfeiture laws.

#### The Shanghai Times Special Edition

#### Well-known Businessman Arrested on Money Laundering Charges

Guangzhou—Just before dawn this morning, heavily armed police officers descended on a palatial home in a quiet suburban neighborhood and arrested a prominent businessman on charges of laundering more than US $ 100,000,000 over a period of 5 years. In a well-coordinated plan, several other teams of police raided the man's offices throughout the city and seized large amounts of cash. Officers were seen carrying computers, books, records and boxes of files to waiting vans, a process that took several hours. Well-known as much for his flamboyant life style as his classy, up-scale shopping malls, the man is being held without bail at an undisclosed location.

# 4. Money Laundering Schemes

### A. Structuring ("smurfing")

Smurfing is possibly the most commonly used money laundering method. It involves many individuals who deposit cash or buy bank drafts in amounts under the $10,000 reporting limit. In some cases, a bank employee is co-opted to help keep the process from being disclosed to the authorities.

### B. Legitimate Business / Commingling of Funds

Money launderers take over existing businesses that typically handle a lot of cash. Examples are restaurants, bars, nightclubs, hotels, currency exchange shops, cheque cashing services, vending machine operators, car washes and laundromats. The illicit proceeds are easily mixed with the normal revenues of the business.

### C. Loan back

A money launderer provides an associate with a specific amount of illegitimate money. The associate, then, loans the same amount back to him or her along with all the appropriate loan and security documentation. This creates the illusion that the funds are from a legitimate source. The launderer then makes regularly scheduled interest and principal payments on the loan to re-enforce the legitimacy of the scheme.

### D. Asset purchases with bulk cash

Money launderers purchase big ticket items such as cars, boats, planes or real estate for cash. In many cases, launderers may use the asset personally but will distance themselves legally from it by having it registered in someone else's name.

### E. Phony Car Lease Scam

Criminals purchase a car with dirty money and then pay a leasing company to arrange a phony lease agreement. The leasing company claims to be the owner of the car and "leases" the car to a nominee of the criminal. If the car is seized, the lease agreement allows the company to recover the car by asserting "innocent owner" status. The leasing company then secretly returns the car to the criminal.

### F. Reverse flip

A money launderer may find a cooperative property seller who agrees to a reported purchase price well below the actual value and then accepts the difference "under the table". For example, the money launderer may purchase a property worth $ 2,000,000 for a reported $ 1,000,000, secretly passing the balance to the cooperative seller in cash. After holding the property for a period of time, the launderer sells it for its true value of $ 2,000,000.

### G. Diamond Industry "Checks for Cash"

Criminals purchase customer checks from diamond dealers with dirty money. In many places, diamond dealers are not subject to the same record—keeping and reporting procedures that financial institutions are. Since they deal in relatively large sums of money with little or no documentation, diamond dealers are prime targets for money launderers.

### H. Underground Banking

Sometimes called "parallel" banking, these systems are highly efficient methods of transferring money around the world. The best known among them are the Chop, Hundi and Hawallah banking systems of certain ethnic communities. There is no conventional paper record of the transactions.

These systems do not require the actual movement of money. Instead money is paid to someone in another country in the local currency of that country by drawing on the reserves of the overseas partner of the local Chop, Hundi or Hawallah banker.

The system is dependant on considerable trust and great simplicity—the money launderer places an amount with the underground bank—the identifying receipt for a transaction being something as innocuous as a playing card or post-card torn in half, half being held by the customer and half being forwarded to the overseas Hawallah banker. The launderer then presents his receipt in the target country to obtain his money, thus avoiding exporting cash out of the country and virtually eliminating the risk of detection.

### I. Chinese Flying Money

In this variation of underground banking, corporate accounts are used to remit money to and from Asia on behalf. For a fee, a Chinese trader in a foreign country arranges for funds deposited with him by a local businessman to be made available for withdrawal from another trader in China. The accounts would then be settled by the two traders through the normal process of trade. Their transactions are very difficult to detect because they are essentially paperless.

### J. Black Market Peso Exchange

Money brokers in Columbia and other South and Central American countries purchase money in the United States from money launderers. The brokers then deposit the funds they have bought in US bank accounts. Businesses in various countries outside the US would buy from the money brokers checks drawn on those accounts to pay for goods and services purchased in the U.S.

### K. Securities, commodities and futures brokers

In its simplest form, this scheme involves a broker taking in cash and delivering securities in bearer form in exchange.

In a more sophisticated version, the money launderer simultaneously buys and sells the same commodity, currency, stock, etc. They settle the buy contract in cash and receive a broker's cheque for the proceeds of the sale. Their only cost is the small amount of commission that they pay on the two trades. The cheque and sale contract create a paper trail that legitimizes the source of the money and is usually enough to satisfy all but the most persistent tracker.

## L. Casinos

Casinos and gambling establishments are particularly attractive to money launderers. Cash can be deposited with a casino in exchange for chips or tokens. After a few turns at the table the player can cash in the remainder for a cashier's cheque which can be deposited in any bank account.

## M. Purchasing winning lottery tickets

A lottery ticket wholesaler contacts other wholesalers or lottery vendors to identify winning ticket-holders. The wholesaler will purchase the winning ticket for the criminal at a price 20% to 50% greater than the face value. The money launderer presents the winning ticket and claims the prize. The premium he or she pays over the face value of the ticket is the "cost" of laundering the money.

## N. Other methods

- Currency exchanges

    Currency exchanges provide a service that permits individuals to buy foreign currency that can then be transported out of the country. Money can also be wired to offshore bank accounts anywhere in the world by these exchanges.

- Telegraphic transfer of funds

    Wiring money from one city or country to another without actually carrying the money.

- Postal money orders

    Exchanging cash for money orders and then shipping them out of the country for deposit.

- Travel agencies

    Exchanging cash for travel tickets, especially airline tickets.

- Credit cards

    Overpaying credit cards and keeping a high credit balance that can be turned over to cash at any time and place.

- Refining

    Individuals change small bills into large ones which are usually done by visiting a number of banks so as not to arouse suspicion. The purpose of refining is to decrease the size and weight of large quantities of cash.

# 5. The Money Laundering Process

Money laundering is not a single act but is in fact a process that is accomplished in three basic steps: placement, layering and integration. These steps can be taken at the same time in the course of a single transaction, but they can also appear in distinctly separate forms as well.

There are also common factors regarding the wide range of methods used by money launderers when they attempt to launder their criminal proceeds. Three common factors identified in laundering operations are the following:

- the need to conceal the origin and true ownership of the proceeds;
- the need to maintain control of the proceeds;
- the need to change the form of the proceeds in order to shrink the huge volumes of cash generated by the initial criminal activity.

### A. Placement

This is the first stage in the washing cycle. Money laundering is a "cash-intensive" business. Illegal activities like drug dealing on the street generate huge amounts of cash in small denominations. The options available to the money launderer are:

- placing the money into the financial system or retail economy, and
- smuggling it out of the country.

The aims of the launderer are first to remove the cash from the location where it was acquired so as to avoid detection from the authorities and then to transform it into other forms of assets, such as travellers cheques, postal money orders, cars, jewelry, real estate, etc.

### B. Layering

In this stage, the money launderer tries to conceal or disguise the source and ownership of the funds by creating complex layers of financial transactions. The objective is to make an audit trail impossible to follow.

Typically, layers are created by moving the money in and out of the offshore bank accounts of bearer share shell companies through electronic fund transfers. Generally speaking, there is not enough information disclosed on any single wire transfer to know how clean or dirty the money is. Moreover, there are over 700,000 wire transfers circling the globe daily representing well over US $ 2 trillion. In view of the sheer volume and the high degree of anonymity, the chance of a single transaction being identified as laundering and then being traced back to the original owner is minimal. Wire transfer systems allow legitimate businesses, individual banking customers and criminal organizations to enjoy a swift and nearly risk-free conduct for moving money amony countries and around the world.

Along the way, the money launderer may insert complex dealings with stock, commodity and futures brokers to further confuse authorities who try to follow a paper trail.

### C. Integration

This is the final stage in the money laundering process. The money is integrated back into the legitimate economic and financial system and assimilated with all other assets. Integration of the "cleaned" money into the economy is accomplished by the launderer making it appear to have been legally earned. By this stage, it is exceedingly difficult to distinguish between legal and illegal wealth.

Methods popular to money launderers at this stage of the game include the following:

a. Money launderers establish companies in countries where the right to secrecy regarding ownership is guaranteed. They have those companies grant loans to themselves or their legitimate businesses out of the laundered money—a perfectly legal transaction. And what is more, they will further increase their profits by getting a tax deduction for the interest payments that they make on the loans.

b. By sending false export-import invoices over-valuating goods, the launderer can move money from one company or country to another. The invoices verify the "legitimate" origin of the monies placed with financial institutions.

c. The simplest method is for the launderer to transfer the money by wire to a legitimate bank from a bank that he or she owns. Ready-made shell banks ("off the shelf banks") are easily purchased in many tax havens.

### Cyber-payments

Cyber-payments are transactions that occur over the Internet or through the use of smart cards. Cyber-payment systems are designed to provide people with immediate, convenient, secure and potentially anonymous means of storing and transferring the money. The speed which makes the systems efficient, and the anonymity that makes them secure are very attractive features for money launderers.

The Internet is one of the greatest opportunities for laundering because of the total lack of traceable transactions and the use of encryption software that make transactions totally secure. Connecting to anywhere in the world is easy and making cross-border transfers of money is simple.

Smart cards are another device which money launderers can use to conceal the source of illegitimate funds. These cards contain a microchip which stores value on the card. They are "recharged" (money obtained legally or otherwise is added to the balance stored on the card) by putting it into a special slot in an ATM. The problem for the authorities and the benefit for money launderers is that smart cards can be used without leaving any physical evidence.

## 6. Preventing Money Laundering

The primary purpose of organized crime is to make profits. Like any business, the purposes of profit are to enjoy it and re-invest it into future activity. For the organized criminal, however, profit close to the source of the crime represents a particular vulnerability, and unless the criminal can effectively distance himself or herself from the crime, which is the source of the profit, he or she remains susceptible to detection and prosecution. Therefore, illegally obtained cash and profits need to be laundered to make them appear legitimate.

The biggest source of illicit profits comes from the drug trade, a highly cash intensive business. In the case of cocaine and heroin, the physical volume of banknotes received is much larger than the volume of drugs themselves. In order to rid themselves of this large burden, it is necessary to use the financial services industry, and in particular, deposit-taking institutions.

**Choke points**

There are certain "choke" points in the money laundering process that the launderers find difficult to avoid and where they are most vulnerable to detection. These points are:

A. The point of entry of cash into the financial system;

B. Transfer of the cash through and from the financial system;

C. Transfer of the cash out of the financial system; and

D. Cross-border flows of cash.

The entry of cash into the financial system, known as the "placement" stage, is where the launderer is most vulnerable to detection. The large amounts of cash involved make it extremely difficult for it to be placed into a bank account without raising suspicions.

---

### Statement of Principles

The Statement of Principles covers all aspects of money laundering through the banking system, which is depositing transferring and/or concealing money obtained from illicit activities such as robbery, terrorism, fraud or drug dealing. The objective is to prevent those engaged in money laundering from using the banking system for that purpose.

a. Know your customer

Banks should try hard to determine the customer's true identity, and have effective procedures for verifying the fact that new customers, whether depositors or borrowers, are honest, and that the information they give is true and complete.

b. Comply with laws

Bank management should ensure that:
- business is conducted in conformity with high ethical standards
- laws and regulations are being adhered to
- services where there is good reason to suppose that transactions are associated with money laundering activities. are not provided

c. Co-operate with law enforcement agencies. are not provided

## Elective Course B Money Laundering 选修内容B 反洗钱

### People's Bank of China—Anti-Money-Laundering Guidelines

■ Financial institutions should:
- create specialized anti-money laundering positions in their branch offices and carefully define their responsibilities of those positions;
- formulate internal operating procedures for identifying and preventing money laundering;
- establish and improve internal controls relating to anti-money laundering and report such mechanisms to the PBOC;
- formulate internal rules and operating procedures for payment, establish and improve internal controls relating to anti-money laundering, and report such mechanisms to the PBOC for the record. Such rules and procedures are to be reported to the PBOC;
- establish and improve internal mechanisms of responsibility for anti-money laundering;
- have dedicated staff record, analyze and report large-value and suspicious foreign exchange transactions;
- establish or designate relevant internal departments to specialize in anti-money laundering efforts and equip them with personnel as needed and
- assist judicial and/or law enforcement agencies in combating money laundering.

■ Financial institutions should not:
- open anonymous accounts or accounts with obviously false names for customers and
- engage in unfair competition that may run counter to anti-money laundering efforts.

■ Employees of financial institutions should:
- be on the lookout for suspicious transactions;
- carefully scrutinize large-value and/or suspicious transactions;
- report to local public security authorities immediately if, after analyzing suspected transactions, immediate criminal investigation appears to be warranted and
- not disclose any information on anti-money laundering activities to their customers and other outsiders.

# 7. Customer due Diligence—Know Your Customer

The risk of being an unwitting participant and even facilitator in a money laundering scheme, can be reduced by following due diligence measures such as the following:

a. Clearly identify the customer.
b. Use reliable documents along with outside data and information to independently verify the identity.
c. Identify the beneficial owner of money and other assets.
d. Take reasonable measures to verify the identity of the beneficial owner.
e. Take reasonable measures to understand the ownership and control structure of the business customers.
f. Obtain enough information to fully understand the purpose and intended nature of the business relationship.
g. Conduct ongoing due diligence on the customer and the underlying business relationship.
h. Carefully scrutinize transactions undertaken throughout the course of that relationship to ensure that the transactions being conducted are consistent with your knowledge of the customer, his or her business and risk profile, including, where necessary, the source of funds.
i. Pay special attention to all complex, unusually large transactions and unusual patterns of transactions which have no apparent economic or lawful purpose. Examine the background and purpose of such transactions. Seek help from outside professionals (police, lawyers, accountants).

---

### Money Laundering Prevention Tip

Ask yourself the following questions:
- How well do I know this customer?
- Do I fully understand the transaction which the customer wishes to complete?
- Am I comfortable with this transaction?

- Does the transaction make sense, considering the customer's profile?
- Is this a usual method for conducting other similar business transactions?

## 8. Effects of Money Laundering

Money laundering has far-reaching social and economic sequences:

- It makes crime pay. It allows drug traffickers, terrorists, smugglers and other criminals to expand their operations. This drives up the cost of law enforcement and health care (e.g., treatment of drug addictions).
- It has the potential to undermine the financial community because of the sheer magnitude of the sums involved. The potential for corruption increases with the vast amounts of illegally obtained money in circulation.
- Laundering diminishes government tax revenue and therefore indirectly harms honest taxpayers and reduces legitimate job opportunities.

## 9. Case Studies

### China Breaks Up 155 Black Markets for Money Laundering in 2004

China broke up 155 underground banks and black markets for illegal foreign currency trading involving 12.5 billion yuan (1.51 billion US dollars) in 2004, a government report said on Thursday.

"About 110 million yuan in cash was seized and 460 bank accounts holding 42 million yuan were frozen," said Zhang Jing, vice director of economic crime bureau under the Ministry of Public Security at Thursday's press conference.

The campaign against money laundering, which started from April last year, was participated by Ministry of Public Security, The People's Bank of China and the State Administration of Foreign Exchange (SAFE).

## 9. Case Studies

### A. Autos for cash

In New York City, the owner of a Mercedes dealership accepted more than $30 million in cyber-payment-laundered drug proceeds in exchange for luxury automobiles. The drug proceeds were initially pooled as cash in Panama, loaded in increments of $20,000 each into merchant Smart Cards issued by a Panamanian bank and taken by courier to Europe for deposit in a London bank account.

The money came back to the US through wire transfers purported to represent business transactions between the Mercedes dealer and a European investment group. The automobiles were delivered to a variety of drug cartel leaders in Colombia, Mexico and Panama.

### B. Internet e-cash

In searching the house of a known cocaine dealer in Coral Gables, Florida, police seized three kilograms of powder cocaine, $24,000 in currency and a computer whose hard drive revealed electronic purse software containing more than $240,000 in stored e-cash value. A spreadsheet revealed a history of more than $7 million in Internet-based e-cash transactions between the Florida dealer and a money broker linked to Mexican drug—money laundering.

Two individuals arrested at the Miami International Airport were found to be carrying over 300 large denomination Smart Cards issued by a Mexican bank, all of which had been altered to store more value than their bank-imposed limits.

### C. Friendly merchant

In Phoenix, Arizona, a Suspicious Activity Report from a bank reported that a small grocery store which had historically averaged $5,000 to 8,000 per week in Smart Card deposits had recently been processing Smart Card transactions at a rate of more than $80,000 per week. Under questioning by authorities, the grocer admitted that for several times a week an individual would come to his store with a bag filled with $20 to $100 denomination Smart Cards which had been accepted for drug purchases by local drug traffickers.

The grocer would download the value stored on the cards to his bank account by running them through his merchant point-of-sale terminal. The bank in turn issued certified e-cash coins to the grocer.

The grocer would then transmit the e-cash coins via the Internet based upon instructions received from the drug dealer. Funds were never forwarded to the same destination twice.

The grocer received a 4% commission on all transactions.

### D. Smart cards

In San Diego, California, undercover narcotics officers reported that drug dealers in the area were beginning to offer discounts of 10 to 15% to customers who paid with Smart Cards.

The rationale given was that the cost of money associated with laundering for Smart Cards was less than half of that for cash and far less risky.

### E. Drug trafficking and money laundering destabilize Mexico

**March 22**

In New York, a nationally known trader in international stock funds warned that because of the continued social and economic instability, Mexico may soon have to be put on the economic danger list. Within an hour, the value of the Peso had fallen 10% against the US Dollar. Several mutual funds specializing in Mexican and Latin American stocks began to suffer from panic selling.

**March 24**

In Washington, the President of the IMF identified money laundering as the major source of Mexico's Peso instability problem and the major impediment to financial reform in Mexico. He announced a draft ed, IMF-led plan to bolster the Mexican economy, contingent on Mexico's passing an array of executive orders and legislation which would bring the Mexican cyber-payment system up to the US and E. U. standards for currency security and anti-money laundering practices.

The Washington Post reported that a major Mexico City bank was under the control of a drug cartel and was deeply involved in fraudulent activities that were undermining the security of the Mexican cyber-payments system.

The absence of any Mexican action on the IMF proposal gave the impression that the Mexican Government was politically paralyzed. High level rumors claimed that the drug cartel was trying to negotiate a formal peace treaty with the Mexican government and was insisting as the price of its support that the President reject the IMF's proposed cyber-payment modernization plan.

**June 4**

US authorities intercepted and decoded a message between two drug cartels. The message expressed alarm about the near success of the negotiations with the Mexican government and concluded that "Operation FIRE GOD" should be launched as soon as possible. The principal objective of FIRE GOD was later found to replace existing Mexican national and state governments with administrations friendly to the cartels.

**June 30**

In London, England, the police arrested six prominent Bond Street financiers in connection with a drug cartel money laundering operation. The brokers had planned to take control of the United Kingdom's third largest Internet service provider which was to become an integral part of a new money laundering operation to replace the drug cartel's primary European money laundering infrastructure and its historical reliance on currency smuggling and the international wire transfer system.

**July 4**

In Switzerland, intelligence obtained from connections in banking system indicated that the drug cartels were planning an economic destabilization plan aimed at replacing the current Mexican Government. The plan was to manipulate the Mexican stock market, the Mexican national cyber-payment system and the value of the Peso on world currency markets. Cartel funds obtained in the destabilization operation and other cartel funds in Mexican banks at the time were to be transferred immediately to European and Asian financial institutions in anticipation of severe Mexican economic instabilities.

**July 9**

US authorities were unsuccessful in persuading the Mexican government to close the Mexico City bank that was involved with the Coral Gables Southern Palms Bank in fraudulent cyber-payment and smart card-related activities.

**July 8**

In Moscow, drug cartel representatives finalized the procedures for a new money laundering operation: The Colombians would deliver US Dollars to a mafia-controlled Russian bank for which they would receive bulk packages of $100 Smart Cards. The Smart Cards would be express-mailed to a bank in Yakutsk and deposited in the account of a Russian/Colombian joint venture mining company. The funds would then be wire-transferred to a bank in St. Petersburg, Florida and then on to the Swiss account of a cartel front company ostensibly involved in international mining.

**July 14**

In Panama City, Florida, a major drug cartel safe house and communications center was captured by police. Examination of computer records found there revealed fund-transfers of more than $200 million to buy political support within the Mexican government.

Several major Mexican and US banks detected a massive outflow of currency from Mexico. By that afternoon, the Mexican stock exchange had suspended trading after a collapse of value in excess of 8%.

In turn, the value of the Peso fell by nearly 10% before a massive intervention by the Mexican central bank.

In Washington, the Secretary of Treasury announced that the Mexican Government was "showing signs of panic" over the country's financial situation and was prepared to radically restrict the flow of currency out of Mexico, including draconian restrictions on cyber-payment transfers.

The Secretary also noted that drug cartel's Operation FIRE GOD included a massive effort to flood the Mexican economy with counterfeit e-money as part of an effort to subvert the cyber-payment system.

**September 26**

In Mexico City, the Mexican government declared a bank holiday and temporarily closed the stock exchange. The Mexican government's effort to staunch the hemorrhage of currency out of Mexico was failing.

**September 28**

In Washington, A joint meeting of the National Security Council and National Economic Council was called for to discuss the escalating of Mexican crisis and the possibility of the US undertaking new and urgent measures to thwart the drug cartels' ongoing destabilization campaign.